# DEVELOPING DIFFERENTLY

A Guide for Parents of Young
Children with Global Developmental
Delay, Intellectual Disability, or Autism

## Dr Joshua Muggleton

Foreword by Tony Attwood

**Jessica Kingsley Publishers**
London and Philadelphia

First published in Great Britain in 2022 by Jessica Kingsley Publishers
An imprint of Hodder & Stoughton Ltd
An Hachette Company

I

A CIP catalogue record for this title is available from the British Library and the Library of Congress

ISBN 978 1 78775 997 8
eISBN 978 1 78775 998 5

Printed and bound in Great Britain by CPI Group

Jessica Kingsley Publishers' policy is to use papers that are natural, renewable and recyclable products and made from wood grown in sustainable forests. The logging and manufacturing processes are expected to conform to the environmental regulations of the country of origin.

Jessica Kingsley Publishers
Carmelite House
50 Victoria Embankment
London EC4Y 0DZ

www.jkp.com

'A book for parents that places the human being at the centre of thinking, explains strategies, and talks about what really happe[ns] I thoroughly recommend this book. It makes good advice pract[ical] and doable.'
— *Gina Davies, speech and language therapist [and] founder and owner of Attention Autis[m]*

'This is the book that I've always wished the families I work w[ith] could access. Friendly, accessible and comprehensive. I recomm[end] it to any family with a neurodivergent child.'
— *Dr Max Davie, consultant community paediatri[cian]*

'As a parent, I often struggle to find the time or energy to read. *De[vel]oping Differently*, however, was engaging from the outset, and it [was] easy to navigate to specific sections relevant to my family's needs [for] information and advice. Muggleton's writing is relaxed, respec[tful] and relatable, with some humour thrown in for good measure w[here] appropriate. I believe it will bring comfort and support to many w[ho,] like me, are navigating the journey of parenting a child or child[ren] with additional support needs.'
— *Elaine Scougal, postgraduate researcher (Augmentative [and] Alternative Communication) and SEN pa[rent]*

'A gentle and encouraging guide for parents, *Developing Differe[ntly]* does a brilliant job of laying out in plain language all of the comple[xity] and nuance of years of knowledge and experience from research [and] clinical practice. Dr Muggleton's sincere empathy and insight [into] the experiences of the families he is writing for is clear on every p[age.] This feels like a book that parents will return to again and agai[n.'] — *The Cerebra Network for Neurodevelopmental Disor[ders]*

'Engagingly written and full of wisdom and warmth, this b[ook] expertly sets out our understanding of what enabling a child labe[lled] 'different not less' looks like. Drawn from the experiences of c[hil]dren, families and professionals, as well as research, it is authe[ntic] and encouraging. A wonderful read that feels like having a kno[wing] friend by your side reminding you what you're doing right, ra[ther] than someone at your shoulder telling you what you're doing wro[ng.'] — *Tony Osgood, author of* Supporting Positive Behaviou[r in] Intellectual Disabilities and Aut[ism]

*To the children in my life...*
*...and to the grown-ups who run after them*

# Contents

# Foreword

Joshua and I both enjoy the many successes and achievements that can be made by developmentally delayed children and their families, when properly supported. I began my specialisation in this area of Clinical Psychology more than 50 years ago, while Joshua has come to it more recently, bringing a new perspective and enthusiasm. I read his book with great appreciation of his ability to perceive the perspective of parents and children developing differently. He offers wise advice to parents on how to manage their new roles, including coping with and guiding children through difficult behaviour and strong emotions, and facilitating the acquisition of abilities that are seemingly so easily acquired by typical children.

One reason I enjoy working with very young autistic children is the fact that the degree of Autism in pre-school years is not necessarily an accurate predictor of future ability and lifestyle. I am frequently delighted with the degree of progress I see in adults I first consulted with as preschoolers. If only we could have seen into the future when they were very young – sometimes their progress has exceeded all our expectations.

Joshua describes six key steps to achieving a successful outcome and I will add another suggestion from my personal experience: the child's personality. They may be extremely brave and tolerant of adversity, never surrender to the challenges of their Autism, and possess a sense of humour and charisma that is so appealing to parents, teachers and therapists.

Parents of developmentally delayed children have much to learn. Sometimes, unfortunately, they may consider the rate of progress in their child as a measure of their own parental competence, rather than being due to the complexity and depth of the developmental delay. They can also be worried about how they will cope with the daily challenges and stresses. Joshua describes the first key step as self-care, explaining that this is to ensure each parent has sufficient energy to implement and coordinate the various programmes. It is important that parents recognise their own expertise regarding their child. I say to them that since it takes about three years to achieve a PhD and they have been closely observing their child for more than three years, they have an honorary PhD in the study of their child. They will know what is likely to work and what probably won't work.

There may also be concern regarding how much time they should devote to intervention programmes. There is an optimum level that varies over time; not enough and progress will be inhibited, while increasing beyond the optimum level will show diminishing returns. Double the intervention does not necessarily double the achievements. Experienced professionals can provide advice on the optimum level of any intervention programme.

Parents will learn a new language. When children have difficulty with spoken communication, they use their behaviour to communicate their thoughts, feeling and needs. The mannerisms have a message and parents learn to translate these mannerisms in order to have a 'conversation'. They constantly observe their child, looking for behaviour patterns and the triggers for specific behaviours, such as the child being overwhelmed by certain social and sensory experiences and reaching the end of their capacity to cope. Parents can then consider environmental rather than behavioural modification, making appropriate adjustments and accommodations according to how their child perceives their world. Parents will also need to acquire resilience, learning to remain calm when experiencing the critical comments of naive members of the public, especially when their child is having a meltdown in public. It is important to retain a sense of dignity and composure, despite what may be running through their mind.

There are many sources of information on children who have developmental delay. While the relevant professionals are an obvious source, there is also the internet and marketing. There are unfortunately, entrepreneurs who will take advantage of parents' motivation for progress, perhaps even a cure, and the advertising is very convincing. It is important to be objective and seek advice before embarking on an expensive programme that is not evidence based. It is also important to remember that sometimes the wisest and simplest advice is from other parents of similar, and perhaps older, children, as they have authenticity and comparable experiences.

There will be successes and milestones that are taken for granted by parents of typical children but are worthy of great celebration for parents of a developmentally delayed child. This can include behaviours such as sleeping through the night or being reliably toilet trained. An ability that once seemed so elusive will be achieved and can be enthusiastically celebrated.

And last, but by no means least, it is important to simply have fun together, with no expectation to learn but simply to enjoy the moment. Parents may take photographs of specific achievements, such as completing a jigsaw or a LEGO® model and create an achievements book that can be enjoyed together and shared with other family members.

Whether you are a parent or a professional, you will enjoy Joshua's engaging and informative style, and so many developmentally disabled children will want you to absorb his wisdom.

*Tony Attwood, PhD, Adjunct Professor at Griffith University, Queensland, and author of* The Complete Guide to Asperger's Syndrome *and* Asperger's Syndrome: A Guide for Parents and Professionals

# Acknowledgements

This book wouldn't have been possible without the hundreds of children and families I've been privileged to work with. Their stories constantly inspired me and challenged me when writing to think 'is this actually practical?', 'have I addressed that?' or 'what would *they* get out of this?' This book is for you, and I couldn't have written it without you.

Similarly, I wouldn't be in a position to help if it was not for the many teachers and mentors I've had since I set out to become a Clinical Psychologist back in 2008. In particular, Dr Louise Connor, Prof Tony Attwood, and Dr Katrina Johnston have taught me so much and helped me to become the clinician I am.

I'm very grateful to all the (many!) parents and professionals I have sent copies of this manuscript to read, and who have provided detailed feedback. This includes Jacqui Brew, Elaine Scougal, Aimée Fletcher, Tracy E. Watson, Vicki McLean, Clare Truman, Hollie Burnett, Zoe Claisse, Claudia Grimmer, Charlie Malloy, Rona Noble, Jo McCabe, and in particular Katrina Johnston who was critic, proof reader and peer reviewer rolled into one. Equally, a huge thank you to Nata, Beth-Ross Gilles, Fiona Mitchell, Ion Wyness, and Tony Attwood for allowing me to use some of their examples or anecdotes in this book.

Most importantly though, I want to thank my partner, who for the last three years has put up with me scurrying off to my office with a coffee and headphones while explaining that I need to keep working on the book else I won't finish it. Her patience, understanding, and support on this project have been unending, and for that I'm forever grateful. Thank you.

# INTRODUCTION

When I go to work, I sometimes get to tell colleagues about my children's successes. 'One of my children today came out with the funniest thing', 'One of my children was so excited to show me their new favourite toy', or 'One of my kids managed the whole night in their bedroom'. Strictly speaking, I'm not *actually* a parent to any of these children. However, in my job, we get to know kids and their families really well, and when one of our kids has a success, we feel so incredibly proud of them and want to boast about their successes.

I'm a Clinical Psychologist, working in a small team for children with Intellectual Disabilities. The children I see all have either a Global Developmental Delay, or an Intellectual Disability, although most also have some combination of Autism, ADHD, genetic conditions, Epilepsy, physical health conditions, or brain injury. I also have a diagnosis of Autism myself, and have siblings with the condition – you might say it's the family business. The work I do is quite varied. Sometimes I'm working with parents to understand and support their child. Sometimes I'm doing specialist assessments to work out if a child has a neurodevelopmental disorder such as Autism, or an Intellectual Disability, or just to figure out how a child's brain works best. Sometimes I'm just in the background providing advice to the team working with the child and their family. I may only work with these families for a period of weeks or months, and some children who I assess I may only see for a day. However, each time, I'm privileged to be let into the lives of these children and their families, often at critical or emotional times, to help them achieve the very best for their child. I'm incredibly proud of their achievements, but I also see how difficult some of the challenges they (and their parents) face are, and I try to do my best to help them.

## WHERE IT BEGINS

I mentioned that part of my job is assessing children with neurodevelopmental disorders – finding out whether the way a child thinks is different to everyone else. When I've done my assessment, I'll have a meeting with parents where often I'll explain to them that 'actually, there *is* something different about Johnny...'. This is where our journey begins.

Notice that I said that Johnny is *different*. **Different is not less**. Different may mean that the world is a harder, scarier, and less predictable place for them. It may mean that learning new skills, being in social situations, paying attention, solving problems, communicating or any number of other skills are harder for them. But every child I meet is still a remarkable individual with *so much* to offer. If life were a video game, their copy would have the difficulty level set to 'expert', with no tutorial level. But they all have their own personalities, quirks, interests, likes, and dislikes, and they all have something to bring to the world, sometimes in the most powerful ways. Our job, as parents and professionals, is to try and reduce that difficulty level for them, find a few cheat codes, and give them the support they need. **Our job is to find out how to help them get the most out of the world, and allow the world to get the best out of them**.

I say 'our' job because, as a professional, there are limits on what I can do. Any Clinical Psychologist will tell you, there isn't much you can achieve in one hour of therapy every two weeks: this is just planning. Real change happens outside the therapy room. This is even more true for the children I see. The younger the child is, or the more difficult they find language as a way to communicate, the less I can do in therapy with them one-to-one. Actually, only a minority of my work is directly one-to-one with a child doing what most people think of as 'therapy'. Instead, the majority of the work I do is with parents. Together, we try and understand their child, create the right environment for their child, improve their relationship and communication with their child, and try and teach their child new skills so they can be all they can be.

However, **I can't help a child alone**. In my work, I always need parents as my co-therapists. Parents are my eyes and ears, gathering information about their child. Parents know their child far better than I ever will, so I need them to bring along their expert knowledge, and I can bring my understanding of child development and how kids learn so that we can think about what we can do to help. I need parents to manage and change things in their child's environment, to look out for certain signs, to try out new techniques and teach new skills. I can't do it without them.

## WHY I WROTE THIS

Parenting isn't easy (...and in other news, it turns out the sky is blue), and parenting a child with a Global Developmental Delay, Intellectual Disability, or Autism can be even harder. However, hard does not mean complex. Actually, a lot of the parenting strategies are quite straightforward once you get your head around them. Often, parents come to me with a fantastic understanding of their child as a person, but are becoming increasingly frustrated and disheartened as they just can't seem to help their child: they just keep having meltdowns, lashing out at their siblings, or hurting themselves. When the parents and I have analysed the child's behaviour, reminded ourselves about the way their child sees and processes the world, often we find the answer is blindingly simple, but is something the parents and I had forgotten to check, maintain or do consistently enough for long enough.

I think that is really exciting! It means that **if we get the basics right from the start, and maintain them, we can reduce a lot of a child's difficulties**. With the right knowledge, environment, interactions, response, and understanding, we can reduce a child's anxiety, build confidence, and develop skills. The end result is a child, parents, and siblings living a much easier, happier, and fulfilling life.

## HOW TO USE THIS BOOK

In the future, I hope this is a book you can dip in and out of for reference, but for your first read, please read it in order. I have set out this book based on what I believe to be the six key steps, with each building on the other:

**Step 1: Acceptance and Self-Care** is my first priority with any family. While the first question I ask parents is usually about the child, the first question I *want* to ask is about the parents. If you are going to be my co-therapist (and, let's be honest, the one of us doing most of the work), we need to make sure you are in the right place to do it. There is no point doing anything else in this book until we check on you and how you are managing, and if needed, make some changes to ensure you are doing ok and have the headspace to be the parent you want to be. Even if you are fine, thinking about what it is you do to look after yourself and your relationships is important, so we can make sure we keep this protected so you stay that way. Likewise, sometimes coming to terms with a diagnosis can be difficult. When we get stuck on that, it makes it hard to properly put yourselves in the mindset of your child and work out how to help. However, if we take the time to think about how you feel about your child's difficulties, then we can start thinking about how we can help your child.

**Step 2: The Right Knowledge**: We learn how children develop, what to expect from them, and how they experience the world from watching children and thinking about our own experiences as a child. However, when you have a child developing differently, this might not work. It can be harder to understand *how* your child is developing differently, what that is like, and what we should expect. So, we need the right knowledge about how children develop, and how they can develop differently, so that you can parent your child effectively. So in the first half of this step, we'll look at various neurodevelopmental disorders and what they mean. In the second half, we'll look at some theories about child development that will be important knowledge to have as we go through the rest of the book.

**Step 3: The Right Environment**: Children (particularly young children and children with limited language) learn so much simply from their environment. Exploring their environment will teach them that leaves are green and pizza tastes yummy, but they will also learn skills by observing others, learning the routines of the days and weeks, and seeing cause and effect. The environment is also the cause of (and solution to) huge amounts of anxiety, confusion, and over excitement. After all, their environment was built for children developing typically, not children developing differently. If we get the environment right it can go a long way to making a happy child who is calm and ready to learn.

**Step 4: The Right Interaction**: One of the most fun and influential aspects of a child's environment is *you*! Well, you and other people. You are interactive, mobile, and have a huge amount of control over what happens to your child. However, even parents of typically developing children can struggle to know how to interact and play with their children. Children who develop differently can need a slightly different approach to interaction, but it needs to be in the right environment, with the right knowledge to back it up.

**Step 5: The Right Response**: Let's be honest, even the most angelic child is going to have behaviours you don't like, or that they don't do enough of. The right response to behaviour can help your child to learn and improve skills, as well as improve their self-esteem and confidence at the same time. However, we've got to know how to interact well with our child in order to get the best out of them, and ensure they are in the right environment, in order for our responses to be effective.

**Step 6: The Right Understanding**: Getting the right understanding through working out the function of behaviour (working out why your child is doing what they are doing) comes last. It is an important skill, but the better steps 1–5 are practised and maintained, the less you'll need to use it. Often, analysing the function of behaviour is a way of *pinpointing what we have missed* from the earlier steps, or that we got something wrong. Equally, while steps 1–5 should reduce your child's anxiety, sometimes we identify that anxiety is driving the behaviour, and we need to help your child to manage and overcome anxiety.

**Bonus chapter: Sleep**: You probably don't *need* to read this chapter at the end, but it will help. Sleep is often a HUGE issue for kids developing differently, and while there are some specific things we can do around sleep to help, we actually apply a lot of the strategies we've learned in steps 1–6.

**Bonus chapter: Siblings**: Similarly, this chapter can be read at any point but will probably make most sense after you've read steps 1, 2, and 3. Here I look at some of the difficulties that can occur when parenting children, whether developing typically or developing differently.

The bonus chapters and appendix can be downloaded from https://library.jkp.com/redeem using the code YJXGEFU

## RECOMMENDED READING

Throughout this book, I mention quite a few different resources – so much that I've put a list of all of them (plus a few extras) in the online appendix. However, there are a couple that I refer to more regularly and deserve a mention here.

*The Incredible Years* by Carolyn Webster-Stratton (Incredible Years, 2006) is a fantastic guide to parenting young children who are developing *typically*. Her book uses many of the same principles, and covers some of the same topics, as this book but from the perspective of parenting typically developing children. If you want to apply what you learn in this book to your other children, it is definitely worth looking at.

I'll also mention it a few times in this book as a source if you want to go into the nuts and bolts of specific topics in more depth. However, remember that it was developed for parents of children developing typically. Therefore, when translating across to kids developing differently, keep in mind:

- **Reasonable expectations.** We can't expect a child to do something they aren't yet able to do. Our kids have more varied profiles of things they can and cannot do, so it can take some more thought as to what we expect of them.

- **A little less conversation, a little more action, please.** Some strategies in *Incredible Years* are quite verbally based, and may well be too verbal or abstract for some of our kids. Focus on the 'doing' and 'showing' bits, and think about ways to make the 'telling' bits more visual.

- **Logical consequences.** These should be used rarely at the best of times, and there are additional considerations before we use them with your child. Please read step 6: The Right Understanding before applying logical consequences where I'll discuss this more.

*Child Development: An Illustrated Guide* by Carolyn Meggitt (Pearson Education, 2012) is a book I take with me to every clinic. It is a fantastic, visual guide to how typical children develop in different areas (motor, speech, social skills, etc.) over time, and has lots of strategies for supporting child development. I'll talk more about child development later in the book, but highly recommend it as a companion reference when reading this book.

I'll also mention several times the website www.nhsggc.org.uk/kids which is a great resource, packed with lots of easy to read, practical information, and well worth bookmarking and exploring as you read this book.

## DISCLAIMER

As with all books you read, please remember that the information in this book (and the supplementary online materials) is not a replacement for a trained medical or healthcare professional, who can get to know your child and provide tailored advice to your child and situation. Always consult a doctor or other appropriate qualified healthcare professionals on any matters regarding your or your child's health and wellbeing, and in particular on any matters which may require assessment or intervention.

In this book and supplementary online content, I recommend a number of books, resources, websites, and videos which parents and I have found helpful. While I've taken reasonable steps to ensure these are of high quality, I don't guarantee this. Further, information published in earlier or later editions of books, resources, or websites will not have been seen by me. I receive no benefit, financial or otherwise, from recommending these resources.

Right, that's it, I think we're ready. Let's get started!

# STEP 1: ACCEPTANCE AND SELF-CARE

How often have you found yourself doing the same thing over and over, sure that there *must* be a better way, but feeling too busy to stop and find it. In life, sometimes it can feel like we are too busy fighting fires to stop, take a moment, and realise we haven't called the fire service or turned our hose on properly.

I know I feel like this at times. Sometimes at work I feel so stressed out and overwhelmed, but rather than take a step back and look at what I'm doing and what I can change, I dig my heels in and work harder, not smarter ('maybe if I bang my head against this brick wall a little bit harder I'll get somewhere...'). When we get like this, we start to develop tunnel vision, and all we can see is the problem that we can't solve. We start to lose sight of other ways we could do things, of what is important. We don't see other solutions, and when people point them out to us we can be reluctant to try them. Other solvable problems start to cause problems because we don't have any time to devote to them, and our mood starts to tank.

This step is about taking a step back, looking around us, and taking the time to think 'is there a better way?'

## ACCEPTANCE

I think every expectant parent, no matter how good or tough their life is, wants their child to have a better life than they had. They want them to have opportunities they didn't have, to not make the mistakes they made. Sometimes, we have visions of this expectant bump in mum-to-be's belly becoming a doctor, lawyer, astronaut.

Other times, we imagine them having their own family, and us being grandparents watching on and sneaking the grandkids sugary snacks. We think about their first day at school, about receiving glowing school reports. We think about all their firsts – their first playdate, their first party, their first sleepover, their first girlfriend or boy-friend. We can't help but make grand plans for our children – and why shouldn't we? They have the world at their feet, and we get front row seats to their life.

Then the vision starts to change. Maybe it is at birth when the doctors rush your child away for tests, or because they are very premature. Maybe when they are a toddler you start to notice that your child isn't quite responding like all the other kids. Maybe your partner asks you whether it is ok that Mary still isn't talking. Maybe it is a teacher asking you to come in after school for a quiet word, because they are worried Simon isn't progressing as well as the other children. Sometimes parents (understandably) find it hard to see these difficulties, even when they are pointed out – it is not the sort of thing you want to hear. Other times, parents are the first to spot any differences, but can sometimes have trouble getting others (including, sadly, professionals) to take them seriously, while they lie awake at night worrying. Then after referral after referral, months on a waiting list, and pages of forms to fill out, I come along, and after a while I tell you that your child has a neurodevelopmental disorder.

For some parents it comes as a shock. In that moment, I'm chang-ing that vision they had of their child's future. For children who think differently, but have lots of language and are able to work out how to adapt to use their differences as strengths (including many children with Autism or ADHD) that picture might not look too different from the one their parents imagined. It might be a bumpier ride, and their child might need to do things a little differently or need specific supports, but there is an expectation that they will be independent. It can even be an advantage to be the person who thinks differently from everyone else. For other children, who are developmentally behind, with limited language, who are more sig-nificantly impacted by their condition(s), the future can be much less certain. Some things parents had imagined for their child, such as living independently, may be much more challenging to achieve, or may even be out of reach. For a lot of children, particularly younger children, we don't yet know what their future will be like. This is really hard for parents to hear, and letting go of that vision they had and starting the process of building a new one can be difficult to do.

For some parents, getting the diagnosis is a relief. It's confirming a long-held belief. They have always known their child is different, and sometimes it is a battle because nobody listened or took them seriously. However, even then, for some, it can still be a shock to hear the diagnosis. Sometimes, even though they knew all along, part of them wondered if they could be wrong. Hearing it confirmed can still be emotional, as it means letting go of that vision they once held.

Lastly, some parents have always known their child is different, and for them the diagnosis is a mere formality. Some of these parents have lived with a working or provisional diagnosis for some time, so came to terms with the likely diagnosis long ago. Other parents may not know what 'diagnosis' fits their child, but they know who their child is, and what their differences are, that vision they have had of their future has changed and developed as their child has changed and developed.

All of these experiences (and everything in between) are normal – there is no 'wrong way' to experience your child's diagnosis. For most parents I see, the diagnosis is the start of a process of coming to terms with the diagnosis, acknowledging their child's differences, and (particularly for those with children more significantly impacted by their differences) letting go of that vision they once had.

A lot of parents identify with the idea of the five stages of grief (denial, anger, depression, bargaining, and acceptance), and I've seen it play out in my clinic. I've worked with parents who think there is no point coming to see me as they are sure there is nothing going on, or who, even after I've given their child a diagnosis, are sure I'm wrong so get a second opinion. Sometimes there is (often justifiable) anger at how difficult getting to the point of diagnosis has been, and why wasn't this picked up or their child supported better earlier? There can be feelings of hopelessness, sadness, or guilt – that somehow this was *their* fault. I've had long conversations with parents who have questioned everything they did or didn't do from before their child was conceived to today, thinking they must have done something wrong, and desperate to work out what it was. Most parents I work with are determined to find the right support to help their child.

This is great when it comes with realistic expectations of what support can and cannot achieve. However, I've also met parents who have started to think that if they *just* find the right intervention, if they *just* work hard enough, their child might be 'cured' or 'catch up'.

Lastly, we get to acceptance. To understanding your child as different, but not less. We get to a place where you can let go of that picture you had, and are ready to build a new picture of hopes and dreams based on your child, and their unique strengths, difficulties, qualities, and personality. We realise that, yes, your child can absolutely make progress, learn new skills, and develop: we can *always* be ambitious about our children. However, they will always be different, this is who they are, and that isn't going to change.

Reaching acceptance is important, because if we hold onto the idea of our child being just like every other child, then it is going to get in the way. It is going to make it harder to change our approach to something that works for *them*, rather than for other children. It is going to mean we create unfair or unrealistic expectations of them, leading us to feel disappointment, and our child to feel failure. Not fully accepting the reality of our child's difficulties can make it harder for us to understand them and make decisions on how to support them. Ultimately, if we keep chasing this vision of how we want our child to be, keep focusing on it, trying to keep it alive, we end up ignoring who this wonderful child we have right in front of us really is. We won't see their needs and wants, their strengths, and their qualities. Instead, we just see differences in terms of what they can't do, and start to feel increasingly helpless, ineffective, and inadequate.

This isn't helpful.

There is a poem, which you can easily find online, called 'Welcome to Holland' by Emily Kingsley.[1] It is about a mother's experience of coming to terms with the fact their child is different, and that the plans she had for her child are going to be different from reality. Please go and have a read, or if you prefer, if you search for it on YouTube you can see short videos with the text and relevant pictures

---

1    I like to show parents this poem early in their acceptance journey, as it often resonates with their feelings of unexpected change, and a new language to learn, but that things are going to be ok. This is not to say that our kids could be 'put somewhere else' or on the outskirts (say in Holland), just that early on that process of adjustment can feel like landing in another country.

flashing up (although I always get teary when I watch it – you have been warned!).

The reason I like it is that it is about a *different* future for our children. Yes, we need to come to terms with this, and even grieve for that future vision we had for our child, and the fact the future is now different, perhaps very different. You might grieve for a vision of what you thought family life was going to be like. That actually, this parenting business is going to be harder than what you originally signed up for.

**But we don't need to grieve for our child.**

Our child is still there – they haven't been taken away. They are a child, not a diagnosis. Yes, they are developing differently, but there is *so much more to them than this*. We have a wonderful young human being in front of us, who still has a future ahead of them, filled with exciting experiences, new adventures, skills to learn, and friends to meet. They are unique, with their own personality, likes, and dislikes. They still have *so much potential*, so much to give, and we get to have a relationship with them. Why would we grieve about having such a wonderful human being in our lives?

It is important to understand where you are on your journey. If you've already come to terms with your child's diagnosis, and how the future you perhaps once imagined might be different, then great! But don't worry if you don't feel like you're quite there yet. Grief and coming to acceptance takes time, especially when we are so busy with life we don't take the time to process. It is also perfectly normal to return to the grieving process every so often. Sometimes seeing another child their age doing something they can't do yet can bring up those feelings, and we might have to work through them again – that's ok, and perfectly normal.

When working with parents who are feeling 'stuck', we've found it helpful to take some time to acknowledge the future we might have imagined, how it has changed, and explore all the thoughts and feelings that went along with this. There are lots of different ways to do this. A lot of people find it helpful to talk to their partner, a friend, or a professional about this, but other people prefer to write it down as a story or letter. However you choose to acknowledge and let go of that past vision, it is important you set aside time to do it somewhere comfortable and private. If you are doing it by talking with someone, it's also a good idea to tell them you want to do this, so you get the time and 'permission' to make it all about you.

When I do this with parents, I find our conversations follow a similar pattern. It is like telling a story with a beginning, middle, and end. In the beginning, we talk about how they discovered they were expecting a child, and all the feelings and emotions they had, their thoughts about what their child would be like, and the future they imagined for them. In the middle, we talk about when they first realised there might be something different about their child, the worries this caused, and the journey that took them from there to where they are now. We talk about all the obstacles that they overcame, and what (and who) was and wasn't helpful. We talk about what it was like to actually get the diagnosis for their child, what it felt like, what it meant to them, the questions they had, and what's happened since. Finally, at the end, we talk about where they are now, and their hopes and expectations for the future. Often, there will be lots of unanswered questions, as it is often hard for professionals to say what a child's future will be like. There may also be a lot of difficulties – children developing differently can be challenging to parent, particularly when they are stressed or struggling to learn skills.

Throughout our story, I think it is important to talk about all these difficulties, and the impact they have on us. However, it is just as important to *not forget the positives*. These shouldn't be platitudes, like 'but there is always someone worse off' or 'I should be grateful'. Talk about things that are real to you: talk about your child, not just their diagnosis – their unique personality, their qualities and abilities, their smile. Talk about all the things they have already overcome, despite their difficulties, and the strength of character that shows. How these qualities, abilities, strengths, and difficulties make your child who they are. Talk about the laughs, the fun times, and the positive experiences you've had with your child, particularly if they wouldn't have happened had they not been different. Talk about how they are part of your family, and what they bring to it. Talk about how much *you* have learned and grown through the experience – about how much strength of character you've had to show to get this far, and what you've had to overcome. Where you are right now with your child may not be easy, and it may not be where you thought you'd be, but there are still lots of positives about how far you've come, and the young person you are going on this journey with. This isn't about putting a happy gloss on all the hard stuff – the hard stuff is really hard, and we're not trying to minimise or discount that. Rather, we're making an effort to ensure we see the good stuff too, and acknowledge that even with all the hard stuff, good things have come out of it.

I do meet parents who are really struggling to find the positives. This is often because their child's behaviour is so extreme, the parent's wider circumstances are so difficult, or their mood is really low. That is understandable – life can sometimes be really tough. If this is you:

1. Try and see the child behind the behaviour. Your child is *so much more* than their behaviour. Think about what they are like on good days, or before things got difficult. That child is still there, and hopefully we're going to bring out more of them as we work out how to teach them new skills, and make their lives a bit easier to manage.

2. Get help. We'll talk about this later in this step (see 'Getting support' section). This could be help with bills, with practical home support, help for your child, or help for your own mental health. Getting help is not a sign of weakness or of being a bad parent – it's the sign of a strong parent who has the self-awareness to know when they need more people on their child's team.

In this chapter, I've tried to introduce the idea of acceptance, and that it is a perfectly natural process to go through. I hope I've also given you a bit of a road map for how to navigate acceptance, but everyone experiences it differently, so you might have your own way of getting there – that's fine too. I've only scratched the surface in this chapter, so if a year down the line from diagnosis you or your partner are still feeling 'stuck' and are struggling to come to terms with your child's difficulties, then it is important to seek help. This will not only help you feel more positive and successful in your parenting, but will also help you put into practice the kinds of ideas, strategies and supports suggested in this book, and that professionals might recommend. Your GP, local parent support groups or charities, and registered counsellors may be able to help you, or direct you to someone who can.

## KEY POINTS

✓ Parents experience the diagnosis of their child in lots of different ways – there is no right or wrong way to feel about your child's diagnosis.

✓ Accepting a diagnosis often means letting go of or changing the vision we once held of our child's future so we can see our child for who they are.

✓ It is ok to grieve for that vision of your child's future, but remember – **your child is still here**! They haven't changed or gone anywhere, and they **have so much to offer**!

✓ If you're finding it hard to process your child's diagnosis, try talking it through with someone or writing it down. Make sure you don't just focus on the hard stuff, and include the positives too.

## YOU ARE ENOUGH

I believe parents always want the best for their children. There is something about the bond between parent and child that drives you as parents to go to the ends of the earth for your children, to do whatever it takes, even to risk your life for them. It truly is a force of nature inside you. Usually, this force is helpful. It drives you, motivates you, keeps you going. However, there are times this force starts to work against you.

I often meet parents where their desire to do the best for their children has driven them to feel incredibly guilty about, well, everything. Guilty that they didn't do that exercise the speech and language therapist recommended today. Guilty that they didn't do the morning routine quite right so their child had a melt-down. Guilty that they couldn't find the energy to play with their child. Guilty that they didn't ask for a referral, meeting, or report sooner. Guilty that they didn't argue harder, or get the result they wanted for their child. Guilty that they didn't spend the money on a toy or piece of equipment for their child. Guilty they weren't able to comfort their child and make them feel better. Guilty they are spending all this time focusing on one child and spending less time with their other children. Where is all this guilt coming from?

The immovable object has met the unstoppable force. **We cannot make everything perfect for our children** yet we have this force within us driving us to do our very best for them. If 'our very best' means setting realistic expectations of ourselves and our children, working towards them, and accepting that there will be good days and bad days, then that is helpful. However, when 'our very best' means that we end up trying to change things we cannot change (our child, their school, the law, the healthcare system, the laws of physics), or be the perfect parent (with unlimited time, energy, patience, forgiveness, and who doesn't need to sleep), then we're going to expend a lot of time and energy on generating a monumental amount of guilt and exhaustion.

What can start to happen, particularly when a child has really significant challenges that are very hard to manage, is that it can all start to feel impossible. When we've tried our best and kept trying and trying and trying and it still isn't enough, sometimes that force of nature inside us starts to stall. We feel hopeless, helpless, overwhelmed. This can generate even more guilt – the sense that no matter how hard we've tried, we aren't able to help our child. We might even find ourselves thinking 'what kind of parent can't help their own children?'

One of my good friends, Nata, is a Clinical Psychologist who specialises in working with children. She also has three young children of her own. You might think that being a child psychologist, she'd have got this parenting business sorted. After all, part of her job is giving advice to parents on ways to adjust their parenting style to suit their children's specific needs and difficulties. She has spent years studying children, child development, and different parenting approaches. When you see her in clinic or in a meeting, she seems like the most 'with it' and 'together' person in the room, and these insights on children and parenting seem to just flow out of her.

When I go to visit Nata at home, however, it is a bit of a different story. I'm greeted at the door by a rather harassed looking Nata with one child clinging onto her, another making a mess with the paints, and the third asking for toast. When we get to sit down (well, *I* get to sit on the kitchen stool, while she frantically re-makes the toast as her child wanted it cut into triangles not squares, whilst making us both coffee and trying to hold a conversation), she remarks to me, as she often does, that when it comes to parenting 'the guilt is real!'

At work, Nata gives parents expert advice on how to help their children get to sleep – how to set up a bedtime routine and their child's bedroom, how to separate, how to manage night-time waking. However, when it comes to her own kids, sometimes she just doesn't have the energy to put that into practice. Nata knows all about how to set and keep boundaries with children, how to keep your cool, and how to get them to sleep, but is she always able to follow it? No. Sometimes it is all just too much, and she either can't, or doesn't have the energy, to follow her own advice. She has these high expectations of herself, because she wants the very best for her children, and she wants to be the best mum she can be. However, Nata is also a human being, who has permission to make mistakes, who needs sleep, who gets hangry, and who does not have infinite patience. Because she is human, she falls down and can't meet the standards she has set herself, and so she feels guilty.

So, why have I just publicly embarrassed one of my friends? It isn't for fun (that's just a happy coincidence). First, I shared this story (with Nata's permission) because when you feel guilty, it can so often feel like you are the only one. Like you are the only failure in a sea of successes: 'Surely other people are able to do this? I must be the exception'. I hope this shows that you are not alone in feeling this way. Nata is one of the best psychologists and mums I know: if she can't live up to these expectations she has of herself, with all the training, knowledge, and experience at her disposal, then how can I, anyone else, or (most of all) **you** expect you to be able to do it, especially when you have the additional challenges of bringing up a child developing differently? That just doesn't seem fair.

The second reason I shared this story is that guilt can very easily turn into shame. When we feel ashamed, we don't want to tell anyone, we want to hide it, we want to pretend it didn't happen because we feel we will be judged really harshly by others. This can lead us to minimise how much we are struggling, make it harder to ask for help, or sometimes not tell the whole truth – all of which can make it harder for other people to help you help your child.

But let me ask you this – do you judge Nata? Would you give her a hard time? I doubt it. What would you say to Nata if you could see she was feeling guilty about her parenting? Seriously, write it down, or say out loud what you'd tell her... Now, is how you would talk to Nata different to how you talk to yourself about all the things *you* feel guilty about? If you're like most people, you'll be kind and empathetic to others, but really hard on yourself, which makes us feel more all the more ashamed. However, if we can be brave enough to (like Nata) admit that we aren't the perfect parent, we'll probably find others feel able to share it too, don't judge us as harshly as we judge ourselves, and all of a sudden it isn't such a big a deal and some of that guilt gets lifted.

Lastly, I shared this story because I think it is really important that you as parents know that we the 'professionals' understand that there is a big difference between giving advice and following it. You aren't going to be able to follow everything in this book all the time, and that is ok. That doesn't make you a bad parent, it makes you human.

You are enough – that doesn't mean you are everything your child will ever need. It takes a village to raise a child, and that is particularly true for children developing differently. But you are enough to be their parent – the most important person to your child. You don't have to be perfect. You don't have to be superhuman. You don't have to do everything. You don't have to prove your worth.

## KEY POINTS

✓ Sometimes, our desire to do our best for our children leads us to set unrealistic expectations of ourselves, creating guilt. This is especially true when our expectations involve us changing things we cannot change, or coping with things we cannot cope with alone.

✓ When we feel guilty, it often feels like we are the only one struggling, but we are not. We can feel ashamed, and judge ourselves much more harshly than we judge other people.

✓ You have to be superhuman to be perfect, or to do it all without asking for help. However, you are enough to be your child's parent – the most important person to them.

## VALUES

In life, we tend to think in terms of goals – things we want to achieve. We set goals for how much we will spend each month, what qualifications we will achieve, tasks we want to accomplish today. Who knows, you might even have a goal of reading a chapter of this book today. Our whole education system teaches us to set goals and then try to meet them. We even teach our kids tools to set better goals ('SMART' goals are still seared into my brain from secondary school!).

The trouble is, goals are pretty poor motivators, and don't tend to make us happy. Think about it, what happens if you meet your goal of getting the shopping done today? Do you feel a sense of pride? Purpose? Satisfaction? Or just relief? How long do those feelings really last?

I wanted to be a Clinical Psychologist since I was about 17. I sat my A levels (two years), went to university (four years), got my Master's degree (one year), got a job as an Assistant Psychologist (one year), won a scholarship (eight weeks), and earned my Doctorate (three years). Each of these achievements were increasingly competitive to get into and difficult to complete. There were many tears, sleepless nights, and days when I just thought 'why the hell am I doing this to myself?' I remember I regularly thought 'I'll be happy/satisfied when I achieve my Doctorate', or 'I'll stop working as hard once I achieve my Doctorate'. You'd have thought that after 11 years working towards the goal of walking across the stage to receive my Doctorate, to finally qualify as a Clinical Psychologist, that I'd be over the moon and with a huge grin on my face for days...

...Nope, I was already half way to achieving another goal (buying a house), and working compressed hours so I'd have time to write and research what would eventually become this book. I was happy for a few hours, and I'm proud of what I've done. But after 11 years of blood, sweat and tears, the satisfaction that I imagined I'd feel was a lot smaller. Was it really worth it?

And that's the problem with goals. The success we feel is fleeting, and we end up on an endless treadmill of moving from one goal to another. We always say 'I'll be satisfied when I just achieve this goal'. We're like the donkey with a carrot tied to a stick just out of reach to keep it plodding along – never *quite* getting the carrot. And that's when we achieve our goals. What if we *just* miss it? Suddenly all that hard work becomes worthless because we came up short, and we feel awful. It doesn't matter if we were close – we *failed*.

But, there is an alternative to goals: values.

Values are very different to goals. Our values are things we choose that are important to us. They tell us how we want to lead our lives, the direction we want to take, guide the decisions we want to make, and how we want to behave. Values are never 'completed' or 'achieved' like goals are. Instead, we can simply choose whether to do something that is consistent with our values and what is important to us, or not.

Think of it like this: Let say you start in London, and you follow your (somewhat odd) value of heading west. Following this value may mean you travel to Dublin – have you 'finished' your value? Well, no, you can keep heading further west. So you do: you go through Reykjavik, New York, Los Angeles, Hawaii, Sydney, Delhi, Budapest, and eventually back to London. After months of heading west, you are back to where you have started, and yet you can still keep heading west. Does this mean you've failed – after all, you've ended up right back where you started? Not at all – with values, it isn't about where you end up, it is about what you do. In this case, it doesn't matter where you end up, it is about the journey you took. Goals might be 'markers' along your way, cities you visited, things you did or achieved – that's fine. I'm not saying you can't have goals. But the important thing isn't how many cities you visited, or goals you achieved. What is important is that you kept traveling west.

Ok, this might sound a bit airy fairy. Let's make it more concrete.

| Goal | Value |
|---|---|
| I want to get the shopping done today | I want to provide for my family |
| I want to lose a stone | I want to be healthy |
| I want to get a promotion at work | I want to do my best at my job |
| I want my child to have friends | I want to support my child to grow and develop |
| I want my child to stop misbehaving | I want to help my child be part of the community |
| I want my child to get more support at school | I want what is best for my child |
| I want my child to stop having meltdowns | I want to help my child to manage in the world they live in |

Can you identify with any of these? It's a bit of a shift in mindset.

It seems everything in life teaches us to set goals, and work harder and harder until you get there. That puts us under a lot of pressure, and can be really demotivating when we miss our goals or don't think we'll achieve them. Values tell us what direction to take – doing what is important and meaningful to us, even if it is hard. Importantly, when we follow our values, even if we don't achieve everything we wanted, even if it is hard to do, *we feel we did the right thing.*

Let's take the 'I want my child to stop misbehaving' example. I think every parent feels like that sometimes. Now, you can have that as a goal if you like. However it's going to be a pretty hard goal to meet – *all* kids will misbehave. Likewise, it is quite a negative goal – you're trying to stop something, and it isn't even something you can control directly. I think I'd get quite frustrated and beat myself up a lot if I had this goal – I'd end up begging and pleading with my child to *please just stop* misbehaving. Whenever my child misbehaved, I'd feel like I'd failed.

However, what about 'I want to help my child to be part of the community'. This is a value because it is never 'achieved' – there is always more you can do to help your child to be a bigger part of the community. Plus, there is no time limit which means you can't fail – you can work on it, leave it be and come back to it, but you've never 'failed'. Part of that value might be reducing misbehaviour, but if your child is playing up it doesn't mean you've failed. You've still worked on helping them be a part of the community, and that is what is important – you can still look back and know you did what was right, even if it didn't end up how you wanted. Plus, values are much more flexible than goals. For example, even if you can't change their misbehaviour, there are still other ways to move towards your value. You might go litter picking with them, encourage them to share, or support them to bake a cake for the school bake sale – all things that still help them be a valued part of the community. Long story short: values help us focus on *doing what is important to us*, rather than getting caught up in what we do or don't achieve.

Let's find out what your values as a parent are.

I'd like you to imagine it is ten years into the future. It is a few weeks before World Parents' Day. For months, children and families have been sending in videos to the UN to nominate parents they believe to be exceptional, who have gone above and beyond to be truly amazing parents and made them the person they are today. Out of the blue, you receive an official looking letter through your door. It is from the UN, telling you that you've been nominated, and asking you to attend the grand finale.

In that envelope are your tickets, and a few weeks later, you fly to New York, and are put up in a swanky hotel. The press keep calling your phone wanting to interview you, so you're keeping it switched off. The next day is World Parents' Day. That evening, you get in a chauffeur driven car, all dressed up, and are driven to a huge venue. There are TV crews and journalists lining either side of the red carpet, taking your photograph and asking to interview you. You walk up to the entrance, surrounded by celebrities who have come to watch the ceremony. You get in and find your seat, and the event begins. Stephen Fry comes on stage and makes some funny quips before introducing a stream of celebrities, each announcing different awards. The 'Best-ist Brother', 'Superb Sister', and the 'Greatest Grandparent' awards come and go. Then, finally, it is time for the main event. Parent of the Year. A celebrity comes on and announces the four nominees, before finishing with 'and the winner is...'. The lights go down, and a video starts playing on the big screen. It is your children. They are showing to the world why they nominated you for parent of the year, what it is you do that makes you such a special parent. What is in their video? Take a few moments to really think about that.

I'm thinking that video probably didn't feature things like a video of your house always being kept perfectly tidy, or your kids saying 'she was never late to pick me up from school'. Instead, I reckon they said things like 'Mum takes the time to understand me', 'Dad worked really hard to get me the support I needed', or a video of you and your child spending time doing their favourite game together. These are examples of excellent values – understanding our children, working to support them, and spending time with them. I'm sure you've got your own too.

Sometimes, following our values can be hard to do, and mean doing things we'd rather not. For example, 'supporting your child' might mean taking time off work to attend school meetings, time that you'd rather spend on family holidays. Trying to 'understand your child' might mean trying to remain calm when your child is having a huge meltdown because you gave them the wrong spoon. However, when we stop, think, act according to our values, and remind ourselves why these things are important to us, doing things that might otherwise be hard becomes a lot easier.

When I was in clinical training, I decided for various reasons that it was important to me to live a healthier lifestyle. This was not my only value, but it is one that was a high priority for me. I decided the way to follow this was to run every Monday, Wednesday, and Friday. Now, in case you hadn't guessed, running in Scotland, in winter, in the dark, and in the rain, is not fun. On my first few runs, I hated it. I tensed up, gritted my teeth, and spent the whole time thinking about how much I hated what I was doing. I just wanted it to be over.

Then, one evening while the rain was lashing the windows and I was lying on the sofa, I saw it was time for a run. I really didn't want to go, but I reminded myself that being healthy was important to me (despite yesterday's pizza box still on the coffee table), and also *why* it was important to me, why I had chosen it as a value, why *I wanted to do this*. I suddenly found it much easier to get off the warm sofa and out into the cold, dark, wet Scottish night. It still wasn't fun, but it wasn't nearly as hard. All that energy I usually used tensing up, beating myself up and thinking about how much I hated it, I could instead put towards actually running. That night, I achieved my best time, and actually noticed how the sensation of my body moving and working could actually feel good (plus, by this time my feet were too numb from the cold to hurt...). This wasn't an easy decision, it was an unpleasant activity, but when I held onto my values, it was easier to do.

Let's put that into a parenting example. Most parents will recognise the experience of having a screaming child in the supermarket who is upset because they've not been bought a bar of chocolate on display by the checkout. You know if you give them the bar of chocolate, they will come to expect it, and that next time you say 'no', you'll have to do this all over again, only it will be even harder to say no. You might know that not giving in, sitting with the screaming and all those eyes staring at you while you try to pack up your groceries and your child throws things on the floor in protest, is going to be so, so uncomfortable, but it will teach your child that they can't scream to get what they want. If you have a value of 'I want to help my child be part of the community', for you and your child, that might mean them learning what is and is not ok, and that this behaviour isn't going to get them what they want. When you hold onto that, and remember *why* it is important to you, it becomes easier to sit with that screaming.

This is the power of values – they *motivate us*, they drive us forward by focusing us on what is important to us. Goals, on the other hand, often motivate us by threat of failure. We also tend to feel good (or, at least, better) when we do something that chimes with our values, even if it is hard to do. There will be plenty of hard times ahead (as well as plenty of good ones too) so having a good grasp of your values and what sort of parent you want to be can be really helpful in getting through those tougher times.

We can't always follow our values. For example, the value of 'providing for my family' might contradict the 'spending time with my family' value. If you followed the 'spending time with my family' value to the extreme, you might give up your job, which (while fun) might leave you unable to pay the bills. Likewise, if you followed the 'provide for my family' value to the extreme, you'd be working all hours and quickly burn out and get to spend no time with your family. So sometimes we have to compromise, or work out which value is more important when. For example, you might decide you want to put your value of spending time with family first for a while, so work fewer hours, even though it means you have to cut down on the holiday budget.

Equally, while some people parent alone, others have co-parents, be they partners, grandparents, or close friends. Those people might have different values to you, but it is important for your kids that you work together. Therefore, you need to talk to them, to find out, honestly, what their values are as parents (and in life) so you can work out which are shared, and where you can compromise, so you can both parent together effectively.

If you want to know more about how we can use values in parenting, have a look at *The Joy of Parenting* by Lisa Coyne and Amy Murrell. They talk about how we can use Acceptance and Commitment Therapy to help us take a mindful, values-based approach to parenting, and make tough decisions and sit with the uncomfortable thoughts and feelings that sometimes come with them.

## KEY POINTS

✓ Goals are *either* achieved or failed. We feel awful when we fail, and when we achieve them, the satisfaction is often short lived.

✓ Values are *never* achieved or failed. Values tell us what is important to us, and guide us on how to act and what decisions to take.

✓ We can choose to act according to our values: we can remind ourselves *why* something is important to us, and when we do, hard things become a bit easier to get through.

✓ It is important to take time to be aware of what your values are as a parent. Holding onto these values will help you prioritise and do things when times are tough.

## LOOKING AFTER YOURSELF

Parenting is hard, and it is even harder when you have a child who is developing differently. I can tell you in this book (and therapists can tell you in clinic) what to do, but it is *pointless* if you are not able to do it. Parents aren't invincible, and all parents will experience some physical or mental health problems, if not now, then in the future. They might be acute (short-term things which can be fixed, like a broken leg, or short-term stress), or chronic (long-term conditions, such as Diabetes, Arthritis or Depression). Parents with physical and mental health problems can still be fantastic parents, but it is an extra thing they have to cope with. What about dealing with divorce? Being a single parent? Having to move house? Losing a job? All these things are surmountable, but they make parenting harder

I meet lots of parents who say they are 'coping' – is that you? To me 'coping' sounds like something you do for a while to get through a hard spot, not something you can keep up long term. It can sometimes be parents' way of telling me they aren't looking after their own health and wellbeing because they want to (or need to) focus all their energies and attention on their child. While that sounds admirable, mental and physical health issues can emerge if you aren't looking after yourself, and they *can* be a big barrier to being the parent you want to be if you aren't getting help.

Parenting is a marathon, not a sprint, and everyone around you (your family, the professionals involved, and most of all your child), need you to be able to keep running. If you want your child to be a priority, **you need to look after yourself**, and (where needed) get some help. You are the most important person to your child, and we can't help your child without you. That is why *you* are our first priority.

More often than not, *you* will be the therapist to your child: you'll be the person who manages their environment, their schedule, and their meltdowns, ensures everyone has up-to-date information on how to get the best out of your child. Often, I and my colleagues won't work directly with your child; we'll be working through you, giving you strategies, interventions, or exercises to do at home. However, unlike me, you don't get to go home and switch off come 5 pm. You don't get annual leave, sick days, or flexible hours. You might not have colleagues you can go to when you've had a really bad day and need to talk. Instead, you have long hours, and you're on-call during the night. You also have to be chef, policeman, nurse, chauffeur, secretary, and parent, sometimes for multiple children, and might have a regular job to hold down as well. All these things mean **if you do not take care of yourself, you *will* burn out**.

Have you had any of these difficulties recently?

- Problems sleeping – lying awake at night even when you're exhausted? Worrying, thinking of what you'd like to say or do to someone, what you should have done?

- Reduced appetite, or comfort eating? Either not eating because 'I don't have time', or 'I've not earned it', or just not feeling hungry? Or the opposite, and comfort eating to make yourself feel better? (This is my personal go-to.)

- Relationship or friendship problems? Are you arguing more? Has your sex life died, you're talking, or just you're 'going through the motions'? Do you not have the energy or motivation to 'make an effort' to see people and do nice things?

- Lack of energy – feeling tired all the time? Even simple things start to feel like a mountain to climb? Or alternatively, are you like me and start trying to fix everything, thinking if I just solve one more problem, things will all be better?

- Trouble focusing or concentrating, and forgetting things? Have you noticed yourself making silly mistakes you don't usually make? Has your performance at work (or even your driving skill) slipped? Mind going foggy, or simple decisions starting to feel too much?

- Low mood, feelings of hopelessness, or guilt? Are thoughts of 'I'm a crap parent', or 'I can't keep doing this' starting to creep in? Or worse, do you believe them? Do you find yourself wanting to just shut yourself off from people? Do you feel desperate for someone to ask you what is wrong, but don't feel worthy or that it is ok to say what is wrong?

- Anxiety? Worrying a lot about things you cannot control, and wouldn't usually worry about? Do you find yourself getting really stressed and worked up at just the smallest change, the slightest hitch?

- Anger, frustration, and lack of patience? Maybe you find yourself snapping at your kids, your partner, your friends, or your boss, which makes you feel even worse?

- No longer doing or enjoying doing things you used to enjoy, such as hobbies and seeing friends?

- Using substances to get by? Are you using energy drinks to keep going during the day? Alcohol at night to help you sleep or unwind? Smoking, or using other drugs to manage?

If any of these are sounding familiar, then *something needs to change*. Burnout is a slippery slope, and the earlier you catch it and act to stop it, the easier it is. It is easy to think when we're starting to burn out 'I don't care about me', 'I'm not important', or 'yeah, well maybe I *should* burn out – that'll show 'em'. *That's not going to work*. If you are burning out, something needs to change *now*. You, and the people around you, need to look after you, so that you can look after your children. You're running a marathon not a sprint, and all good marathon runners have a support team. The good news is that it is never too late to change things or ask for help.

If you don't see any of this in yourself, that's great! It sounds like you already have a routine which ensures you take care of yourself as much as your children and family. However, let's not get complacent: burnout is sneaky, so it's important to recognise what it is you do which helps protect you from burnout, and ensure you keep prioritising those things.

If you are struggling with self-care, there are lots of things we can do to take care of ourselves. We'll never be able to do them all perfectly, but give them a try and work out what works best for you. When I say try, I mean give it a *proper go*. Pick something, and give it a go for at least a month. If it isn't working, think about if you maybe need to take smaller, more manageable steps, or alter something about the way you're going at it. It is ok to find these changes difficult, to change your plan, or after a month conclude that this form of self-care just isn't for you right now, and try something else. As long as you can look back and honestly say you gave it a proper try, that's fine. However, these aren't pills – they take a while to have an effect, and often the first couple of weeks they can feel like a chore, like they are more effort than they are worth, and they can take a while to 'get into'. But, as they start to become a habit and become less of a chore, they become easier, more enjoyable, and more helpful. Often, people don't notice the benefit of them until they are gone, so if you notice you're getting more stressed or not sleeping as well, see if you've let something in your self-care routine slip, then start it up again!

**Diet**. Boring as it is, having a balanced diet with plenty of fruit and veggies (and avoiding processed food) can really help. Likewise, cutting back on sugar and caffeine can help with sugar and caffeine highs and crashes. I'm not saying you have to live on lettuce, carrot sticks, and hummus – treating yourself to a takeaway, glass or two of wine, and bar of chocolate are also part of self-care.

Take small steps – think about replacing a couple of food items with something a bit healthier – that mid-afternoon chocolate bar could become an apple, for example. You could try cooking things in a healthier way (boiled potatoes rather than mashed?), or (as in my case) buy a multipack of small chocolate bars (rather than one big one that, once opened, has to be finished even though it was meant to last the week!).

**Exercise**. Anyone who read my first book, *Raising Martians*, knows *exactly* how I feel about PE and exercise, so I never thought I'd write this but, here it goes...

Exercise is good for you.

There, I said it. Exercise isn't just good for our bodies, it can have a *huge* effect on our mood and wellbeing. Exercise releases endorphins, improves our physical and mental health, and helps us manage stress. In fact, a big part of why I started running during my clinical training was to manage stress. Exercise also *gives* us energy. I often hear people say 'I don't have the energy to exercise', but if you start exercising, your body will adapt to it and *give* you more energy.

There are lots of ways you can go about this. I got into running by using Couch to 5k (lots of apps, free and paid for are available for this), which really helped me do it in manageable steps and get into a weekly routine. Some people find the community around Parkrun (www.parkrun.org.uk) every Saturday morning helps them get into and keep up running (whenever I've been, they are a lovely bunch). I know people who love walking, and have a friend where, instead of sitting eating coffee and cake, they will go for a long walk to talk. You can also do things with the kids too (surprising, I know!) – go and play football, tig, frisbee, etc., or just simply run about. Kids can be great exercise instructors because they never seem to run out of energy (particularly the kids with ADHD) so they'll probably be able to keep running about for longer than you can. For other kids, you might really value spending time doing a walk together, trying to join in with a sport they enjoy, or simply playing on the swings, slides, and see-saws at the local park together. The best bit is you get that smug feeling when you go into work the next day and say 'Yeah, I'm good thanks, I played frisbee with my kids last night. What did you do? Netflix again?'

**Sleep**. This is sometimes the hardest to get, particularly with young children, or children developing differently, which can often affect sleep–wake cycles. Most adults need 7–8 hours of uninterrupted sleep most nights to be able to function (although there is a lot of variation in this). We can get by without our personal minimum sleep for a time, but eventually it will catch up with us.

Often, lack of sleep is one of the biggest predictors of whether a family I see will be successful in managing behaviour, and so it is one of the first things we tackle. If for whatever reason you're not able to get your 7/8 hours, we need to get creative. If there are two of you, could you take it in shifts – one person gets to sleep through the night uninterrupted one night, while the other is 'on call' to deal with things that come up, then switch the next night? If you're a single parent, is there a relative who can sleep over a couple of nights a week, so you can catch up? What about any friends? Can we find you a time to catch up on sleep during the day? Also, make sure you look at all the sleep hygiene stuff I talk about in the bonus chapter on sleep, which is available to download from https://library.jkp.com/redeem using the code YJXGEFU. It applies to you as much as it does to your child!

**Hobbies**. Netflix is not a hobby. Sleep is not a hobby. By hobby, I mean something *active* (something where you do something, make something, something where you feel a sense of achievement or accomplishment, where you enjoy the learning process or already feel mastery over it) rather than something passive like watching TV or sleeping. Reading, sports, collecting, researching, making, gardening, etc. can be hobbies if they are enjoyed, and doing them (once you get into them) makes you feel good. You don't have to do hobbies alone, but we want to try and ensure that (as much as possible) if you are keeping up a hobby as part of self-care, you are not 'on duty' when you're doing them. For example, it is fine to do cross stitch with your child if they enjoy it and don't need too much help and supervision when you do it with them, but if you're spending your time teaching them and solving their problems, you're not doing your hobby, you're parenting.

**Downtime**. There is a time and a place for Netflix and computer games, and this is it. You absolutely need downtime, time to just zone out, escape, let your brain wander, and to not have any demands. However, for some parents, this can be hard to find, while for others it can take over.

A few hours of this a day would be great, but if you spend *all* your self-care time doing this, it is just going to make you feel tired. What is more, we don't really 'live' in this time – we're just switching off from life. We aren't doing things, or making memories. It means when the next day you look back at what you did, you don't remember the down-time, you remember the other stuff. If that other stuff is filled with hard work, self-doubt, frustration, sadness, or other negative stuff, there isn't going to be any positive self-care memories to balance it out.

On the other hand, there are parents who really struggle to find any downtime – after all, parenting is a 24/7 job. At these times, just being able to grab ten minutes of downtime is a *huge achievement*. Again, see if you can negotiate with a co-parent, family, or friends to see if you can schedule in some of this downtime so you have a min-imum amount to look forward to. When we do get those moments, a) well done for finding them, and b) make sure you use them. Think about what will help you make the most of those ten minutes – a cup of tea? Reading a book? Listening to music? You've earned these ten minutes, so you've got the right to enjoy them! Remember to give yourself permission to not do the dishes or other chores during this time. Yes, they need doing, but do they really need to be done *right now*? Or can we say that these precious few minutes of downtime are going to be spent on you, and the dishes can be done later.

**Holidays.** Holidays are important! I've seen parents transform from zombies to humans after just a few days on a hot beach away from the kids. The chance for parents to focus on them, on their needs, on their relationship, and on their wants not only does wonders for their mental health, physical health (they often come back looking years younger and tanned!), and relationship, but it is also great for the kids. The parents have more resilience to deal with the difficult situations, more patience for when a child is upset, and more deter-mination when they are trying to resist a child's tantrum because they want a chocolate bar. Family holidays are great too, especially those where the kids have enough to do to entertain themselves for short periods, or where there is stuff to do that everyone loves and can enjoy. However, a parents-only holiday can be particularly powerful, especially when you are exhausted.

Ok, so that sounds great and all, but not everyone will be able to afford, or be able to get away from the kids long enough for, a holiday in the sun for a few days. That's fine – a holiday might not be that big. It might be a day trip, overnight at a hotel or cottage, or a long weekend. It doesn't even have to be far away. However, getting some time away is important, and we may need to get a bit creative on how we go about getting it. Can friends or grandparents come and stay at your house to look after the kids (so they get to keep their own bed) while you have a weekend or day away? After-school clubs (for many parents I work with, the best thing since sliced bread) are a great way to extend the school day, and make it easier for working family and friends to help out. For example, if they can pick up the kids after their after-school club, feed them, and put them to bed, sleep over, then get them back in school, you've got yourself a mini-break! From dropping the kids off at school (breakfast club, anyone?) to picking them up the next day, you're on holiday, even if it is just a half hour drive away. Even if all you can get is an evening away for date night, or taking a day off work so you have the time they are at school as downtime for you, that can still help recharge your batteries.

## KEY POINTS

- ✓ You are the most important person in your child's life – we need to take care of you if we're going to take care of them.

- ✓ Look out for signs of burnout, and if you recognise it is starting, take action.

- ✓ Try out different self-care strategies, and find what works for you.

- ✓ Prioritise self-care. It is often one of the first things to be 'cut' when things get tough.

- ✓ Build self-care into your daily or weekly routine.

## LOOKING AFTER YOUR RELATIONSHIPS

So far, I've just talked about self-care that you can do by yourself. However, your relationships with others are also an important part of self-care.

Have quality time as a couple. If you're lucky enough to be sharing the parenting journey with someone, you've got a great resource to help you. You've got someone who can understand, listen, and be there for you. Having quality time with a romantic partner is one of the best forms of self-care for both of you.

However, relationships don't maintain themselves. Remember all those fun memories you made when you first met and started dating? Yes, there was a spark of excitement from the unknown, but there was also lots of *effort*. You went out and did things, you went out for meals, or made meals at home *together*. You had time to talk to each other, learn about each other. However, sometimes life starts to get in the way. Tidying, cleaning, working, cooking, parenting start to take up so much time. You and your partner start becoming colleagues who share a bed, rather than a romantic couple. Suddenly you're not that couple who were going to take on the world together, hand-in-hand; you're both just trying to get through your own lives, and the 'togetherness' is lost. So we need to make time to get these things back, to be a couple again. Sometimes that is as simple as treating yourself to a nice ready meal from the shops, a bottle of wine, a dessert, a candle, and setting aside time to actually talk over your meal. Get a puzzle book to do together, play a game, do shared interests, or just talk, but whatever you do, make the time to connect. Even if it is just snuggling up on the sofa together watching TV, without any phones or tablets (so you can actually *watch* together). All these things don't cost a lot, and don't take much effort, but they can help you maintain your relationship and look after each other.

Regardless of how it happens, the result of a poorly maintained relationship is that you stop being able to support each other, or even worse, stop being able to be around each other. Your ability to use all these great parenting strategies you've devised or learned about starts to falter, increasing the stress, and making the situation with your partner even harder. When you see that happening, it is important to get things back on track. There are lots of organisations out there offering relationship advice and counselling, but one I will mention is Relate (relate.org.uk) who are one of the largest providers and who have some free resources.

One common issue I come across sometimes is when parents are at very different stages in their acceptance journey. Sometimes one parent will have come to terms with their child's particular difficulties, grieved if they need to grieve for the old ideas about what life might have looked like, and come to see all the wonderful aspects of their child, and be ready to help them. However, the other parent finds it hard to acknowledge their child is different. Sometimes this is because the other parent has attended fewer of their child's appointments, or has not spent as much time with them (for example, if they don't do the school run, or they work full time), so perhaps doesn't see the extent of their child's difficulties. Sometimes parents have a coping strategy of 'if there is a problem, I fix it', which can be helpful in some situations, but can make it harder to accept that your child has a difficulty that you can't 'fix'. Whatever the reason, often differences in acceptance can lead to a disconnect in how parents are trying to parent their child (e.g. 'why are you using those symbols, she doesn't need those!', 'he's just got to get used to routines changing at short notice, now come on', 'she's fine! She'll catch up').

Another common issue is when one parent attends most of the appointments, and the other parent is unable to. This means one parent is getting all the information and strategies, but the other has to hear them second hand, so (despite their co-parent's best efforts) might only get the crib notes, and nuances and important bits might have been missed. This can be really hard for that other parent as when they try to implement the strategies, they aren't as effective, or perhaps don't work, when they do for their co-parent. This can lead to them feeling less empowered to help their child, or even resentful that their co-parent seems to be doing so much better than they are, despite them trying so hard.

However it happens, when this happens, if parents as a whole are being inconsistent (one parent using one approach, and another parent using another), this can result in children acting up, a lot of stress for parents, and a lot of tension and frustration in their relationship.

When the root of this is acceptance, and understanding that your child is different, then I think we need to encourage your co-parent to start that process. I often suggest bringing them along with you and your child to see your child's Paediatrician/Psychologist/Speech and Language Therapist, etc., so they can hear from the horse's mouth exactly what the diagnosis is and what the difficulties are, and have an opportunity to ask the questions they perhaps aren't able to ask you but have been turning over in their head. The chances are that your child's health professional will have been in this situation before – let us be the ones to give them the information directly, explain why their child is behaving as they are, answer their questions, and (if needed) be the bad guy and tell them that actually your child *does* need these strategies. Attending appointments together (even if only a few) is also a great way to help both parents feel skilled at supporting their child, ensure you are both being consistent with each other, and both feel like equal members of your child's team.

A lot of places (such as the NHS and charities) run parents groups for children developing differently. These are often fantastic, as even if you already know all the strategies, getting to meet other parents on that journey can be really helpful – especially for those working full time who feel a bit disconnected from what is going on. Sometimes these groups can also help with coming to terms with your child's diagnosis when they've not been able to attend many of their healthcare appointments. I also find they are particularly helpful for dads, as it is harder to talk about your child's difficulties in 'male' culture, and this might give them a chance to make some guy friends who 'get it'. There are even some fathers groups out there for just that reason.

Lastly, some relationships, despite people's best efforts, just aren't meant to last. Whether you and your child's other parent(s) are in a relationship or not, you are still your child's core team, the most important people in their lives. Staying on friendly, good, or at least civil terms can make a huge difference, particularly for kids developing differently, as consistency (which you'll hear a lot about) is so important for your child. Keeping communication open, focusing on the values you all share, and remembering that you are still a team (perhaps even with new team members in the form of step-parents) is really important in doing this, if at all possible.

## KEY POINTS

✓ Make time for your partner and your relationship. It is easy with everything going on to just go through the motions and let the relationship fizzle. Putting in a little bit of thought and effort and creating some quality time together can go a long way.

✓ If one parent attends most appointments and/or spends more time with your child, the other parent may not have as much information or support to understand your child's needs, and accept their differences. Try and ensure both parents attend some appointments together.

## LOOKING AFTER YOUR FRIENDSHIPS

It is not just relationships which need looking after; friendships also require maintenance, and can also form an important part of your self-care. For the parents I see, it often seems like friendships are one of the first things to go when they are starting to find parenting more difficult. It is understandable why. It is hard to go out for a nice coffee with Claire when Adam can't sit still for more than two minutes, and ends up spilling someone else's latte. It is hard to justify going out to the pub with Bill from work when your partner is having running battles trying to get Izzy into the bathtub.

However, it is important you get regular time with friends. This time doesn't need to be spent 'opening up' about stresses and strains – it is good to have the ability to do that, but friendships shouldn't be *all* about that. Spending time having general chat, playing sports, or just catching up can all be just as beneficial to our wellbeing – it doesn't have to be serious chat. Even when it is serious talk, sometimes talking to friends about their problems and being a sounding board for them can also help us feel better and more able to manage our own problems. If you *do* have friends you're able to open up to and talk with about your stresses and strains, that is great. They are someone removed from the situation, but who knows us and how we think and work, which can be really helpful in giving us a fresh perspective, or even just letting us vent a little. However, try and balance that with other chat too.

During tricky times, it is easy to feel resentful of a partner going to spend time with friends, or guilty about doing it. *Talk about it*, and come up with a plan. If on Wednesdays Mike stays home with Izzy and does the bath to let Sarah go have coffee with her friends, then on Fridays Sarah manages the kids so Mike can go play footie with his friends. It is important that both parents get this time, as well as plenty of time with each other.

For all parents, but particularly for single parents, it might also mean being creative with how you see your friends. Can you get as much from seeing a friend via Zoom or on the phone as you can in person? Do you have to 'go out' to see friends, or could you agree that, actually, so that Adam doesn't get over excited, you just do coffee at your place each time? Maybe you want to go with a friend and their kids to the park? Great! But can we go to one Izzy knows, and take separate cars in case Izzy needs to go home early? A little time, effort, and honesty to work out how you can take part and keep these friendships going pays real dividends in the long run.

Sadly, sometimes people just don't 'get it'. It is a real shame when this happens. Sometimes friends aren't willing to put the effort in when you need to draw on them for some support. Maybe they aren't able to be flexible to see you at slightly different times or different ways to work with your child's needs. Maybe they just don't understand your child and why not having fish fingers on a Friday has upset your child so much that you need to cancel at short notice. Good friends will stay – they'll *want* to learn and understand. Even if they can't fully understand your child, they will at least make the effort and try and understand your experiences. However, sadly many parents have told me they have lost friends because their friends can't (or don't try to) understand their children or their experiences as parents. Other parents have said that because their friend doesn't get it, they have to put a lot of work in to accommodate both their child and their friend's needs, and it just isn't worth the effort for what they get out of the friendship.

I take the view of quality over quantity – better a few good friends who you know understand you and your child and where you can have a meaningful friendship, rather than lots of friends who you don't see or talk to much, and can't really talk to. If you do have those friends who do get it, then it is really important to invest your time there to keep those going, so both you and your friend benefit from it.

Lastly, while you may lose some friends who don't get it, there is also a chance to make good friends with parents who really do – because they are going through it too. When I run parents groups, meeting other parents is often what parents value more than me droning on about visual communication for 90 minutes. Look for local parents groups or play facilities that cater for children with additional needs. This can be a great place to meet other parents with similar experiences, and a great way to strike up friendships with people who don't care that Adam can't sit still in the coffee shop, because their daughter Katrina can't sit still either!

## KEY POINTS

✓ It is important to put time and effort in to maintain friendships. This may require both you and friends to think creatively, and adapt how you connect.

✓ Friendships can be a useful space to decompress, but even if you can't or don't want to, just spending time chatting or doing things with friends is really important.

✓ Some friends might not 'get it'. If they don't, and they aren't able to try and understand, then you may find you lose a few friends. However, you may also make great friends with other parents of children with similar difficulties who do get it.

## GETTING SUPPORT

I've talked a lot about the need to take time for self-care, and to maintain relationships and friendships. But, of course, there isn't always much time, energy, or money to go around. Sometimes, with a bit of thought, we can work out how to get the most bang for our buck – find things where investing a small amount of time/energy/ money will give us more in return (such as taking time to ask for help, or staying up late to work on our child's sleep, so long term we can get better sleep ourselves), or ways of doing things that are less time/energy/money consuming than how we currently do it. However, when you sit down, you might realise *you can't* do it all. That's ok – nobody is expecting you to be super-mum or super-dad every day. This is where we need to get support in.

There is *no shame* in saying 'I need help'. Honestly, sometimes it seems like the hardest thing to do at times, especially when it comes to parenting – it's so personal. Sometimes people can feel that they are failing as a parent if they have to ask for help. **You are not**. Asking for help does not make you a bad parent. Children (but particularly children who develop differently) can be hard work, and getting extra support is not a sign of weakness. Equally, you should absolutely ask for help *before* you need it. All too often I see parents asking for help once they are burnt out, which then makes it so much harder to help. Services can spend hundreds of thousands of pounds in social care support, health care support and educational support because things have come to (or come close to) crisis point. However, if parents said a year earlier 'we don't have the time to meet our child's needs *and* do the basic self-care we need to do to allow us to keep meeting those needs' (and, if services listened), the whole thing could be averted much more easily, with a lot less stress, and for less cost.

Now, as you may have noticed from my slightly sassy use of brackets in the last paragraph, I'll admit that getting this support early is sometimes hard. However, you should *absolutely* ask for it. I will always stand by parents and argue until I'm blue in the face that **you are entitled to support that allows you to take care of yourself**, because taking care of you means taking care of your child.

Often, the first line of support isn't through services, it's through family. Grandparents, particularly in younger families, can sometimes take on a caregiving role to allow their own children some valuable downtime. Trusted friends can do the same, perhaps as part of a playdate arrangement. When you do look at what social services or social care can provide, take a little time to know your rights. For example, in the UK, your child is legally entitled to a social work 'assessment of need', and that should absolutely look not just at their needs, but also the needs of the people supporting them (also known as *you*!).

Charities, advocacy organisations, and Citizens Advice are all really useful people to contact to ensure you know exactly what you and your child are entitled to, what sorts of supports are out there, and how to navigate the ins and outs of the different hoops you might have to jump through to get support.

**Do not assume that just because a professional handed you a few leaflets that that is all the support available**. Almost every week I learn about a new organisation I want my clients to know about, and just as often I forget to mention one or other support they could have accessed. Finding out about what is out there in your area for you and your child is something you'll have to do for yourself and keep doing, because it will keep changing.

Sometimes, it can also be hard for friends or relatives to understand (or for us to explain) our child's difficulties. Maybe you've told them Adam has ADHD and Autism, but they think Autism is like Rain Man or Sheldon Cooper. Maybe they know Rona has an Intellectual Disability, but they think you mean a Learning Difficulty like Dyslexia. It can be particularly hard when the people who don't quite get it also have (or feel they have) what I call 'parenting privileges' – the ability to hand out treats, telling offs, rewards, and consequences. For example, someone thinking ADHD just means the child is badly behaved and needs 'a good telling off', which they are then happy to give them, and which only makes matters worse because they *don't get it.*

Equally, one of the difficulties with enlisting relatives for help is that they too can sometimes have to go through that same acceptance (and sometimes grieving) process. They might have had ideas about what it would be like when their grandson or nephew came over for the holidays, and suddenly it isn't like that. For older relatives, there can sometimes be a generational difference. This is not always the case and I've known many families where nana and grandad are completely understanding and on board. However, as I write this on the train, behind me are an older couple talking about how all the classes now seem to have kids with ADHD, Autism, Learning Difficulties and challenging behaviour, but that these things didn't happen when they were at school. I, on the other hand, am trying to resist the urge to turn around and give them a half hour lecture on the history of neurodevelopmental disorders and why they are wrong. As a parent, chances are you've immersed yourself in everything you can find out about your child, their condition, and how to help. You understand your child and their difficulties on a level nobody else does. However, everyone else won't have done that, so it is all new to them, and they are struggling to make sense of your child and their behaviour in terms of their existing (and sometimes faulty) knowledge.

Hopefully, however, these family members will be keen to learn – that's great! It means you can cherry pick the best resources you've found to help them understand your child (if only there was a book you could give them...), so they can get the knowledge they need fast. I also highly recommend creating a communication passport for your child. In fact, I'd argue such a guide is virtually essential for anyone involved with a child with additional needs, especially those taking on caregiving duties. The idea is that we write a guide, written on behalf of your child, on how to understand them, their needs, and how to respond to them. Hopefully, anyone who picks it up and takes the time to read it and digest it can (without even having met your child before) quickly get up to speed on how to support your child and get them at their best. I'll go into this in more detail in the section on 'Consistency' in step 5.

Some great supports can be found in schools. Often people think that schools are just about education, but they are often the first place services can get involved, and so they often host lots of supports too. For example, some schools can give you great information and support on using visual communication strategies, or set up morning or bedtime routines. They might run breakfast or after-school clubs, which can help you get a bit more time to spend with your other children, your partner, or just looking after yourself. Schools can have access to basic mental health supports, and have lots of ideas for where you can access other support services, and may even be able to make referrals. If you find yourself struggling, you should absolutely talk to your child's school.

Of course, I know parents who have a difficult relationship with their child's school, particularly if they feel their child isn't being treated according to their needs or level, or isn't getting the right support. I'd really encourage you to try and form and keep a positive relationship with school (and perhaps try and bite your tongue at those meetings when you feel like banging your head on the desk because nobody seems to be listening). You should absolutely be persistent, insistent, and hold people to what they say (and ensure you get it written down!). You are there to advocate for your child after all. However, keeping the relationship positive will make everything so much easier in the long run. If you are really struggling with school, look into getting an advocate. Lots of charities and organisations offer advocacy services – someone who knows all your and your child's rights, and can be the bad guy at the meetings, so that you can keep a good working relationship with your child's school. Think of them as your hired 'muscle', while you get to play the ever so reasonable mob boss making an offer they can't refuse...

Health services can also help. The trouble sometimes is working out who it is you need to speak to, particularly because child neurodevelopmental services tend to be pretty small, or can be spread across lots of services. It can mean that your friendly GP or family doctor doesn't know about a service, or isn't sure who to refer to. Generally in the UK, Paediatricians (particularly Community Paediatricians) are a good place to start for younger kids developing differently. Older kids I see might also come through child and adolescent mental health services (CAMHS). Health services can also help with things such as communication (Speech and Language Therapy), sensory and motor difficulties (Occupational Therapy or Physiotherapy), mental health/behaviour (Clinical Psychology), and feeding (Dietetics), among others.

Equally, remember to look after your own health. Go to your GP – they may be able to help or refer you to a specialist, and may also know a lot about other local services and how to access them. If you have a chronic problem, it is still worth going to your GP every now and then so they can keep an eye on it, and so you can ask if there are any new supports – even if they can't prescribe a pill to take away the issue, they might be able to help you live better with it.

Lastly, there is social work. Most families I work with (who, in fairness, are often the families who have children with the most challenging and complex needs) have a social worker, and these social workers are often a real lifeline to families (and to me as a member of your child's team). They can help find pots of money for funding, help identify services that might be able to provide some support at home, get support for you to have a night away (or for your child to have a night away) so you can get some respite, come up with some befriending services for your child or their siblings, find community organisations that might be easier for you and your family to access because they are particularly accommodating (or specifically set up) for kids with additional needs. In fact, they are so useful that if a family comes to me who doesn't have contact with social work, often one of the first things I discuss with parents is getting social work involved.

I sometimes think there is some stigma around social work too. People think that social work is for families which are 'falling apart' or 'from the bad neighbourhood', etc. Well, my family had a social worker, and I was brought up in the heartland of the middle class (the suburbs of Surrey), and I turned out ok (...I think). In fact, they were really important in getting my parents a little bit of help so they didn't burn out looking after four kids developing differently, and could have some time together. They organised someone to come in for a couple of hours a few days a week to give my mum a much needed rest, and for my parents to have a long weekend away a few times a year so they could get a bit of a break together. Of course, the support social work offers will vary by area and by country, but I would highly recommend at least *considering* asking social work for support. Why not make enquiries to learn about what they do in your area? Speak to other parents of children with similar needs and see what they say about them. Remember – social workers often specialise, just like doctors, so a social worker working with adults may offer very different things to one working with families.

Social work often seems to be seen as the 'bogey-man' by parents, as they fear social work are going to take their kids away. This does happen – I'm not going to lie about it. When parents ask me 'are they going to take my child away from me?', I can never promise them that they won't as that isn't something I can control. However, in my experience (at least in the UK), this is a *real* rarity. **Social workers want to keep families together**. That's their job. I've never met a social worker who got into this job because they want to take kids away from their parents. On the very rare occasions they have done it, I can see how agonised they are in doing it as an absolutely last resort. Instead, every social worker I've ever met has done everything possible to support families and keep them together. Even the less helpful social workers I've met are less helpful due to having too much to do and not enough time to do it, rather than because they are 'trigger happy' to take kids away from their families. If you're still a cynic, the cynical argument I make is this: it costs *far, far* more to take a child away from parents and look after them (especially if the child has additional needs and needs a highly specialist home setting) than it does to support parents to support them at home.

## KEY POINTS

- ✓ Don't be afraid to ask for support – it isn't a sign of weakness, it's a sign of strength.

- ✓ All children with a disability or 'in need' in the UK are entitled to an 'assessment of need', which includes the needs of those supporting them.

✓ Extended family can be a great support, but may need time and help to learn about your child, and be able to support them as well as they need.

✓ Schools have lots of information and links to support – they aren't just about education.

✓ Through your GP, you may get referrals to healthcare professionals such as a Community Paediatrician, Clinical Psychologist, Speech and Language Therapist, Occupational Therapist, Physiotherapist, Dietician, etc., all of whom can help your child in different ways. They can also help you!

✓ Don't be afraid of social workers – they are in the business of supporting families and keeping them together, not taking kids away from parents.

# STEP 2: THE RIGHT KNOWLEDGE

So, hopefully now you and the rest of your child's team are feeling on top form, or at least have a plan for how you are going to look after yourselves. Next, we need to prep you with the right knowledge – and we've got a lot to cover!

In this next step, there are lots of different topics – each of which could be a book in themselves. I'm not going to go into detail on these, as if they are particularly relevant or important, you'll find plenty of other books or online resources going into them in greater depth. What I'm going to do is focus on the basics (what you *need* to know), and what it means for your child. Think of these as your crib notes before going into an exam, rather than a complete textbook.

To start with, we're going to talk about a few neurodevelopmental diagnoses (a label we use to say a child has a specific pattern of strengths and difficulties we commonly see) that you might come across, and some things that often go alongside them. We'll then talk about the idea of ESSENCE to bring these ideas together. Next, we'll talk about different aspects of how children develop, as that will inform a lot of our work later on. Finally, we're going to look at the theory behind anxiety, a perennial issue in my clinic.

Remember, however, that **all children are different**. This is true for typically developing children, but even more so for our children who develop differently. Therefore, what I talk about might not be a picture-perfect description of your child – and that is ok. These are general principles of child development, and brief sketches of several common conditions. However, I'd still encourage you to read every chapter. Even if you think a chapter isn't going to be relevant. As we'll learn, neurodevelopmental disorders can (and often do) overlap with each other, so you might recognise something about your child in unexpected places. Equally, when reading about child development, while some bits may seem way off in the future for your child and not relevant, it is still helpful to know where you're going.

When you go on to read up more about some of the conditions mentioned, you might come across terms like 'neurodiversity' and 'neurotypical'. *Neurodiversity* is the idea that *all* brains are different. In the same way that human beings are diverse in their personalities, races, genders, and heights, they can also be diverse in how their brains work (how they understand things, what they are good at, and what they find difficult). *Neurotypical* refers to the 'majority neurotype' – people who are typically developing, and whose brains work the same way as most other peoples' brains. Some people, however, are '*neurodivergent*' meaning their brain works in a way that is different from most people's. Within this, there are lots of 'minority neurotypes' – people whose brain thinks differently in a specific way. For example, an Autistic person could be said to have an 'Autistic neurotype' – an Autistic way of thinking that is different to how most people think. Likewise for ADHD and other neurodevelopmental disorders we will talk about in this book.

Neurodiversity is often combined with the social model of disability, which points out that what is disabling to someone are barriers in society (such as lack of adaptations, lack of understanding, or stigma) rather than a person's differences. Combined with the idea of neurodiversity, this be used to help society understand, value and accept people developing differently for who they are; recognise their strengths as well as their difficulties; and realise what they can add to society, rather than seeing them as someone who can't do something.[1] This is a really important idea, but sadly not one I've

---

1    Indeed, neurodiversity suggests that the term 'neurodevelopmental disorder' is unhelpful as 'disorder' suggests there is something 'disordered' about the person, and does not recognise the strengths of that person's neurotype. In this book, I tend to refer to children as 'developing differently', as it doesn't refer to any one diagnosis, and (unlike 'disorder') doesn't suggest that there must be something 'wrong' with a child. However, I will use the term 'neurodevelopmental disorder' when referring to the formal medical diagnoses, as this is the medically correct terminology at the time of writing.

got space to cover in this book. My focus is on helping you (rather than society) to understand and support your child. However, this is a concept you will almost certainly come across in your reading, and one worth considering, particularly when trying to advocate for your child, or help others to understand your child.

## UNDERSTANDING AUTISM

Autism is probably the most well known out of the conditions I'll cover, and the area where there are probably the most books and resources available. Because it is well known, it is often the diagnosis people (sometimes wrongly) jump to if they think their child might be developing differently, so we need to be clear about what Autism is and is not.

I explain Autism to children (including siblings) using an idea I learned about from Tony Attwood and Carol Gray. To paraphrase:

> There are five senses, aren't there? You can see, hear, touch, taste, and smell. But there is also a sixth sense – the social sense. It helps us understand how other people might be feeling, and what they might be thinking. It tells us how to make and keep friends, how to play together, how to have conversations. However, some people have difficulty with one of their senses, don't they? Some people are blind or partially sighted. Other people are hard of hearing or deaf. What sorts of things do you think might help them? Maybe white lines on steps so they are easier to see? Someone to guide them around the school? Having things written down, not just said? Now imagine you have a difficulty in the social sense. What sorts of things do you think might help them?[2]

I love how creative children can be when given this explanation of Autism, which both helps them see Autism as a part of everyday life, and at the same time encourages them to think about how they can help an Autistic person – without even using the word 'Autism'. It also encapsulates the core difficulty of Autism: understanding 'the social sense'.

---

2   Carol has taken this concept and turned this into a fab lesson plan you can buy: *The Sixth Sense II: Sharing Information about Autism Spectrum Disorders with General Education Students* (Future Horizons, 2002).

If you are a young child with difficulty understanding others' thoughts, feelings, or motivations, then you might struggle to understand why you should take turns, why the rules others make up should apply to you, and why on earth you shouldn't win! You might not realise that what you are saying or doing others might see as rude, or might hurt their feelings. You also might struggle to recognise or predict others' emotions. For example, is my friend shouting because they are excited or angry? Maybe I know my friend wants to play with this toy, but I might not appreciate how upset they are, or what that feels like when I take it because I really want it. That might also make it harder to make and keep friends – to respond to their feelings and their interests in the way they expect, or to know when they are being friendly and when they are lying or making fun of you, or how to manage fall-outs. Incidentally, Autistic people can also have trouble recognising their own emotions too, meaning emotions can sometimes appear suddenly rather than as a slow build-up.

If you have difficulty with the social sense, you might struggle to fully grasp what others are trying to say. When someone walks into the office in a huff and says 'I'm fine', you *know* that's a lie because that social sense of yours tells you that is a load of crap and they are either angry or upset, but an Autistic person might either not pick up these non-verbal cues, or they might be less sure how to interpret those cues given the person just said they are fine. If a teacher says your name and gives you a look, you know they are giving you a warning, but an Autistic child might not get this and think they are about to be asked a question.

Autism can also make it harder to express yourself (especially when it comes to emotions). If you find people so hard to understand, you might not have as much motivation to interact, communicate, and (for some young children) learn language. Or, when you interact, you might find that people aren't responding how you are wanting, expecting, or in a way that is motivating for you. If you're struggling to add things like tone of voice and eye contact, it might make it harder to make your points, indicate that it is someone else's turn to talk, or that you want to start talking. This means it can become so much easier to be misinterpreted, misunderstood, or not even listened to!

Not picking up on this social sense can also cause a lot of anxiety. If you don't know what others' thoughts, feelings, or motivations are, it makes it harder to know what they are going to do, or how they will act. This problem is compounded by people without Autism having an awful habit of changing their mind or their plans, being emotional and erratic, and following these weird social rules that nobody has written down (such as 'it isn't socially acceptable to hug your primary school teacher, but it is ok to hug mum', or 'it is socially acceptable to be more casual and tease your boss a little on a work night out, but not back in the office the next day'). I often describe this as being a bit like your first day on a new job. You don't know anybody, you aren't quite sure how everything works yet, you don't know the unwritten rules of the office (such as the fact everyone knows that the desk just on the left as you walk into the hot-desking area in room A at work is *my* desk, even though nobody is meant to have assigned desks), who is in charge, who not to pi** off, who you can have a laugh with and who you can't. Your first few days, you're nervous that you're about to make a mistake, or put your foot in it by telling the wrong joke to the wrong person.

So what would you do with that sort of anxiety? As we will learn, what most people do when they are anxious is to try and control things, and keep things the same. So guess what? That's what Autistic people do. Same route to school, same foods for dinner, everything in a certain place. Even if you are feeling less anxious, having that order and certainty can help keep you feeling relaxed – the world becomes a predictable and safe place. Equally, if you have difficulty with the social sense, you might find things or facts more interesting than people. In fact, without those pesky social distractions, you can become very knowledgeable, and find collecting facts and objects soothing – creating order in a chaotic world.

A lot of Autistic people also have a lot of sensory interests and aversions, and they are part of the diagnostic criteria for Autism. However, lots of people (especially people developing differently) can have these too, so I've written a separate section on sensory stuff later on in this step: 'Understanding sensory sensitivities'.

Autistic people can have a number of unique strengths too. These are quite variable, but common examples include:

- loyalty

- attention to detail

- honesty

- thinking in a systematic way

- an affinity for children or animals

- efficiency

- a great knowledge of specific topics

- being extremely persistent and determined.

However, Autism is a *hugely* variable condition. Plenty of Autistic people are highly articulate, have their own family, friendships, and are highly skilled at what they do. While I've talked about lots of difficulties – this does not mean Autistic people *can't* do these things. For example Autistic people can and often do understand others thoughts, feelings, or motivations. However, for many, it requires more effort, it isn't as 'automatic', and they may be more prone to making errors. Therefore, while they might have to work a bit harder to fit in with a non-Autistic world, to most people they seem like everyone else. Indeed, many Autistic people find Autistic traits advantageous. Often, what this group wants and benefits most from is people just understanding and accepting them for who they are, and that they think in a different way to other people.

However, there are many Autistic people who find themselves impacted to a much greater extent, and need a much greater level of support. This can be due to the particular way their Autism presents, the difficulties that come with being Autistic in a world built by and for people without Autism, or because they have another neurodevelopmental disorder as well, which makes it harder to learn strategies to work with their Autism. This is particularly true of those who also have an Intellectual Disability. Therefore, it is not just whether a child is Autistic or not that it is important, we also need to consider their developmental level, the way Autism presents for them, what support they have, and any other conditions they have too.

I think it is really important for a child and family to get to know their Autism – how it presents for them. When I do this with parents, I use the NHS Inform (www.nhsinform.scot) page on Autism. This has a really nice overview of what Autism is, and how it presents at different ages. I'll go through and think about which bits of the many presentations do and don't fit with their child to build up a picture of their Autism. It is also has some great myth-busting material, and goes into more detail on things like how Autism presents differently in girls, what causes Autism, and warnings about so-called 'treatments' for Autism.

If you want more information on Autism, I recommend looking at the NHS Inform page and the National Autistic Society (www.autism.org.uk).

## KEY POINTS

✓ Autistic people have difficulty with the 'social sense'. This can make communicating (both with and without words) and understanding other people (their thoughts, feelings and motivations) harder.

✓ Autistic people can have particular interests, need for routines, or other ways of creating and cataloguing order in the world.

✓ Autism is highly variable – some people require little to no support to be completely independent, while others (particularly if they have other difficulties too) require much more support.

✓ Autistic people have strengths too, such as loyalty, eye for detail, perseverance, and honesty.

✓ Two great resources to read up more about Autism are www.nhsinform.scot and www.autism.org.uk.

## UNDERSTANDING INTELLECTUAL DISABILITY

I need to start off by explaining Intellectual Disability (sometimes called a Learning Disability) and Learning *Difficulty*. A lot of people confuse these, or talk about Learning Difficulties rather than Learning Disability because it sounds kinder, which I completely understand. However, there is a *big* difference between an Intellectual or

Learning Disability and a Learning Difficulty, and we need to be clear on the difference.

A Learning Difficulty, or technically a *Specific Learning Difficulty*, is the name for a group of conditions that interfere with learning. These include:

- Dyslexia (difficulties with reading)

- Dysgraphia (difficulties with writing)

- Dyscalculia (difficulties with numbers and their patterns).

People with a Specific Learning Difficulty are unaffected in their intelligence. The difficulty isn't in their overall ability to learn, it is in *one particular way* of learning.

For people with an Intellectual Disability, their intelligence *is* affected. People with an Intellectual Disability have an IQ (a way of measuring overall intelligence) below 70. Only 2% of the population have an IQ of 70 or below. For those of you who don't like numbers, imagine 100 children (in the UK that is a little over three mainstream school classes). Line them up in order of their IQ, with the lowest IQ at the front and the highest IQ at the back. On average, the first two children in the line will have an IQ of 70 or below.

People with an Intellectual Disability also have difficulties with adaptive behaviour. Adaptive behaviour is a fancy way of saying 'skills people learn in order to live independent lives'. This isn't about stuff a child learns in school. It's about things like being able to order off a menu, tying shoe laces, cleaning and dressing themselves, using the toilet; right through to more advanced stuff like organising holidays, making and evaluating choices, and managing bills (stuff we'd only expect people to be able to do when they are adults). Like with IQ, people with an Intellectual Disability are in the 2% of people who find these skills most challenging to develop and put into practice.

Put simply, we do an IQ test to measure the *ability* a child's brain has for learning and problem solving. We do an adaptive behaviour test to measure *what the child has actually learned so far.*

There is no denying that people with Intellectual Disabilities will face significant difficulties – their IQ and adaptive behaviour tests spell it out in black and white. People with Intellectual Disabilities will have difficulty gaining the sorts of qualifications most teenagers have when they leave school, and may well need extra support in employment, self-care, and managing a house. People with Intellectual Disabilities may need legal protections too, as they *can* have difficulty making informed decisions on how to spend their money, about their health-care, or about where to live. Some may never learn to talk.

*But* an IQ test only measures a small part of who a person is. They do not measure a person's capacity for creativity, kindness, determination, or honesty. It doesn't measure a person's capacity to love, work hard, or be a friend. In fact, in my experience people with Intellectual Disabilities are some of the nicest people you'll meet. Yes, their IQ may make some of these things harder, and learning new skills will always be a challenge for people with Intellectual Disabilities. But that does not prevent them being a valuable part of their community, and contributing to society. It does not stop them having experiences, and living happy, healthy lives. Depending on their level of Intellectual Disability, they may have successful long-term romantic relationships, be valued team members at work, and (just like everyone else) people with an Intellectual Disability can keep learning new skills, albeit more slowly, to become increasingly independent. Their IQ may define their disability, but people with an Intellectual Disability are so much more than their disability!

So what is life like for a child with an Intellectual Disability? Well, learning *anything* suddenly becomes much harder... and think about how much there is to learn – how to walk, talk, use the toilet, and that's before we even get to school!

Ok, learning how to move about and use the toilet is important. However, communication is, in my experience, the biggest issue. Language is really complex, which makes it hard to learn. So let's imagine you don't have language – you can't read, write, or talk, and you don't fully understand gestures. How would you let people know you are hungry? Tired? Don't want to do something? Chances are, you'll start communicating using your behaviour. You start to bash things, throw things, do whatever it takes to get someone to notice and give you want you want or need.

A child with an Intellectual Disability may be able to crack the code of language. However, just because they are able to use language doesn't necessarily mean they fully understand it, or use it how we'd expect. They might say 'I want a cookie', but they might have picked up that phrase and really mean 'I'm hungry' or 'it's lunch time', so you can't take it at face value.

But language isn't the only thing. I mentioned earlier that Intellectual Disability also affects a person's ability to make decisions. For example, a child deciding whether it is safe to cross the road, a teenager working out whether to spend £20 on food or Pokémon cards, or an adult whether to spend £100 on rent or takeaway. This involves understanding cause and effect, often on quite complex matters. For example, how much money you have in your bank account could be hard to grasp – it is just a series of numbers, not cold hard cash in your hand. What is easier to grasp is that I have lots of bank notes in my wallet, I can go to a cash machine and keep getting more bank notes, and I want a takeaway, so why not get one? Thinking about how much money will be left in the account and when the next rent payment is due may be challenging for a person with an Intellectual Disability to weigh up.

While some people with an Intellectual Disability may never develop language to understand these decisions, plenty will. With the right support, they may be able to make many of these decisions, although some may still need other people to be given legal power to ensure the decisions they are making are safe and in their best interests. For example, someone to ensure bills are paid and that there is food in the fridge, and having a separate account (without an overdraft) which the person can use for spending money on things they want.

To help the parents I work with get into the mindset of their child, I often ask them 'I know Joe is 12 years old, but in terms of his learning and development, how old do you think he is?' We then compare this age, say, 8 or 9, to what most other children are able to do at that age (I use Carolyn Meggitt's book *Child Development* that I mentioned in the introduction for this). Often, Joe is actually developmentally younger than his parents thought – he can't yet do a lot of things 8 or 9 year olds can do. When we keep going back, we might find that developmentally, his skills are more like that of a 6 year old. However, it is important to remember that while 12 year old Joe may be developmentally at the age of 6, and may understand things in the same way as a 6 year old, *he is not 6 years old!* He has 12 years of experience to draw upon. He has the body, size, strength, and hormones of a 12 year old. He is also seeing what other 12 year olds are doing and perhaps wanting to do the same. He also has the rights, challenges, wants, and needs of other 12 year olds. It also doesn't mean that he will always be mentally at the level of a 6 year old, or that he will always be 6 years behind his chronological age. Just like everyone else, he will learn and develop, but Joe, like other children with Intellectual Disability, will learn at a slower rate. This means he will keep learning and developing, but it also means that the gap between Joe and his peers will get bigger, at least until his peers stop developing new skills.

For people with an Intellectual Disability, it can be incredibly frustrating trying to communicate their wants and needs. No wonder they have tantrums or meltdowns – so often *we just don't listen* (or at least, not in the right way). It can also be hard for them to understand what we are saying – we have an awful habit of using far too many words, far too many big words, and saying far too much too quickly and all at once. Life can be really confusing for these kids.

For example, we might say 'we're going to Gran's today, but we need to go to up the motorway to the supermarket to get some petrol first', but from this they only take in 'Gran' – the rest is too much, too quick, with too many big words. As a result, your child may think 'why are we driving this way – we never normally go this way to Gran's, where are we going?' and get really upset. They may hear mum in the front of the car saying 'supermarket' but they might not know what 'supermarket' means – they might recognise the Tesco, ASDA, or Aldi logos on the shopping bags, so know when they see them that is where they are going, but you've not brought any bags with you as you're just going for fuel. On the way there, a child with an Intellectual Disability may not understand how the world works, and so doesn't get why (for example) we can't stop the car on the middle of the motorway to look at the cows in the field, or why with a shop literally FULL of things to eat within eyesight, you wouldn't go in there to get some of it, and instead pull up then almost immediately drive away – what was the point of that?!

This is why our job is so often about good communication, routine, and teaching new skills. When we do this, we help the world become much more predictable and understandable to our kids, and help them take part in and influence the world they live in.

## KEY POINTS

✓ A Learning *Difficulty*, such as Dyslexia, is a difficulty with one specific part of learning.

✓ An Intellectual Disability (also known as a Learning Disability) is where a person has an IQ (ability to learn) and adaptive behaviour (life skills) that are significantly impaired.

✓ An Intellectual Disability can make a lot of things harder, including communication, understanding how the world works, understanding cause and effect, making decisions, etc.

✓ It can be helpful to work out a child's developmental age – the age most children have the skills they have. However, children will have the experiences, needs, wants, and challenges that come with their actual age.

✓ There is *so much* more to a person than their IQ. An IQ doesn't measure a person's kindness, creativity, warmth, or empathy. IQ defines an Intellectual Disability, but an Intellectual Disability does not define the person.

## UNDERSTANDING GLOBAL DEVELOPMENTAL DELAY

Global Developmental Delay is a diagnosis given to children who are very delayed in at least two of these areas:

- using and understanding language

- working out how to control their body, such as being able to pick up a grape (a fine motor skill) or walking (a gross motor skill)

- their social and emotional skills (such as making friends and learning how to self-soothe)

- their play and adaptive behaviour (such as developing increasingly complex play, and learning how to feed themselves)

- their cognitive development (learning skills, solving problems, understanding concepts).

Usually, kids are identified quite early on (within the first four years of life) as having a global developmental delay. However, Global Developmental Delay as a *diagnosis* is a bit odd. I tend to think of it as a 'holding' diagnosis. It means that the child is not developing at the rate we would expect, and we need to keep a close eye on them. Some kids catch up, but for other children, this is the first sign of what will later be diagnosed as an Intellectual Disability, Autism, ADHD, or another neurodevelopmental disorder. Because it is a temporary diagnosis, there is frustratingly little research on this condition. Likewise, there is often a lack of information given to parents on what this means and what you can do.

Global Developmental Delay means your child is delayed in their development, and delayed enough for people to be concerned. The good news is that this label (should) mean that healthcare and education professionals are keeping a close eye on your child, and offering therapy or strategies to help boost your child's development. For example, Speech and Language Therapy to help your child develop language or other communication skills; Physiotherapy or Occupational Therapy to help your child develop their motor skills; time in a small, supportive nursery or play group setting to help your child develop social, emotional, play, and cognitive skills.

But of course, there will be plenty you can do to help your child too. There are lots of books and resources with ideas for how to help your child develop (again, I love the Meggitt book) – just remember to do activities based on where your child is in their *developmental age*, not by how old they are. Equally, if you are not already linked into these services, go to your GP and ask for support and advice for specific strategies to help with your child's development.

However, you need to remember that these are strategies that can *help* your child's development; this does not mean they will 'cure' your child's developmental differences. If this is the first sign of Autism, an Intellectual Disability, or some other condition, lots of help to boost your child's development won't stop them having that condition – your child's brain is just wired that way. However, that doesn't mean we shouldn't put strategies into place – even if your child has these difficulties, early interventions will still be helpful. A parent who does lots of early intervention to stimulate their child's development and whose child then goes on to have Autism or an Intellectual Disability isn't a failure, and they didn't do anything wrong. In fact, they will have given their child a head start in challenging their difficulties.

Importantly, if your child still has a diagnosis of Global Developmental Delay by the time they are 8, it is time to ask your GP or Paediatrician why they still have the diagnosis. Global Developmental Delay is meant to be an early years diagnosis. There isn't a clear line as to when a Global Developmental Delay diagnosis needs to be reviewed or should 'expire', but for me, 8 is (in *most* circumstances – there are a number of factors which would make me want to wait longer) when I'd expect there to be a plan to remove or replace the diagnosis. Delaying replacing a Global Developmental Delay diagnosis isn't fair to the parents or the child, as it holds them in limbo, and can mean they don't meet criteria to access certain services. So, if you are wondering why your child still has this Global Developmental Delay diagnosis, never be afraid to ask your child's healthcare professionals. A good healthcare professional will have a good reason for waiting which they can talk you through, or be willing to discuss the appropriateness of a Global Development Delay diagnosis and what other assessments might be needed now they are older.

## KEY POINTS

✓ Global Developmental Delay is a 'holding' diagnosis – it means your child is significantly delayed in at least two areas of development.

✓ Some children with Global Developmental Delay 'catch up', but others don't, and will get a diagnosis of a different neurodevelopmental disorder.

✓ Global Developmental Delay means people have identified that your child may need closer attention and more support to develop. There is plenty you can do at home too to support their development, but if your child does not 'catch up', **it does not mean you have failed** – if they have an underlying condition, the support won't change that, but it will give them the best possible start.

✓ If your child is 8 years old and the Global Developmental Delay diagnosis has not yet been replaced with something else, talk to your child's doctors as to why they still have the diagnosis, and if a more long-term diagnosis is needed now.

## UNDERSTANDING ADHD

When looking for ADHD (Attention Deficit Hyperactivity Disorder), clinicians look for three key things.

The first is inattention. Now, lots of kids can struggle to pay attention and listen when people are talking or giving instructions (particularly if they are talking about boring stuff, as so many adults do...). However, a child with ADHD will be far more distractible than other children their age, to the point where you have to keep what you are saying really short and direct else they'll be onto something else. They might struggle to start or finish what they are doing (even if it is something enjoyable) because they keep getting distracted. Getting distracted can also mean a child with ADHD is more likely to lose things or be forgetful. Given all these difficulties, it is no wonder that kids with ADHD can start to avoid tasks – it can be so hard for them to get to the end of them!

Have you ever had one of those days when life chooses to pile it on? You've got a to-do list a mile long, people constantly interrupting you, and a jam-packed schedule. As the day goes along, no matter how many coffees you have you start to let stuff slip. You find it harder and harder to listen to people, and find yourself drifting off into thought when people are talking to you. You'll start to forget things, and think you have done things when you haven't. You say you'll add things to your to-do list then forget to add them, leave activities half-finished (or don't even get started on them) because you get called away and forget to come back to it. You put your phone down and end up leaving it behind. When you do get some time, you'll see a big job you really should do, but feel you just can't face it, and start to avoid it and do other little jobs instead. These are the days I try to remember when I'm trying to understand what it is like to have the inattention side of ADHD.

The next is impulsivity. Impulsivity is that 'impulse' you get to follow your emotions and punch that person who just said something insulting to you. To say 'Really?' in a surprised tone when a colleague tells you they've lost weight. To buy that chocolate bar you see by the checkout. To do that thing you know you really shouldn't but... whoops now we've done it. Usually, when we get such an 'impulse' to do something, our brain gives us a few moments of thinking time. It puts the brakes on and says 'do you *really* want to do that?', and we get a moment to decide before we act.

For kids with ADHD, they aren't given those precious few moments to pause, think, and decide – or if they do they are much shorter. That can mean they blurt out answers to questions in school, keep talking and talking and talking in conversations, perhaps say or do things that (on reflection) they know they shouldn't but they had the impulse to do it and didn't get a moment to 'pause' and stop themselves. It can mean they have difficulty when they have to wait their turn or work with others as part of a team. Impulsivity effects emotions too. When someone stands on your foot, you might feel a flush of anger, but you get a chance to take a deep breath and reason with yourself that it was an accident, which stops you reacting. A child with ADHD on the other hand might not get that chance, and so react really strongly to things that (to other people) seem really minor, as they get carried away in the emotion before they even get a chance to try and manage their emotions.

How many times have you done something, and then as soon as you've done it thought 'Oh no, why on earth did I do that? I *knew* it was wrong'. Like saying something you know you shouldn't? It is a really awful feeling. That is your brain not giving you that thinking time, leaving you to act impulsively. Worse, when you've said or done something, it is often embarrassing, hard to backtrack or difficult say sorry – so you might feel you need to cover it up or defend it, even though it's actually not something you wanted to do in the first place! Now imagine that happens to you constantly, on a daily basis.

Finally, clinicians look for hyperactivity – a child who cannot sit still, who is always squirming, moving, running, bouncing, climbing, jumping, talking, and seems to have an infinite supply of energy. The most common descriptions I get from parents of younger kids are 'like he's got a motor running inside him' or 'like he's the Duracell bunny with fresh batteries'. The older kids with ADHD, while less physically over active, tend to describe a feeling of restlessness, agitation, that they can't settle.

While all three of these difficulties (inattention, impulsivity, and hyperactivity) often occur together (in what is sometimes called the 'combined subtype'), they don't have to. Some children have an 'inattentive subtype', also known as Attention Deficit Disorder, or ADD. For these kids, their main difficulty is focusing their attention and dealing with distractions. These kids can still have *some* difficulties with hyperactivity and impulsivity, but they aren't as significant. This is more commonly seen in girls, and children with this subtype can sometimes be overlooked as they tend to fly under the radar. It tends to be hyperactivity and impulsivity that leads kids to inadvertently get into trouble, but children with the inattentive subtype may be able to stay in their seat and manage their behaviour ok. However, they might be really struggling to focus on the teacher (so they might start to fall behind in class), be disorganised or always running late, and keep leaving things behind. Less commonly, some kids have the 'hyperactive-impulsive subtype'. For them, their biggest difficulties are thinking before acting, and being constantly on the go, but it is easier for them to manage distractions and focus.

A lot of the difficulties kids with ADHD face are related to differences in a part of their brain called the frontal lobe, and the connections to and from it. This is the bit of the brain that, among other things, helps us to focus our attention, and that gives us those few moments of 'thinking space' before we act on our impulses. For children with ADHD there are several medications which can help, but medication is only part of the answer – parenting strategies and supports are also important.

A colleague of mine, Beth, once described it to me like this: imagine the frontal lobe of a child with ADHD being an engine running out of fuel, so it's not working very well – coughing and spluttering along. Medication puts fuel into the engine and helps it run a lot better. It sometimes takes a few goes to find the right fuel (i.e. medication), and there are a few kids who don't find a medication that works for them, but if you find it, the child finds it much easier to focus and think. This can be great, and allow kids to get the education they deserve, and get on better with their friends and teachers.

The trouble is, for children who have ADHD *and* another neurodevelopmental disorder, it sometimes isn't that simple. For some of our kids with ADHD and something else, the engine is *built differently*. This means that for some of these kids, medication *might* not make as much of a difference, because their brain is just wired differently. Your child's doctor will be the best person to consider if medication might help your child, but this should always be a joint decision with parents and your child (if able).

There are plenty of other books out there for parents of children with ADHD (such as *Taking Charge of ADHD* by Russell Barkley (Guilford Press, 2020), or *Late, Lost and Unprepared* by Joyce Cooper-Kahn and Laurie Dietzel (Woodbine House, 2008)). However, a lot of kids developing differently have difficulties with impulsivity, inattention, and/or hyperactivity without having ADHD. Therefore, we need to be aware of what these difficulties are like and the effects they can have, so we can understand our kid's difficulties and how to help.

## KEY POINTS

✓ ADHD is defined by three key symptoms – hyperactivity, impulsivity, and inattention. While all children might be very active, impulsive, and struggle to focus their attention, for kids with ADHD these difficulties are significantly greater than for their peers.

✓ Inattention is struggling to focus on something, and getting distracted really easily.

✓ Impulsivity is not having those crucial few moments before doing something where your brain asks you 'do you really want to do that?' before acting.

✓ Hyperactivity means being on the go, full of energy, always talking, running, jumping, climbing, moving.

✓ Medication can help some kids with ADHD, but some kids with ADHD and other conditions may be less likely to respond well to medication. Your child's doctor will be the best person to advise you on if ADHD medication may help your child.

## UNDERSTANDING SENSORY SENSITIVITIES

Children who develop differently experience the world differently. They can be more sensitive (hypersensitive) or less sensitive (hyposensitive) to certain senses.

People who are hypersensitive will often avoid sensory input, because it is too much. If you want to experience this, wear a thick blindfold for five minutes, then go outside on a bright summer's day and take the blindfold off. For a few moments before your eyes adjust, you're hypersensitive to light – your eyes are physically taking in too much information, and it feels really uncomfortable. To manage this, you might close your eyes, look away, look down, wear sunglasses, or anything to get away from all the bright light and make it manageable. When a sense is hypersensitive, it is like this sense 'has the volume turned up'. It makes tastes more intense, smells more overpowering, sounds louder, sights brighter, and pain more severe, for example. So, when a child is hypersensitive to a sense, what is fine for you may be really uncomfortable, even painful for them, and so they will try to get back to a comfortable level by getting away from it. It's like walking into a nightclub with a hangover – the music and lights are just too loud and you want out NOW!

The alternative, hyposensitivity, can also be imagined this way. Think back to when you had a really bad cold, and you were all stuffed up. Chances are you'd have been struggling to taste anything. After a while, you might want a really spicy curry, or lots of salt and vinegar on your fish and chips just to help you taste *something*. You're seeking out lots more sensory input, because you're not getting enough. When a child is hyposensitive, they 'have the volume turned down'. That means tastes are bland, smells are faint, sounds are quiet, sights are dull, and pain doesn't register as much. A child who is hyposensitive is going to try and seek out and relish these sensations because life without them is dull!

At school, we learn there are five senses – touch, taste, sight, smell, and hearing. These are actually the five *external* senses. There are also internal senses. There is the *vestibular* sense – this is your sense of balance. If you stand on one leg and close your eyes, it is this sense that keeps you upright. There is also the *proprioceptive* sense. This is about being aware of your body in space – how you are moving, how much you're contracting your muscles, etc. If you close your eyes and touch your nose, you've used your proprioceptive sense to work out where your nose is in relation to your hand, and how much force to use to ensure you're not punching yourself in the face or poking yourself in the eye. There are lots of other internal senses too, such as *pain* and *hunger*, as well as the sense that tells you when your bladder or bowels are full.

Each of these senses is independent, so while one might be hyper-sensitive, another can be hyposensitive. Equally, while each one of these can *tend* to be set at a certain level of hyper or hypo sensitivity, this can change depending on, for example, if the child is stressed or upset. These can also change as a child develops, and so you may find effective strategies for managing some sensory inputs change.

Over time, our brain adjusts to the level of input we receive. For example, if you go to a nightclub, for the first 15 minutes or so, the music probably feels incredibly loud. However, over time, your brain gets used to this, and while you know it is loud, it isn't quite as hard to bear. When you leave again, the chances are you'll be speaking in a loud voice and everything will seem really quiet. This is because, again, your brain has to adjust to the new, lower level of sensory input. This process of adjustment is what we call *habituation*.

Sometimes, children who develop differently can take longer to habituate. Do you have a friend whose house smells funny? Maybe they use lots of scented candles, maybe it is an old and stuffy build-ing, or maybe they simply need to work on their personal hygiene. When you visit, you probably only notice that smell for the first few minutes, then your brain kind of tunes it out (unless they smell *really* bad). Your child, however, might take much longer before they get used to that smell (and may comment on it!). The same goes for put-ting on socks and shoes. When you first put on socks and shoes, you'll notice what it feels like, but pretty quickly you'll stop registering the sensation – you habituate to it. However, for a child developing differently, they may keep noticing the constraint of their socks and sweaty shoes for much longer before they habituate, which might feel quite uncomfortable or unpleasant.

In the next step on the Right Environment, I'm going to talk a lot more about sensory processing, and how we need to use our understanding of sensory needs to adjust your child's environment to suit their sensory needs. However, for now, it is enough to know that children developing differently can experience the world in a radically different way from us, so we need to consider what *their* experiences might be, and not assume it will be just like ours.

## KEY POINTS

✓ There are five external senses (sight, taste, touch, smell, hearing), as well as several internal senses (including feeling full/hungry, having full bowels or bladder, pain, etc.).

✓ Children developing differently are more likely to have some senses that are hyper or hyposensitive.

✓ Hypersensitive is when the 'volume' of a sense is high, so a child is trying to block out, avoid, or reduce a sensation so it is comfortable again. Hyposensitive is when the 'volume' of a sense is too low, so a child might not notice things, or be trying to get more of that sense.

✓ Habituation is when our brains try and adjust to a sensation to get comfortable with it. This can take longer for children developing differently.

## UNDERSTANDING PHYSICAL HEALTH

While this book is focused on how our kid's brains develop, it is important to remember the rest of their body too, as this can also affect their behaviour.

One of the most common physical complaints the kids I see have is hypermobility (lax joints). Many people have hypermobility and it doesn't cause them any problems. However, for some people, having looser tendons and ligaments can mean their joints overflex, causing injury to the tissues around the joint, causing pain. Likewise, it can put strain on muscles as they have to work harder to keep joints in place, causing tiredness and pain (which can also lead to difficulty sleeping).

One of the ways we manage this is by pacing. Overactivity often leads to over-working muscles, tendons and joints, and leads to pain. Therefore, we try to make sure that your child isn't doing too much physical activity *for them* – this might be different to other children. Likewise, underactivity will mean losing strength and condition in muscles, and make lower levels of activity more painful and tiring. Therefore, we try to get a balance – not too much activity, and not too little. When working with families, we'll try and work out how much activity is too much for their child, and how much is too little, and try and ensure that each day is getting roughly the same activity level, right in their happy medium zone. The tricky thing tends to be that after a few good days, kids feel better, and so want to do more, which then sets them back as they've done too much. If your child has hypermobility, their GP, Paediatrician, or Physiotherapist will be able to advise you on how best manage this, and how to get their activity levels right for them.

Many children I see also have constipation or diarrhoea. This can make them feel really uncomfortable. On top of this, a child developing differently might have difficulty explaining or showing what is wrong or explaining how they are feeling, especially for things that are 'internal'. Therefore, this communication might come out as behaviour (often seemingly out of the blue). Bowel issues can also create problems toilet training, as going to the toilet could be a difficult, potentially painful experience. The GPs, Paediatricians, and Dieticians I work with are fantastic at looking at what changes in diet might help with these difficulties, if there is a particular thing in food they are struggling to process, or using food supplements/medicated drinks to help things... *ahem*... bind or loosen. If your child is having any bowel issues, get them checked out, and see if there is anything you can do to improve their bowels, as that might also help with their learning and behaviour too.

Lots of kids hate brushing their teeth, but this can be particularly true of kids developing differently. There are some amazing Occupational Therapists out there with great ideas for what can help – such as special toothbrushes, timers, unflavoured toothpaste, etc. Likewise, there are some dentists who take a special interest in kids developing differently and have great ideas and strategies that can help. However, even with all the best tips and tricks, getting more than a few seconds of teeth brushing can be hard for some kids, leaving children susceptible to cavities. This (and losing baby teeth) can leave kids suffering from dental pain. I also see a lot of kids who grind their teeth, or who have conditions which mean they have poorer enamel on their teeth making them more susceptible to decay, amplifying their risk of dental pain. It is therefore really important we get their teeth checked regularly so we can be on top of any problems that might be starting to develop, particularly for children who struggle to use language, as they may not be able to tell us their tooth hurts. Instead, they will likely show us through their behaviour – such as chewing or biting more, salivating more, or banging their head.

Kids developing differently can sometimes be prone to ear infections. These can be acutely painful. If a child can tell you where the pain is, you can use your over the counter children's pain relief as a starting point. However, if a child doesn't have the language or ability to communicate that they are in pain, or where it is, then (just as with dental pain) they might start banging their head to try and get rid of the pain, or create a new, bigger pain that they can at least control. If you suspect your child is having prolonged ear pain, if it is happening regularly, or if you are in any way concerned, make sure you get your child checked out by a doctor.

Children developing differently can also be prone to Epilepsy.[3] While most people think of seizures as the classic Tonic-Clonic seizure where a person falls to the floor and starts shaking, there are many other types of seizures. For example, absence seizures where a child is apparently unreachable and 'switched off', focal seizures which can involve unusual sensations or repetitive movements, or temporal seizures which can cause unusual behaviours. Often (but not always) children will start to realise when they are about to have one of these

---

3    Plenty of children develop differently and don't have Epilepsy – this section isn't designed to scare you, just make you alert. I do come across a lot of children who have periods where they seem unreachable, and parents are concerned this could be an absence seizure, but after investigation the conclusion is that it is a behaviour/not listening/lost in thought, etc. Nevertheless, it is important that you always take any concerns you have to a doctor for expert advice and possibly so they can investigate further.

events, and be able to sit down or shout for an adult, if they are awake at the time. Likewise, a child with good language and memory will, once they are old enough, know what is happening, what they will be like the other side of it, and what they need to do to try and keep themselves safe and recover properly. However, if a child doesn't have good language, they might communicate this with their behaviour (such as being sleepy, cranky, or trying to get your attention in some way), so we need to be alert not only for any seizures, but also what they do just before a seizure, in case that is part of how they communicate that they feel like they may be about to have one.

You'll have noticed a reoccurring theme with these health conditions: for children with good communication skills, a lot of these difficulties are easier to manage – they can tell you where the pain is, and you can respond. However, for kids developing differently, that isn't always the case – some of our kids have real difficulties with language and communicating, and so they have to resort to behaviour to try and get the message across, or try and distract themselves from the pain. Therefore, we as parents need to be vigilant for any new behaviours which may indicate pain, or a possible health issue that might cause pain.

For these reasons, it is especially important that a child developing differently and with limited communication is under the care of a GP or ideally a Paediatrician. With your help, they can look at whether behaviours could indicate a physical health problem, many of which can be treated or managed. Before I even start working with a child, I always want to check that they've had a doctor (and dentist) check them over for any possible physical health issues, as these could be driving some of the behaviours I'm being asked to help with. Similarly, we also need to remember that if a child is developing differently, they might have sensory issues, such as being hyposensitive to pain. This means they might not pick up that they have a health issue that needs looking at before it becomes more severe.

## KEY POINTS

✓ Children developing differently can be more susceptible to a number of health issues, including ear infections, dental pain, stomach/gut/bowel issues, hypomobility, and Epilepsy/seizures.

✓ Children developing differently may not be able to communicate, may not realise they have a health issue, or may by hyposensitive to pain.

✓ Health issues often drive behaviours, particularly in children who have trouble communicating verbally. Therefore, children should be under the care of a doctor and dentist to regularly check their physical health, and manage any health issues.

✓ Health issues should always be considered first as a possible cause for any new behaviours.

## THE ESSENCE OF NEURODEVELOPMENT DISORDERS

So far, I've talked about Autism, ADHD, and Intellectual Disability as if they are separate things. However, while each condition is different from the other, there are also a lot of areas where they overlap. Lots of children developing differently share a need (or benefit from) for sameness and consistency, have difficulties with communication, or often say the wrong thing, for example. They also have a habit of occurring together – if you have one condition you are more likely to have another. So far, I've just mentioned some of the most well known neurodevelopmental conditions, but I've only scratched the surface – there is also Developmental Coordination Disorder, Language Disorders, Tic Disorders, as well as a host of other conditions (such as Down's Syndrome) which can affect the way the brain develops.

Broadly, there are three big reasons for this overlap.

The first is our genes. There is not an 'Autism', 'Intellectual Disability' or 'ADHD' gene. Instead, there are the countless genes that come together to form the blueprint of how to make our brain. Each person's genes are unique, so their blueprint for building a brain will be unique, but they all follow the same broad pattern. However, there are some genes, some bits to the blueprint, which make it *more likely* a person will have Autism, an Intellectual Disability, ADHD, etc. Interestingly though, a lot of those genes are linked with more than one neurodevelopmental disorder. This means one collection of genes could increase the likelihood of a child having two or more conditions, not just one.

Second is that the brain is very interconnected. In your brain, there are 100 billion cells, each talking to 1000 other cells at 250 miles per hour across 100,000 miles of cable. That is a lot of information being sent and received very quickly, and in very complex patterns. If one area of the brain is a bit different, the effects of this can easily ripple out to other areas.

A lot of neurodevelopmental disorders are associated with quite advanced functions of the brain – areas like executive functioning (how we make decisions and pay attention), communication and language, and social cognition (understanding other's thoughts and feelings, etc.). They are skills which tend to be 'at the top of the pyramid'.

As we grow and develop, we learn new skills. Often, these new skills build on old skills (in the same way that you need to learn to walk before you can do the more advanced skill of learning to run). If one of the skills lower down on the pyramid is a bit different (and there can be a lot of these lower down skills) then that top bit of the pyramid might be a bit different, a bit wobbly, or can't be built – either that new skill is a bit different, perhaps doesn't work in the same way, or doesn't develop. This means that, especially for young kids, we might know they are developing differently, but we don't yet know *how* they will develop, or what diagnosis they will eventually get.

Finally, and perhaps most importantly, **diagnoses are man-made**. People like to label things. So, when they see a group of people who have similar difficulties, they like to give that a label, like 'Intellectual Disability'. However, there is not an 'Intellectual Disability' centre in the brain. God/mother nature/genetics/etc. did not set out to create one specific difference in how a child develops, that we have miraculously discovered and named. All we are doing is grouping collections of difficulties that tend to happen together, and giving them a name – we often don't know what the underlying cause is. When it comes to labelling neurodevelopmental disorders, we are a bit like a young child who goes to the farm for the first time and thinks that everything with four legs is a 'cow', and everything with wings is a 'chicken'. We're right that we are grouping things based on similar characteristics, but our descriptions aren't that useful except for working out what might trample us and what might peck us.

Therefore, rather than asking 'what diagnosis does this child have?', I find it much more helpful to ask 'what difficulties does this child have?' If a child has social difficulties, sure, we might look and see if we can call it Autism. However, the diagnosis itself isn't a support, it is a label – a communication tool.

Diagnoses can still be really useful. They can:

- help access support (in my opinion, support should be based on need, not diagnosis, but that's a story for another day)

- help us work out what kind of supports are more likely to be effective

- help us to research and understand people with similar patterns of strengths and difficulties

- help people understand how a person thinks

- sometimes allow people to accept/come to terms with their child's differences.

However, the diagnosis *itself* isn't going to change anything. That is not to say that getting a diagnosis doesn't make a difference – for a lot of parents, it can feel like a whole world of difference emotionally when I give their child a diagnosis. However, practically, very little changes – it is your child's specific pattern of strengths and difficulties that is important, and that doesn't need a diagnosis.

This is not a new idea. Prof Chris Gillberg set out the idea of ESSENCE (Early Symptomatic Syndromes Eliciting Neurodevelopmental Clinical Examinations) in 2010. He made the point that lots of conditions that I've already mentioned (plus others) present with behaviour and learning problems at an early age, often occur together, often look similar (particularly at an early age), and have similar things which make developing them more likely. Therefore, we need to focus on the child's differences and difficulties across all areas of development and how we help them. Even after a child has one diagnosis, we need to be alert to the idea that they might have difficulties in other areas too. Indeed, I've met some children who don't meet criteria for *any* neurodevelopmental diagnosis, yet clearly have elements of lots of different diagnoses. This isn't to say we should do away with diagnoses – they can still be helpful to have along the way. However, diagnosis should not be our starting or ending point.

Ok, enough science. What does this *mean*? Well, it means that while these conditions are all different, they all have a lot in common, and respond well to the same sorts of strategies. This means I can write one book, but with strategies which will work for multiple conditions, not just one. Equally, it means I'll be focusing more on what a child's *difficulties* are, rather than what their diagnosis is. Specifically, the children I'm writing this for will likely have at least a few of the following:

- need for sameness and difficulty with change

- sensory seeking or avoiding behaviour

- communication difficulties

- difficulties with social skills, friendships, and relationships

- attention or concentration difficulties, and impulsivity.

- difficulty learning

- difficulties with mood (feeling sad, upset, angry, frustrated, stressed, or worried)

- difficulties with sleep

- challenging behaviour – things that hurt/put themselves or others at risk, or that might lead to them being excluded from things they enjoy – behaviours like hitting, kicking, spitting, etc.

Additionally, many of the children I see with these difficulties also have other physical health problems, such as those I discussed earlier.

So, when a get a referral for a child, I'm less interested in what diagnoses they have, and much more interested in what *their specific strengths and difficulties are*. A diagnosis tells me what these are likely to be, but it isn't the same as meeting the child and their parents. Likewise, I'm always sceptical when I receive a referral for a child who seems to have a diagnosis for every letter of the alphabet. Each new label *usually* explains even less of a child's presentation than the label before. In fact, because the child is being bounced from professional to professional and being given label after label, it suggests to me that nothing quite fits – this is a child who either has the wrong diagnoses, or (more likely) won't easily fit into *any* of these neat man-made diagnosis boxes we've made for them.

If you want to learn more about ESSENCE, and the conditions that slot into this way of thinking, Chris Gillberg's book *The ESSENCE of Autism and Other Neurodevelopmental Conditions* (Jessica Kingsley Publishers, 2021) is a great place to start.

## KEY POINTS

✓ Neurodevelopmental disorders all overlap. If you have one, you're more likely to have a second one too.

✓ Diagnoses themselves don't change much – they are a man-made shorthand for describing a particular collection of difficulties that often occur together.

✓ Because diagnoses are man-made, often kids don't fit neatly into our diagnoses. A child might have one diagnosis or several, but a diagnosis never describes everything about a child.

✓ It is much more helpful to look at what the child's difficulties (and of course strengths) are, and work with that. You don't need a diagnosis to understand what a child's difficulties are, and to start supporting them.

✓ This book focuses on a set of common difficulties I see in the kids I work with, and how to support those difficulties, rather than talking about specific diagnoses.

## UNDERSTANDING ATTACHMENT

So far, we've covered some of the things our children developing differently are likely to find difficult. However, while our kids might be developing differently, the *overall* broad pattern of their development will likely be similar to those who develop typically. They might be delayed or stuck, there might be things they struggle to do, and sometimes their development may happen in different ways to most other children. However, even though they are developing differently, their brain is still wired along the lines of everyone else's. Therefore, it is important we understand some of the stages and processes through which children typically develop, as these will guide us for our children too.

The first is attachment. People often make attachment seem really complicated, and try to decipher and define how each child has attached to others. Really, attachment is quite simple.

A newborn baby is helpless, cold, and hungry – it can't even lift its head up. Left completely on its own, uncared for, it will die in minutes. A baby is completely reliant on other people from the start to keep it safe, wrap it up, keep it warm, and feed it.

Newborn babies are good at three things: eating, pooping, and crying. Crying is their first way of communicating. It is their way of saying 'I'm cold, scared, hungry, wet, dirty, hot, worried, unsure, alone, bored, [and everything else you can think of]: *help me*'. We, out of love (and a desire to get a good night's sleep), respond to this cry to try and comfort our baby, and make everything ok. This is the basis of attachment – your child asks for your care and you respond.

From birth, the child starts to learn that if there is something wrong, I can express my feelings (i.e. cry), and somebody will help me feel ok and keep me safe. But that somebody isn't just anybody, usually this starts with one specific person (most often mum), and then grows to include other people (dad, grandparents, siblings, etc.).

The best outcomes for children are when they form secure attachments. This is when the child knows that if they need help, help will always be available to them. This helps children have the confidence that they can go off and explore the world, but to come back to mum/dad when things get too scary. As they grow up, this attachment becomes the model for how they form *other* relationships. For example, a child with a secure attachment learns it is ok to share feelings, trust other people, and ask for help. They also turn this on its head, and become the 'parent' in the attachment relationship. Through noticing how they were listened to, comforted, and helped, they learn how to listen to, comfort, and help others.

Our attachments also help us to manage emotions. Learning how to comfort ourselves and make ourselves feel ok is a really hard thing to do, and is something even adults struggle with at times. As children, we go to our parents when we are upset, angry, or worried, because we don't know how to manage these emotions. We offload our big scary emotions onto our parents by crying, screaming, yelling, etc., and in return, our parents give us a hug, tell us it will be ok, and they make these big scary emotions seem ok. As we get older, we start to internalise this – we do to ourselves what our parents would do to us, so we hug ourselves, snuggle under a blanket, tell ourselves it will be ok, etc. This means it is our job to help our child manage their emotions, and how we do it will help them learn how to manage their emotions in the future.

Attachment tends to be made more difficult by two things. The first is if people don't respond to a child when they cry or need help. The child starts to learn that crying doesn't do anything to help them. This child starts to bottle up their emotions, doesn't show emotions, and as they grow up, starts to think 'I have to be ok, I can't ask for help, I can't show emotion, I just have to get on with it'. In their relationships, they might struggle to share and open up, and can seem non-committal, as they aren't used to sharing their lives and emotions with others. This child might seem to have no problem leaving their parents, but is actually really anxious and trying to hold it together. Likewise, they may not be comfortable comforting others, or feel that people should get on with it like they do.

The second is when people respond inconsistently to the child. Sometimes the child gets comforted when they cry, but other times they get shouted at, ignored, or people cry back at them because the adult can't manage their own emotions at that time. This child is coming to adults with these unmanageable scary emotions and needs, and sometimes they get help, but other times they don't (or things are made worse). This child finds it hard to trust people, but at the same time wants to get close to people, and can often have very extreme emotions.

If you're reading this and thinking 'Oh God, I did that once', or 'Charlie always seems to be distant, did I do something wrong', you can stop panicking:

1. A lot of neurodevelopmental disorders can make children appear more distant, or to have more extreme emotions, even when the child has a great attachment.

2.  There is no such thing as 'perfect' attachment.

3.  Children can form attachments to different people. It doesn't matter who it is – mum, dad, or gran, as long as they can form it with at least one person.

4.  Attachment styles can change over time, particularly in childhood – this means we can improve it!

5.  You are only human. Having a child is difficult, especially when you've got your own mental health problems. The most important thing if you do have these difficulties is to you look after yourself to help you manage your emotions, and if you need it, get some help. That will allow you to help your child with their emotions.

6.  Plenty of adults don't have secure attachments and are still fully functioning adults.

The takeaway from this section is that you need to be in tune with your child and their needs. These might be physical needs (e.g. they might be hungry, thirsty, or tired), or emotional needs (such as worried, angry, or upset). **Our job is to *consistently* meet their needs**, to build a trusting relationship. The hard bit for us is that children who develop differently can find it harder to communicate their needs (and is one of the reasons why I talk about communication so much in this book), have slightly different needs, and have needs that are harder to meet.

## KEY POINTS

✓ Attachment is about a child learning that if I ask for help (whether that is practical help or help managing emotions), I will get it. It is about being in tune with your child and their needs, and consistently meeting those needs to build a trusting relationship.

✓ Attachment forms a blueprint for a child of how friendships and relationships work. It is also internalised and is how a child learns to help themselves.

✓ We can't be perfect parents, so sometimes we might not respond in the best way possible. That is ok. The important thing is that we are striving to be consistent and responsive to our child. If there is something getting in the way of this, or making it a lot harder, we can always get help to support us to be the parents we want to be.

## UNDERSTANDING CHILD DEVELOPMENT

Child development is a fascinating area, but with frustratingly few good, easy to read books on it. Once again, I highly recommend *Child Development: An Illustrated Guide* by Carolyn Meggitt for an easy read overview of how children develop and at what stages. I've also stuck a very basic guide to child development milestones in the online appendix, which can be downloaded from https://library.jkp.com/redeem using the code YJXGEFU, for you to look over as a quick reference, but the Meggitt book can do it far better than I can here.

Before we go any further, I need to make something really clear. Developmental milestones are meant as a *guide*, not as predictions that will be accurate to the day. Think of them a bit like British train timetables – they are a good estimate, but don't be surprised if they are a bit early or late, so you always want to leave plenty of time for your change over. **You should absolutely seek professional advice if you are worried that your child is delayed in their development**. However, as all children develop at different rates it is important not to get too focused on the exact ages these books say skills should appear. Instead, use them to help you know what skills are likely to be developing now and next, what to look out for, and how to encourage skill development.

There are lots of ways to break down child development, but the easiest way is to break it down the same way we did for Global Developmental Delay:

- communication, speech, and language
- motor development (learning to control their body)
- social and emotional skills
- play and everyday living skills
- their cognitive development (ability to learn, solve problems, etc.).

While we think of these as separate areas of development, they will affect each other too. For example, a child with poor social skills might not have much chance to practise more advanced play with other children, which in turn may affect their problem solving skills. Or a child with difficulty controlling their body might find it harder to communicate with gesture or language, which in turn makes socialising harder.

Each area tends to build in a reasonably predictable sequence. It is like building a tower – each new skill relies on the last skill. For example a child needs to be able to form words with their mouth before they can start to put words together into two word pairs to add meaning. Likewise, a child needs to learn to take turns before they are going to understand the concept of winning and losing (otherwise you'll have a child thinking 'but I want to have my turn now, or someone else will win!'). There are a few times kids jump a step (like going from sitting upright to walking, completely skipping out crawling) but this is the exception rather than the rule.

Through studying kids, we've got a pretty good idea of the various 'windows' when typically developing kids should be starting to do what. However, there will always be some kids who develop early, and some later. Child development isn't just about the first five years of life, when all the big 'milestones' parents look out for (first words, first steps, etc.) tend to occur. Children don't fully turn into adults until at least their early to mid-20s (just go to any university town on a Friday night for proof). Throughout that time, there are big changes that happen to their brain and body, and lots of new skills to learn!

When it comes to children developing differently, they are often delayed in one or more of these areas. For example, a 10 year old who communicates with single words, or a teenager who is still really struggling with forming friendships. These kids will keep progressing, but sometimes in a different way, at a slower rate, and sometimes they'll get to a point in their development where they won't progress any further. Before you ask, no, we don't have a way to predict exactly what a child will and won't be able to do. After studying a child for a while, an experienced clinician might make a rough *estimate*, but there are always children who will go further, and children who won't get that far.

This is where having something like the Meggitt book is important. Because all children develop at different rates, knowing a child's age isn't going to tell you much. Give me a typically developing 5 year old and I can tell you pretty accurately what skills they will definitely have acquired, the skills they will be developing, and the skills they won't have developed yet. However, with our kids who are developing differently, their age alone can't tell me what skills they have, or what skills they should be developing. Give me a 5 year old with an Intellectual Disability, Autism, or any of these other conditions and I won't have a clue until I get to know them.

We therefore always need to be referring back to the different stages of child development to track our child's progress, rather than making assumptions. Look at the brief summary of child development in the downloadable appendix (or at the Meggitt book). You'll probably find that rather than one particular age band describing them well, they are sitting across several age groups – different skills are developing at different rates. Go back to our five areas of development, and think about where they are in their development in each of those areas – *what is the latest/most advanced skill they have in each area*? Be honest, rather than optimistic – what can your child do *without* you helping them to do it?

Done that? Now look ahead at the skills that come next (the ones they are maybe starting to develop) and the ones even further down the road. How often do you expect your child to do one of these later skills that they haven't actually developed yet? I know I do it a lot. We see a child who looks 8, and we treat them as such, when actually in some areas, they are maybe 6 or 4 years old. We sometimes ask our kids to do things they can't do yet. We assume they will understand things they can't understand. We put them in situations that require them to have skills that they just don't have yet. This is really unfair for the child as we are setting them up to fail – we *know* they can't do it! But we forget, or make assumptions because we are human. However, with a little work, we can remind ourselves of exactly where your child is in their development.

Psychologists like giving complex names to simple ideas, and Vygotsky did this brilliantly with the 'Zone of Proximal Development' or ZPD. The ZPD is a simple idea. It looks like this:

All the ZPD says is that there are things a person can do without any help, that a person can do with help, and that a person can't do (at least, not yet). We need to build a child's skills from the inside out. We've got to start with what they *can* do. Think about what the next 'step' up from that skill is, and give them the chance to practise that skill with our help. Once they can do that skill independently (i.e. it has become 'can do without any help'), we can look at what the next step is – what has moved into the 'can do with help' bit.

To dust off an old saying, you can't teach a child to run before they have learned to walk. In the same way, there is no point trying to teach me university level chemistry until you've gone back to re-teach me the high school stuff I've forgotten (or rather, never learned – there is a very good reason I'm not a medical doctor). However, time and again, I find parents, schools, and professionals (including me!) assuming what we are trying to teach a child is in their 'do with help' zone, when in fact, it is several steps too advanced.

What happens is this: we look at a child, and work out what skill they lack, and try to teach them that skill. *This is completely backwards!* If the child was capable of learning that skill, and had all of the foundation skills they needed to learn this new one, they would have probably learned it (or at least have started to learn it) already! One of the most common examples of this is a child who 'explodes' at school, and despite teachers and parents trying to help him calm down, nothing is working. So they send him to me to teach him how to calm down. Well, if he was *capable* of calming himself down, wouldn't he have learned it? After all, everyone is desperately trying to support him to do it? Clearly this skill is in the 'can't do yet' zone.

Instead, we need to look carefully at what a child *can* do now, and what series of skills we need to teach them to get from where they are now to where they need to be, and work on them *one by one*. For the above example, I'd start off with checking whether this lad understands emotions. Can he recognise emotions in himself? Does he actually know what people mean by 'happy', 'sad', and 'angry', and relate those words to how he feels? Only if he can do all those things can we start to teach him how to keep himself calm.

Likewise, even if we have a clear plan for what skills we need a child to learn before they get to the skill we want them to have, **they need to be developmentally ready**. A book may say that Iain should be capable of this skill by now but I don't care what a book says – a book doesn't know Iain.[4] I care about where Iain is in his development. Sometimes, kids just aren't ready to develop a certain skill yet. That's ok – child development isn't a race, and children developing differently will develop differently (groundbreaking insight there Josh...). So, all we can do is support where they are now in their development: give them lots of opportunities to practise the skills they can currently do, and currently do with support, so that your child has a really firm foundation to jump up to the next step when they are ready.

## KEY POINTS

✓ Child development milestones/timeframes are a rough plan as to when skills are likely to develop, not a detailed map. What is more helpful is looking at the order different skills develop.

✓ When looking at skills, we can use the Zone of Proximal Development – what your child can do independently, what they can do with some help and support, and what they can't do yet.

✓ We need to focus our attention on supporting our kids becoming

---

4   My first supervisor had a saying that I think is very true: 'the word "should" is a big stick in word form that we use to beat ourselves up with'.

independent in the skills they can currently do with some support. There is no point trying to teach a child a skill they are not developmentally ready for.

✓ Working with a child at their developmental level (even if that is much younger than their age) isn't having low expectations – quite the opposite. It is giving them the best chance to learn and develop.

## UNDERSTANDING HOW CHILDREN LEARN

So, we've looked at what children learn (or are able to learn) as they develop. The next question is how do we teach them? In essence, most of this book is about teaching children skills. However, it can be helpful to understand two of the most important ways children learn.

### Number 1: Modelling

'Stop f**king swearing!'

'I told you to STOP SHOUTING!'

'Oi! Come here [slaps child on the back of the hand]. We don't hit!'[5]

'Give that here [takes toy]. In this house we share, we don't snatch!'

How many times have you seen this happen? Or, for that matter, how many times have you done it? When it is written down, it is easy to see how utterly stupid and counterproductive these statements are, yet in the moment (likely filled with stress and frustration) I can completely get how they come about. It is only when we step back that we can actually see the contradictory messages we are giving our children (and which message do you think they'll remember?).

One of the biggest ways children learn is by watching others and copying them. At only a month old, children will copy you – if you get a baby's attention and smile at them, they will smile back. As children

---

5    This is illegal, ineffective, unhelpful, and not something I support – I'll give you better options later in the book.

get older their copying starts to get more complex. Give a child a doll, and what will they do with it? Hold grown-up tea parties like the ones they have seen you have with your friends? Try parenting it like you have parented them? Teach them like their teacher teaches them? Older siblings (myself included...) start to try to lay down the law among younger siblings trying to imitate their parents (and it feels really unfair when we are told off for it – especially if we think we were right!). Right from the moment a child is born – *you are being watched!*

And it isn't just you. It is your friends, and (later) your child's friends. It is TV characters, video games,[6] the kids on the street they see out the window. Your child is exposed to a world of people doing weird and wonderful things that they see and want to try out for themselves – and frankly, who can blame them?

The fact that our children watch us so closely is fantastic. It means that if we act and treat others how we'd like our children to act and treat others, we'll be well on our way. Job done!

...Except that trying to model that behaviour 24 hours a day, 7 days a week requires endless self-discipline and patience. It isn't just that you have to act perfectly *towards* your child, but also whenever you are *around* your child. Shout and swear when a driver cuts you off on the motorway, or when someone shoves you on the street, your child will see it and copy it. And all this is just about you – what about all the other children and adults your child comes into contact with?!

We'll never be able to model perfect behaviour. Everyone has a bad day when they have shouted at their children that they *just need five F\*\*KING MINUTES of peace*. Even if we could always be perfect ourselves, we can't stop them seeing bad behaviour in others. However, the more we can model positive behaviours such as:

- sharing

- compromise

- listening

---

6   This is also why video games and movies have age certificates. For kids developing differently, it is important you don't just go by their chronological age, but their *developmental age*. Sam may be 15, but if her level of understanding of social relationships, consequences, and right and wrong isn't also 15, then don't give her a 15 certificate game or movie.

- being helpful

- asking

- saying please and thank you

- following house rules

- apologising

- owning our mistakes, etc.,

the better. Same goes for reducing behaviours we don't want our children to copy, such as:

- shouting

- swearing

- rudeness

- hitting

- not following requests (such as when your partner asks you to bring the laundry down and you say 'I'll do it later').

How many of these are things we wish our kids wouldn't do, yet are things we do ourselves? Or things that we wish our kids would do, that we don't do (like following the rules, owning our mistakes, and apologising)?

So, children see all these weird and wonderful behaviours in others that they want to try out (as well as stumbling upon behaviours they haven't seen before). What decides if they keep doing a behaviour or not?

## Number 2: Rewards

The other way children learn is by the response they get when they do something. If they get a positive response, they are more likely to do that behaviour again. If they get a negative response, they are less likely to do it. Common sense, right?

Going back to the example of a child seeing a chocolate bar at the supermarket, asking for it, and mum says no. The child then has a tantrum, and mum gives in. What has the child learned about the 'tantrum' behaviour? More than likely, they'll have started to learn that tantrums get them good things! What about a child who starts to draw with their new coloured pens on the TV? Dad, seeing his precious 52 inch is about to turn into an impressionist painting, leaps off the sofa and bounds over to the child to take the child away to sit on his lap. What has the child learned here? Perhaps that drawing on the TV gets them attention.

Attention, it turns out, is just about the most rewarding thing in the world to a lot of children (and for good reason – attention from parents is incredibly important for your child's development). So, when your child works out how to get your attention I'll bet you dollars to doughnuts they will remember what it was that got your attention, and use it or something similar to it in the future. Usually, when mum is on her laptop working or dad is watching the TV!

Importantly, for all kids, even *negative* attention (such as being told off) can still be rewarding. For kids developing differently, they also might not *understand* that the attention is negative. In fact, it might be incredibly entertaining – Dad is making that funny face again where his face turns that odd blotchy red colour, and that blue vein on his forehead starts to pulse... Ooh and his eyes start to pop out too and he makes his monster voice! How funny!

So far, I've used examples where we have *accidentally* taught a child to do more negative behaviours, but we can also use it for positive behaviours. For example, giving a child lots of attention when they have been playing nicely with their sister for five minutes, or when they put their coat on. Often, these aren't big, impressive, or unusual behaviours, but rather the behaviours we want your child to show on a day-to-day basis. We are trying to catch our kids doing something, *anything* positive we can reward:

- 'Johnny, you're sitting ever so nicely at the table, good sitting!'

- 'Sophie, thank you for getting your shoes, that is really helpful!'

- 'Wow, you're so good at puzzles Adam!'

- 'I love your hair Sarah, did you brush it today?'

Often, people don't think to reward these behaviours. In fact, if I ask parents for examples of what their child did recently that got them praise or a reward, often the child has to do something unusually good to get praise, so the bar is set extremely high. This is particularly true for kids developing differently, when people might be expecting them to do things based on their age, rather than their developmental level. This means kids are more likely to *rarely* get this positive praise, but probably get a lot of negative attention (which, remember, is still rewarding) for doing behaviours you as parents don't want. The end result? Those behaviours you don't want increase.

Of course, the other side to this is punishment. If a child does something we don't like, we can punish them, either by taking away a toy or privilege, shouting at them, or giving 'time outs'. That way, the child will learn to not do those behaviours, right? Wrong.

Here are nine reasons why I don't believe punishment is effective:

1.  The evidence says so. Research on both humans and animals says punishment is a really poor way of stopping undesirable behaviours and increasing desirable ones. It is certainly *nowhere near* as effective as rewards.

2.  Looking back at my childhood, punishment didn't teach me to not do something, it taught me not to get caught (I had ninja skillz!).

3.  Punishment tries to tell our kids what we don't want them to do. However, with our kids in particular, *they might not know what the right thing to do is*. There is no point punishing them over and over again for doing the wrong thing when they don't know what the right thing is! That's like a policeman giving me a fine for not guessing the number he's thinking of.

4.  Punishments usually involve giving a child at least some attention while you 'tell them off' – so can end up making behaviours more likely, not less.

5.  Remember how we just talked about how children watch and copy? Well, have you ever seen a child try to snatch a toy away, telling their parents they're not allowed to do something, or give them a time out? Who do you think they learned it from? When we punish, we model antisocial behaviours, which is the opposite of what we are trying to do.

6. Remember all that stuff about attachment? I mentioned that children look at their relationship with you to teach them how to manage their own emotions. Well, what does it tell the child about managing their own emotions if they are punished for doing something when they are upset? How do you think they feel about coming to you for help if they have made a mistake if the last time they made a mistake they were punished?

7. It costs a lot of 'emotional credit'. I like to think of a positive relationship with a child as building 'emotional credit'. This is a credit we have with your child that we spend when we ask them to do something they don't particularly want to do. The reason they are willing to do it is that they have a good relationship with us, value and enjoy that relationship, and want to please us – they do it because we have 'emotional credit'. Punishments cost a lot of emotional credit (we're asking them to do something they don't like, and right now they probably aren't enjoying the relationship they have with us) for something that probably isn't going to be that effective.

8. Punishment only works for so long. As children get bigger, you aren't able to place them on the 'naughty step'. At this point, we cannot control their behaviour.

9. Punishments can hurt children's self-esteem, and they can start to think that a 'bad child' is who they are, so live up to that.

So, why do people punish? Usually it is for one of five reasons:

1. They don't know what the alternative is.

2. They think it is how children learn.

3. It is how they were taught (I didn't say it *couldn't* work, just that it wasn't effective).

4. It makes the parents feel better (a sense of 'justice' being served).

5. They feel that is what other people expect them to do.

Reasons 1, 2, and 3 are easy to tackle. However, 4 and 5 can be more difficult. Being so frustrated at your child that you *want* to punish them is completely understandable. But if you're finding yourself actually punishing your child because of these feelings, we need to go back to the step on self-care and find ways to manage this, or let it out in other ways. Likewise, for 5, who is this child's parent – other people, or you? Do you want to do what you think will make people stop staring at you, or do you want to do what is right for your child? *It is not easy*, I've had people stare at me in that kind of situation and it feels so, so uncomfortable. However, that is why we need to invest plenty of time in looking after you, so you have the strength to do it. I'm not trying to shame you, or make you feel guilty here – all kids can be really frustrating, and the social pressure in public can be huge. What I'm trying to say is that if these things are influencing your parenting, maybe we need to focus on your wellbeing first so you feel better able to resist these ways of acting.

There are also so many benefits to focusing on rewards rather than punishments. For example, it is great for children's self-esteem, motivation, and perseverance. However, the argument parents often find most convincing is this: when your child is older, say, 15, you can say 'no', threaten, and punish all you like – if they don't want to do something, you can't *make* them do it. You can put a screaming toddler in a pram, you can't do that with a teenager. **If you've used praise and rewards for positive behaviours, your child will genuinely *want* to do these behaviours.** They will associate doing these behaviours as rewarding at first, then as what is expected, and eventually as just part of the routine, needing very little if any rewarding to keep them going.

## Putting it together

Those are the two biggest ways children learn: copying others, and being rewarded for certain behaviours. 'Being told' isn't on my list. This is partly because a lot of the kids I work with either can't understand language, or can't use it very well, and it is often particularly hard for them to understand language if it is being used to describe something they've not done before. The other reason is that language is great for communicating ideas, but ideas are pretty poor as instructions. For example, would you rather a pilot *told* you how to fly a plane while you were sitting in their living room, or *showed* you how to fly a plane and explained what they are doing? Likewise, your child will learn much faster if you *show* them how to play nicely with their sister, rather than just tell them that they need to share. We can absolutely use language with our kids to explain what we are doing, or as part of our praise, but it is best used along with these strategies, rather than by itself.

## KEY POINTS

✓ Children learn by modelling (watching what we do), and whether they get rewarded for doing something (such as with praise or attention).

✓ We are always being watched – we need to try and demonstrate all the positive behaviours we want your child to learn, and reduce bad habits we don't want them to pick up.

✓ The best way to praise is by catching our kids doing the behaviours we want to see more of. It doesn't have to be perfect, or extra special – just a behaviour we'd like them to do more.

✓ We can sometimes accidently reward behaviours we don't want – such as rewarding a tantrum with a chocolate bar.

✓ Attention is highly rewarding, even if it is negative attention (such as being told off).

✓ Punishments don't work.

✓ By rewarding our children for positive behaviours, we are making them genuinely *want* to do these positive behaviours.

## UNDERSTANDING HOW CHILDREN COMMUNICATE

Talking is often really important and emotive for parents. Don't get me wrong, it is important, and we should absolutely try to help our children to communicate in as many ways as possible. However, talking isn't the *only* way to communicate.

Children communicate a huge amount with their behaviour. Screaming, crying, hitting, tantrums, being overexcited, being calm, being happy and smiley, being quiet and sleepy, they all communicate something. Sometimes we automatically work out what a behaviour means ('oh look at Tom, I think he's getting tired'). However, for a lot of behaviour, we don't put much thought into trying to work it out. This can be because a behaviour is so disruptive all we can think about is the behaviour, how to manage it, and how stressed and frustrated it makes *us* feel – we don't think about what your child is trying to say. Other times, we might not even realise our child's behaviour has changed, such as an infant going from singing or cooing in the shopping trolley to quiet and still with a slightly satisfied expression on their face. If we are too busy shopping we might not notice this subtle change, until a certain aroma wafts towards us and we realise that Tom now needs a nappy change.

But communicating with behaviour works the other way around too. Think about it, if your child doesn't understand (much) language, what communication *do* they pick up on? It's *our* behaviour. This means we've got to think carefully about what we do, so we are sending a clear message. Let's say your child has learned that 'when mum puts shoes on me after breakfast and gives me my bag, that means we are about to get into the car and go to nursery'. However, what happens if suddenly we aren't going to nursery, but we are going to the park? Here, we gave the child the same behavioural communication, but something different happened – something unexpected, that they perhaps weren't prepared for. It's a bit like if you go to work and suddenly find out you're doing a different job for the day – you'd feel really out of your comfort zone and anxious.

Another common one is that we get ready for school, but then we take a *different* route. Taking the same route to school is *part of the communication*. It's a bit like when you bump into Fred at the office, you go through the same, 'Hi, how are you? How was your weekend? How are the kids?' You're not remotely interested in any of the answers (and Fred knows it). Fred also knows that even if he had the most awful weekend, the expected answer is anywhere from 'great thanks, yours?' to 'busy, very busy, how about you?' It is a predictable sequence, a back and forth. In the same way you put your child's shoes on, he stands up and walks to the car, you put him in, he watches the trees go by, and you take the same route to school – it's a bit like a conversational exchange, but with behaviour. Suddenly, if you take a different route, the communication has changed. 'Am I going to school still? What are we doing instead? This was not what you said (with your behaviour) was happening!' Even if we then get to school, your child might be thinking 'Ok, we're here, but what else is going to change? What else haven't you told me?'

Even when a child can appear to use language well, we need to be careful – how well a child can use language, and how well they understand language can be very different. I've met children and adults who have gone for decades with people thinking they understand language well, and it is only on formal testing where you check and realise that, actually, they have been muddling through without understanding a lot of what is said to them because people are pitching their language at too high a level, or saying too much at once. In these cases, when the child gets it wrong or misunderstands, people can think the child is being wilfully disobedient or deliberately trying to cause problems if the adults assume the child's understanding of language is fine. In fact, they simply haven't understood, and the fault is the adults', not the child's.

In the case of us driving a different route to school, we might be able to say 'we are going a different way to school today'. Your child might recognise the words 'going', 'school', and 'today', and that together with being in their school uniform with their school bag tells them they're going to school. However, if they've not understood the 'a different way' bit, then they might still get really distressed when you seem to be going a different way.

It is no wonder then that often children's distress, anger and frustration comes from either miscommunication or lack of communication. After all, if the usual road to school is closed, there isn't much you can do about it, even though you might *know* it is going to cause a big problem for your child. Naturally, parents then try and find other ways to communicate.

First, parents talk. Talking is great for encouraging language, and to communicate with children who have developed a good grasp language and can use it easily. However, the younger your child is in their language development and understanding, the less effective talking will be. Also, stress makes communicating with language *much* harder. Even typically developing kids (and adults for that matter) with well developed language can really struggle to properly *listen* to language and put how they feel into words when they are really stressed, upset, or angry.

Despite this, the natural response of parents when a child is stressed is to try and talk – it's our default option as adults. However (even if your child is able to use and understand language) if they are stressed, overexcited, upset, overwhelmed, or angry, then when we use language, we'll be trying to talk to that thinking, rational part of the brain – but that bit of the brain isn't the bit at the controls right now.

Imagine you've twisted your ankle on the streets of Paris and everyone around you is trying to help you but in French. You might have learned enough French to have a holiday, but are you going to be able to think back to your 'conversational French' CD to ask for help and explain what is wrong, or are you going to be too stressed and just shout in English? In fact, are all these voices talking French just going to confuse you and get you more worked up? When things get too much, just like everyone else, your child's ability to communicate will likely take a few (temporary) steps backwards, so we need to adjust.

So, language can be good if a child is developmentally able to use it and is calm. However, clearly we are going to need alternatives. Here, parents often jump to using symbols such as PECS (the Picture Exchange Communication System). I've known parents to go out and spend hundreds of pounds getting thousands of symbols, visual timetables, miles of Velcro, and a brand new laminator, only to find it isn't working.

Visuals are great, but you've got to pitch it at the right level. Children go through three stages of symbolic development.

1. Object level. If we are trying to communicate 'Apple', the child needs to physically see the apple to know what you're on about. So, they might bring you an apple to cut up, or be able to make a choice between a banana and an apple if you physically show them both. As the child advances, they might be able to use a representational object, such as a plastic apple instead of the real one, but it still has to be something they can see and touch.

2. Photographic level. Here, the child might be able to use a photo of the object. However, at the start it has to be *the* object you're talking about. For example, if the photo is of a red apple, it has to be a red apple that they get, or if it is of a supermarket,

it has to be your specific supermarket (the building, not just of a generic 'ASDA' or 'Sainsburys'). As the child progresses, they may be able to use photos of non-identical objects, such as a green apple for *any* apple, or a photo of *a* supermarket, rather than your supermarket, but it is still a photo of something real.

3. Symbolic level. Here, we move away from photos, and start with like drawings, or symbols for 'apple', like those you get in PECS. Eventually, we might be able to progress from illustrations as symbols (i.e. cartoon drawing of an apple) to something purely symbolic for an apple, such as the written word 'apple'.

So, things like PECS (i.e. symbolic drawings) are really not far back from written language. They are great if your child is at that level. They are also good for kids who have good language, but might struggle when stressed. However, for children less advanced in their development, we might need to consider things such as photographs and objects.

Parents often overlook the value of photographs. Sometimes, there is a feeling that there is something 'special' or 'magical' about these symbols, because they are a bit different and it is what they may have seen other kids with additional needs use. Other times, parents can think that symbols might cost a bit, but they will be just as effective as a photo, so why go to all the hassle of taking all those photos, paying to printing them out, and laminating them. However, as we have just seen, photos of the actual objects are much easier for a child to understand than symbols. Equally, taking photos has never been easier with smartphones and online printing, often making these a much cheaper option!

When a child is at the object level, we need... well... objects. This might be showing them options when making choices, but we can also use it for things like cuing into routines. Using objects of reference is when we use an object to cue a routine. For example, it might be showing them their school bag to communicate going to school, a roll of toilet paper for going to the toilet, or their shoes for going out.

The final issue I tend to come across is when people introduce visuals (symbols, photos, or objects) as commands. For example, showing a child a photo of school to say 'get ready for school'. I don't know about you, but if someone tried to communicate with me in a way that was all about telling me what to do, I wouldn't be too keen to learn it or use it! (Maybe this is why I ignore my emails…). Not only do I not like being told what to do, but if I don't understand fully the language yet, then I'm going to end up getting the command wrong which won't feel good.

Instead, it is far better to start using these communication tools for *commentary*, and ideally for things which the child is ok with or enjoys. For example, if Billy hates the supermarket, but loves going to the park, then rather than introduce a photo of the supermarket (which Billy will promptly try and rip up or hide under the sofa), start by introducing a photo of the park when you're getting ready to go there, and en-route. This means the picture is more of a commentary than a command, so Billy associates the photo as meaning 'going to the park', and that this is a way to communicate. However, if we started with the supermarket, he'd more likely see this as a way of giving orders, and not want to use them. We might then start to use symbols as a way to give him choices (choices where we get to choose what the options are!), so they are a way for him to communicate to us and influence his world. Once he has learned lots of fun visuals, and is engaged with this as a way to communicate, we can start to introduce less fun ones as a way of forewarning.

I'm not saying we shouldn't use spoken language – language is a great tool, and one we should keep trying to develop. However, using visuals and our behaviour to communicate won't delay your child developing spoken language. Quite the opposite in fact. When we pair a visual with words, we are communicating in two ways – verbally and with the visual. That means they get two chances to understand what we are saying. If your child understood the visual, they might start to associate it with the language we used, helping to bring on their language skills.

While I hope this brief introduction is helpful, I'm far from an expert in communication strategies, and there is so much more to explore (I've not even touched on signing systems communication, such as Makaton and Signalong, which are also great aids to communication). If you think communication is a particular problem for your child, I'd strongly suggest getting in touch with a Speech and Language Therapist, who will be able to properly assess your child's communication, and tailor the communication strategies to your and your child's needs. There are also lots of apps out there that try to help with communication, many of which are great. However, get advice from a Speech and Language Therapist first. They'll be able to advise you on which will be most applicable to your child, and how to introduce it at home and school most effectively. This means that rather than trying lots of different apps and giving up quickly, we're focusing on just one or two, and using them in a way that is going to be useful for your child.

## KEY POINTS

✓ Spoken language is just one (rather complex and tricky) way to communicate, and it is what we as adults tend to default to.

✓ Our children communicate a huge amount with their behaviour. So do we (although we might not always realise it!).

✓ A lot of distress, anger, and frustration comes from problems with communication – when we aren't getting the message, or your child isn't understanding what is going on.

✓ As well as our behaviour, we can use visuals to communicate.

✓ Children go through three stages of understanding visuals: object level (needing the actual object, or a model of the object), photographic level (needing a photograph of the specific thing, or of a general example of it), and the symbolic level (drawings or symbols, then eventually the written word for what we are talking about).

✓ We have to pitch our visuals at the right level for where your child is at in their development.

✓ Using behaviour and symbols to communicate won't delay your child's language development.

## UNDERSTANDING ANXIETY

Anxiety is going to be a reoccurring theme throughout this book. A lot of the kids I work with experience higher levels of anxiety because the world is harder for them to understand, predict, and engage in. So, let's talk about it.

First off, I should say, I have a pretty broad definition of anxiety. I'm not just talking about a big fear reaction that happens when you see a spider, or hear the in-laws are coming round for tea. In anxiety, I include day-to-day stress, worries, dealing with uncertainty and things beyond your control, managing demands and expectations, etc.

Anxiety is *normal*. In fact (in moderation), it is healthy. Back when we were cave men, anxiety was our body's way of preparing us to fight the sabre-toothed tiger (good luck), run away from the sabre-toothed tiger (yeah, that'll work...), or freeze and hope it hasn't seen or smelled you (ok, all these three options suck, but they are better than not having anxiety and going up and trying to pet the cute kitty, which our anxiety stops us doing). That is why anxiety for a lot of us (kids in particular) comes out as physical – screaming, shouting, hitting, kicking, etc. It is our body being primed to deal with threats, or things going wrong.

The trouble is, the modern world doesn't have sabre-toothed tigers. The things that stress us and cause us anxiety usually aren't physical things, they are mental ones – lack of control, change, unpredictability, people acting in ways we don't like, having to do a task in a certain time, threats of consequences if we don't do something, or memories of what happened in the past. This means our body is primed for *physical* work to resolve the stress, but there is nothing for our body to do. There is no outlet for it.

After pain (always the first thing I consider for any behaviour), anxiety is usually the next thing I look at. Anxiety can create aggression or challenging behaviour, it can create withdrawal, sadness, or hiding under the bed, it can lead to kids not eating or overeating, not sleeping, wetting or soiling themselves – anxiety can come out in lots of different ways.

Our kids are also more likely to be anxious due to the fact they are developing differently. They are kids who are set up for a world that is just slightly different to ours, and so they are always having to adapt and work a lot harder.

There is a concept called the window of tolerance, coined by Dan Siegel.[7] It is a simple idea, but a really useful one:

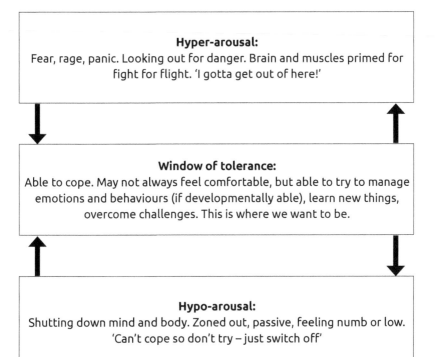

Every day we experience things that stress us, that place demands on us, or that calm us. Most of the time, we can handle these ups and downs fine. We are within our window of tolerance – the level of stress that we can manage without too much difficulty. When we get to the edges of our window of tolerance, when we feel 'yep, things are starting to get too much, I need to look after myself', there are things we can do to bring ourselves back – things like exercise, mindfulness, deep breathing, recognising unhelpful thoughts, doing things that we enjoy, etc., all to keep us within our window of tolerance. This is us doing what psychologists like to call emotional regulation (and that everyone else calls dealing with life). We might also try and reduce the demands on us by delegating, getting more time, or taking some time off. When we are within our window of tolerance, it might

7    Siegel, D.J. (1999) *The Developing Mind.* New York: Guilford.

not always be comfortable (we can still feel stressed, sad, or worried) but we are able to cope.

If, however, things get too much, we get pushed out of our window of tolerance. We can be pushed out the top, and that leads us to feel terrified, angry, overwhelmed. We get into what we call a hyper-aroused state – on the alert for anything and everything that could go wrong, or the smallest hint of danger. Our body is in fight or flight mode, and full of energy to either run away from or fight whatever is making us feel this way. If, on the other hand, things push us out the bottom of our window of tolerance, we get into a hypo-aroused state. Here, we kinda zone out, shut down, switch ourselves off. This is the brain and body getting overloaded saying 'no, too much, I'm outta here. I'm going to protect myself by switching off from what is going on'. We might feel depressed or numb, and will be unmotivated to do anything. Our brains are just trying to ride it out without drawing attention to ourselves or making it worse.

Because our kids are developing differently, it can be harder for them to learn ways to notice and manage their emotions, or they may not (yet) have developed to a point they are able to do this. Because of all the extra things they have to manage being a child who thinks differently, they have a lot to cope with. Finally, they may find it harder to communicate their distress, or ask for help earlier on. This triple whammy makes it easier for children developing differently to be pushed out of their window of tolerance, and is why I see a lot of anxiety, meltdowns, and challenging behaviour in my work.

The good news is there is a lot we can do to help with all of these. There are some specific strategies we will look at to help your child when they are anxious, having a meltdown, or behaving in ways that are not ok. However, the biggest way we can help our child remain in their window of tolerance is by managing their environment, keeping to a routine, and communicating clearly, all of which we have a lot of control over. The impact of getting these right is often underestimated, particularly for kids developing differently. Adults tend to think of managing emotions in terms of talking therapy, mindfulness, deep breathing, grounding techniques, etc. This is because they *already have* the power to alter their environment, so have probably already done what they can to make their environment work for them. Our kids, however, don't have that power, and have a lot of difficulty communicating what they'd like us to do. Therefore, if we get the rest right in terms of our child's environment and the people in it (see the following steps in this book), we'll need fewer of those other more complicated techniques, and most importantly, we'll have happier kids.

## KEY POINTS

✓ Anxiety is normal. It is a natural response that helps us survive.

✓ Children developing differently can experience more anxiety.

✓ We have a 'window of tolerance' in which we are able to function well. We (and our kids) can get pushed out the top of our window into a fight/flight response or out the bottom into a 'shut down' response.

✓ For children developing differently, especially children who do not (yet) have a good grasp of language, the best way to manage their anxiety is with clear communication, routine, and carefully managing their environment to meet their needs.

# STEP 3: THE RIGHT ENVIRONMENT

In the wild, animals have evolved to suit their environment. However, when you go to a zoo, the staff at the zoo have to ensure each animal's environment is specially adapted to their needs. You don't see a lion living in a penguin enclosure with a huge lake in it, and you don't see penguins in a lion's enclosure with nowhere to swim.

We can apply the same logic to our kids (minus the animal enclosures, obviously – our kids aren't zoo exhibits!). Typically developing kids follow a pattern of development suited for the world we have created, so it is usually pretty easy to meet their needs. The chances are their needs were similar to ours when we were their age, and similar to lots of other kids their age. However, children developing differently might need a slightly different environment. We as parents are in the privileged position of being able to shape our child's world. If we make assumptions about what our child's environment should be, we might end up with a child living in an environment which, rather than helping them to develop, holds them back.

The right environment does not *necessarily* mean that your child needs to be in their own special bubble, or that they cannot go to mainstream school. Rather, it means we need to think about what their needs are, and how we can adapt the environment to fit their needs, as well as that of their typically developing peers who they will likely share their environment with. School is a good example of this, and one that parents often ask me about. There may be lots of things that the school can do to make the environment easier for your child, but it also has to work for all the other children too – it is a shared environment after all. Likewise, there may be times that, actually, either the environment or people in that environment just aren't compatible with your child, and all the supports and adaptations in the world aren't going to fix it (a horse won't do well in an aquarium, no matter how much you adapt the aquarium). At those points, we might be looking at special education. Regardless of what environment your child is in, our focus is always on getting the environment right, because if we get the environment right, we give your child the best opportunities to thrive. That is what this section is all about.

## KEY POINTS

✓ Our child's environment plays a huge role in their development and managing their stress levels. Getting the right environment can make a huge difference to a child, so is the first place we start to look to make changes if your child is having difficulties.

## DEFINING YOUR OWN NORMAL

What is the perfect Christmas? If we look at TV adverts, postcards, and TV Christmas specials, it is about having the picture perfect Christmas dinner, miraculously cooked without any stress. It is about children waking up all excited, opening presents as a family, and children actually *playing* with a present before putting it aside and opening the next. It is about extended family coming over and spending six hours together (with the adults getting tipsy and the kids getting hyper) and nobody has any arguments or fallings out.

It's a lovely story, but it is fiction. Nobody has a Christmas like that. And yet, every year, that is what millions of people strive for. Inevitably, it never comes true, and people start to feel disappointed, or start blaming others. Then that makes them even more angry – 'It is Christmas, I shouldn't be feeling like this!' or 'It is Christmas, couldn't they just get along!' It's rather pointless, isn't it? And all of this because they wanted the perfect Christmas.

What if, rather than trying to have the perfect Christmas, people accepted that kids will be kids and open present after present then decide to play with the boxes, and instead of trying to control their kids and start an argument, we just let them do what they're going to do? We know that Aunty Stef and Grandma Liz always end up fighting, so maybe we see Aunty Stef on Christmas day and Grandma Liz on boxing day, rather than hoping they will magically get on for once in their lives? What if, rather than trying to have the perfect Christmas dinner cooked from scratch, we decide that actually spending time with the kids is more important than stressing out in the kitchen, so get it all pre-made from frozen that you can just bung in the oven? Once we let go of this 'ideal' Christmas, it becomes much easier to work out what we *actually want* to spend our time and energy on, and what we can let go because it just isn't worth it. It will be very personal what you can and can't let go of, and everyone will be different, but it makes life so much easier when we work this out.

The same applies to family life. Often people have this idyllic vision of what family life will be like, where everyone gets on, the kids get good grades at school, and nothing bad ever happens. This, just like Christmas, is a fiction. Siblings fight, parents squabble (and sometimes separate), kids get into trouble at school, parents miss out on promotions or lose their jobs, the boiler breaks down, and people get ill. Family life is never going to be plain sailing.

And that is ok. It doesn't mean you're doing a bad job, and it doesn't mean you've failed. Remember earlier in the book when we talked about values? This is when we get to use them. We can remember our values as parents – what is important to us – and use that to decide which bits to let go, and which bits are the ones we want to put our energy into.

Ok, maybe the kids are fighting, but right now health, and in particular focusing on mum getting better from gallstones, is more important than her trying to keep the kids from fighting, and therefore not resting and making herself more ill. Maybe you're not getting that insta-tweet-bookable holiday to Majorca, because mum lost her job, and instead are spending a week going to local attractions as a family, because spending time together as a family is more important than where you spend it.

Just like families with children who develop typically, having a family with a child who develops differently is never going to meet the 'idyllic' vision people might have. Often, however, what we choose family life to look like might be quite different from other families. **Different does not mean worse**, it just means different.

A child who develops differently might not be able to cope with Christmas dinner. There are too many flavours and textures, they are all touching, and there are so many people making noise, and there is the bang of the Christmas crackers – it is all just too much! Rather than trying to force Christmas dinner on them in an attempt to get closer to that 'ideal' people have, everyone might be happier (and it might feel a lot more like Christmas for the child) if they have McDonalds while everyone else has Christmas dinner? (For that matter, I wouldn't mind McDonalds for Christmas dinner either...). Is it more important for you that everyone eats the traditional Christmas dinner, even if there is shouting and screaming, and you don't get to eat or enjoy it because you're trying to force feed a child who is too overwhelmed? Or is it more important to you that you're all together, and McDonalds is just the adaptation to the environment that allows your child to join you?

If Jen doesn't understand the concept of death, and that she isn't going to see Nana again, if she finds change and big crowds hard to deal with, will she benefit from going to the funeral? She should absolutely get to come if she wants to (we are not trying to deny our children opportunities), but if going won't mean anything to her, if it is going to stress her out, then does she need to go, just because all the other grandchildren are there? Would it be far more meaningful to Jen to be supported to grieve in a different way that she can understand and feel safe and supported to do?

Maybe a family holiday is going to Legoland for the 12th time in a row, because 17 year old Zach can go on the LEGO® train over and over and over, and there is enough there to entertain his siblings too. It may not be a traditional family holiday, and yes, people might stare at Zach and wonder why a 17 year old is so excited about a train pretending to be made of LEGO®. But if he, his siblings and parents are able to enjoy themselves, then does it really matter?

Sometimes, these differences can be smaller. It might be that you're still having to make a checklist for 15 year old Jess of what to pack in her school bag each day, and double check she has ticked it all off before she goes, because she isn't able to focus for long enough to pack it herself without this support. Maybe it is not eating fish in the house because Henry can't stand the smell of it. Maybe it is doing most of your food shopping online because Ellie finds supermarkets too difficult to manage.

**Having a child who develops differently means having the courage to create the right environment for them (and everyone else), even when that is different to the norm**. It means defining what is 'normal' for you, rather than using everyone else's 'normal'.

This isn't always easy. Sometimes you might know which choice is going to meet the needs of your family (including your child who is developing differently), but doing it feels uncomfortable because it is different. At times like this, we need to think back to our values as parents. If you look back on this decision a few months from now, will you feel proud of it? Is it an example of those wonderful things you imagined your family saying about you during World Parent's Day? Or was it the easy option that didn't make you feel uncomfortable?

At other times, we can be so caught up in what *most* families do, we do it without thinking about whether it is right for *our* family. Some families eat together, but maybe Anna can't cope with all these smells, and the noise of people eating, and needs to eat separately, or in her own room. Maybe if she was allowed to do this, she'd eat more, and dinner time would be much less stressful for everyone? There may be good reasons why this is not the *best* solution to Anna's difficulties (for example, would headphones help her stay? A different place at the table?). However, often in situations like this, my first question to parents is 'is this something we need to change, or can we let Anna eat by herself?' Often, parents have never thought of this, and just assumed that we had to make Anna conform.

Don't get me wrong, there is a case for 'conformity'. For everything we adapt in their home environment, we have to consider whether 5, 10, 20 years from now that is going to be sustainable? For example, if we don't work out how to help Anna tolerate being around the dinner table, is she going to miss out on opportunities *she* wants (not that we want) later down the road? Is this something your child is going to have to learn to cope with? The answer to that might be yes. If so, then we need to think about if *now* is the right time for you and them to learn to cope with it? Do you and the child have the right skills to develop the ability to cope with this, or do you need help?

Equally, there are other people to keep in mind too, with their own needs. It is all very well Peter having the same spot on the sofa he sits on every day, but is it fair on everyone else if he also dictates where they can sit? Amira might want to watch Frozen for the 100th time, but if everyone else wants to watch something new, it is hardly fair to make them sit through the same movie every night. This is arguably something that Peter and Amira will eventually have to learn to cope with – that sometimes in a world filled with other people, we need to accommodate their needs by sitting somewhere else, or watching Frozen in a different room.

Defining your own normal is easier said than done. Your needs and your children's needs will constantly change, and so will your normal. There will be compromise between the needs of all the members of your family. Often the biggest challenge to creating the right environment is having the courage to be different. This is where holding onto your values, working out what is important and what matters for you can help us find that courage to be different. And, if you can dare to be different, to let go of the idea of 'normal' and replace it with 'what works for us', things become much easier.

Now comes the hard part – we have to put our money where our mouth is and start living by these values, and daring to be different.

## KEY POINTS

✓ Everyone has an idyllic version of what they'd like life to be like. This is completely normal, but it is also a fiction. If we hold onto this too tightly, we'll use up a lot of time and energy trying to achieve the unachievable.

✓ For all families, but particularly those with children developing differently, we need to define our own normal – what does a good family life look like for us? Our values as parents are important in guiding this.

✓ When defining our own normal, we have to balance the needs of everyone in the family.

✓ Doing things differently might mean letting your child developing differently (or your whole family) do things in a way different to most people.

✓ Sometimes, your child developing differently will need to change –

what they are doing now might not be sustainable, or they might need to learn how to do things differently if they are going to be able to do the sorts of things they want to do. If we are going to make this change, we need to ensure it is the right time; that both you and your child have the resources (time, patience, energy) to do it, and you both have the skills to do it.

## WHY ROUTINES ARE IMPORTANT

Routines are important for any child. However, they are especially important for enabling children who develop differently to thrive. Here's why:

First, and most importantly, **routines let children know what is going to happen**. You are the adult in the situation – you know what is going to happen because you can control it, you can imagine what could happen and how the situation might change, and you can communicate this with others. Often, a child who is developing differently doesn't have this. They certainly don't have the same level of control, and a lack of control makes everyone feel anxious. Think about when you're late and stuck in traffic, or on a delayed train – you can't do anything about it, you have no control, but if you're like me your hands will grip the steering wheel tighter, your jaw will clench, and you'll keep looking at that clock.

Your child might also not be able to communicate as well as you. Even if your child can use language to communicate, can they listen and understand everything you say? Or is it just a few key words they understand (which lead to misunderstandings)? If they do understand it, do they understand it when they are stressed? Can they communicate that they are stressed (remember, earlier we talked about how when we are stressed our ability to communicate takes a few steps back)? Did they hear you when you told them but they were really engrossed in a game? Often we can tell children stuff and assume it has been heard, when in fact it hasn't been, or only half the message has gotten through.

This is why routines are so important. Regardless of language, children can learn routines – they learn that after breakfast we do the school run. They learn that we go left at the end of the road to go to the shops, and right to go to grandma and granddads. They learn that they get a snack when they get home from school, but they don't get one after dinner time. They don't need much, if any, language to learn these routines. When we keep to these routines, we are providing our children with a safe, constant rhythm to their lives, minimising their anxiety.

This brings me to the second big advantage of routines. **Routines free up kids to learn**. If a child knows what is going to happen, they then don't have to spend their time and energy trying to prepare for an unpredictable future. This means they are more relaxed and ready to learn and develop their other skills. Routines themselves also teach skills. For example, knowing that at a predictable time they'll be learning to put shoes on, or get a bag ready, means the child is going to learn to anticipate a task they have yet to master, and so not only get regular practice, but a little time to prepare for it.

Third, **routines are *essential* in getting a child to sleep**. Bedtime routines can evolve, and develop with the developmental age of the child, but bedtime routines can start to be introduced from as young as 3 months old. These routines are one of the most important cues for both body and brain that it is time to sleep. When children don't have a routine, I will often hear that the child 'falls asleep on the sofa', 'in front of the computer', or 'whilst playing with their toys' in some other inappropriate place. This is likely a child falling asleep mostly out of exhaustion and being over tired, rather than choice. See the bonus chapter on sleep, which is available to download from https://library.jkp.com/redeem using the code YJXGEFU, for more information about this.

Finally, **routines set boundaries**. They help children learn what is expected of them, and that in life (despite their difficulties) there will be things they are not allowed to do, and things they have to do. This means that building and sticking to a routine will help your child to follow instructions, follow rules, and learn self-discipline. The earlier this is done the better. Establishing a routine when a child hasn't had one can be extremely challenging. Even once established, all children will push boundaries – just think of the terrible twos and teens! However, setting up these routines, modifying them as the child grows so they remain appropriate, and sticking to them is essential.

So what happens if we don't have a good routine? Well, how do you feel when your routine suddenly changes? Let's say, you go to work and suddenly find out your hours have changed – rather than working 9–5, you now work 6–2. Would this stress you out? Even if you were able to sit and plan out your new routine, wouldn't you feel stressed for a few weeks until you got used to it?

What about if you get a new boss who micromanages you. They give you one task to do, then when they feel like it move you onto the next one. You have no idea what you'll be doing at work five minutes from now, and they won't tell you. All they do is tell you what to do right now. Sometimes you don't even get to finish what you're doing! Wouldn't this get really annoying? Wouldn't you start to feel really controlled? If you are a child with poor language skills, or who struggles to imagine the future, this is what having a lack of routine can feel like – stressful! Unlike you, or a typically developing child, they might not be able to ask what is going to happen. They might not be able to understand the logic of what you're asking them to do. As far as they are concerned, they were playing happily and now you are taking them away from something they enjoy, and subjecting them to uncertainty over what is going to happen next. It can feel completely unpredictable and unsafe.

This is why disruption to routine is often one of the biggest causes of anxiety (and therefore challenging behaviour), and is usually behind a lot of the referrals to my clinic. For our kids, even small changes to routines can be highly anxiety provoking. For example, if a child knows 'we always go to Grandpa's after lunch on a Sunday', but this time you go to Grandpa's before lunch, then that could throw them for the whole day. You might think the disruption to their routine would just be the fact you are going early to Grandpa's and that when they are there they will be more settled. Not so. Even after small changes like this, the whole day's routine can be thrown out the window. It can feel like 'you changed one bit of the day's routine, so now anything could happen!', no matter how many times you try and explain everything else is going to be just the same! For example, are you going to Grandpa's after lunch too? What about what they usually do in the morning – when is that happening?

A lack of routine is one of the other big causes of referrals to my clinic. Often, I'll see kids who, for almost the entire day and night (possibly with the exception of school – but not always), are in complete control of what happens. Their 'routine' is whatever they say it is going to be that day and they often get very upset, angry, or frustrated when parents try to take that control away. Rather than their reassurance coming from knowing the routine and trusting parents to follow it, their reassurance comes from being in control of the situation – they are making the unpredictable predictable, they know what is going to happen because they are deciding what is going to happen. There is nothing wrong with kids having *some* control and choice – we want our kids to learn to be independent, to make choices, and take control of their lives, and it is important we build choice into their day. However, when a child has control over a big chunk of time that they aren't developmentally ready for, it can cause significant problems for the whole family, and a huge amount of distress when we ask that child to give up the control they find so comforting. We can avoid that if we get a routine in place early on, and make that the norm. If we get our kids into a regular, predictable routine, we are going to make their lives and our lives a lot easier.

## KEY POINTS

✓ Routines help our kids know what is going to happen, without relying on language, which reduces their anxiety.

✓ Routines help children learn.

✓ Routines help children sleep.

✓ Routines set boundaries.

## TURNING YOUR NORMAL INTO A ROUTINE

While routines are important, they can also be one of the most challenging parts of life to implement. Sometimes, parents can be used to a more freestyle lifestyle – there is absolutely nothing wrong with that if that works for you. Maybe it has to be freestyle due to irregular working hours, or because you like to be spontaneous, and find routines constricting. However, while this lifestyle can work well for some people, it is something children who develop differently can really struggle with.

Other times, parents can want to establish a routine, but when their child resists it, they think it is the wrong thing to do. What I tend to see then is parents and children ending up in a vicious cycle. The child feels anxious because they don't know what is happening – they are out of routine. So, they do what every creature does when stressed, they try and impose control. When parents try and resist this control and impose a routine, their child gets really upset, and in extreme cases, starts harming themselves or others – head banging, biting, or hitting. Parents then back off, and the child stays out of routine, and so needs to be completely in control to create predictability. The result can be a child who cannot accept boundaries, who is sleeping during the day and waking at night, and who is ruling the roost at home. The longer this goes on, the harder it is to change and build in routines, and the more extreme some of the behaviours can be. This is a particular challenge with older kids: you can't just pick them up to make them follow their routine! This is one of the reasons why establishing routines early is so important.

The most common scenario is that parents will have established some kind of routine, but over time, bits have slipped. Maybe their communication of the routine to their child has stopped. Maybe some bits are routined, but others have become more higgledy piggledy. Often parents won't have realised this, but when they sit and write down their routine, they find it is actually quite hard to write down. Or, when they tell me their routine, it is full of 'sometimes', 'usually', 'we used to', etc. That is a sign we need to go back to basics and write down exactly what their routine was, check if that would still work for them, where they are and are not following it, and then modify and re-implement it.

So how do we start designing a routine? Well, a good place to start is writing out what (if any) routine your child currently has, and what everyone else's is. People do this in different ways. Some people like to put in specific times and what happens at those times, while other people will draw out a grid with 24 hours going down the page, and either each family member or each day of the week going along the page. Either way, we need to work out where we are now, and then think about what we want to change first. We aren't aiming for ideal right away – we don't have to change everything at once, but it is good to know where we are aiming for.

While putting in routines can feel daunting, it can also be a great opportunity – a chance to put in place some of what we've talked about in previous chapters. We've talked about the need to dare to be different, to go with what works, rather than what everyone else does. That might mean our routine looks different to what most people's routines are like; it might be odd or unusual, but it needs to be a routine which the whole family can follow.

Obviously, routines change over time. Family routines are not set in stone, and change as the needs of different family members change – new jobs, new schools, new hobbies, and children (and adults!) maturing. However, often we tend to 'fall' into these routines rather than planning them out. We're going to change that.

First off, this routine (or rather, set of routines – one for each family member) has to work for everyone – it needs to be something that everyone can follow. You cannot have one person on a strict routine, and everyone else in a much more laid back routine. I've seen parents try and put their child developing differently on a strict routine, but everyone else on a more laid back one, but in my experience, this is very hard to make work. Every family member's routine interlocks with everyone else's. If one person is late, or doesn't do something, that will have a knock on effect on everyone else, including your child who needs the routine.

This is not to say that everyone else's routine needs to be quite as detailed as the routine for a child developing differently might need. For example your typically developing daughter might not care who takes her to football practice, or what route you take. However, Jimmy, who is developing differently, has a routine where he has his mid-afternoon snack, then dad takes Jenny to football and he does his homework with mum. That means, if Jimmy is going to do his homework, mum needs to stay, and dad and Jenny need to go (it might not matter too much where they go, but from Jimmy's point of view, homework time means only him and mum in the house after snack time). Therefore, your daughter and dad have to be ready to go at the right time for Jimmy's routine to work, and so need to have enough of a good routine themselves to make sure this happens.

Having a routine doesn't necessarily mean doing the same thing every day of every week. It means *having a predictable structure*, but we can build in a little unpredictability into this too. We can have times in the routine when we know *something* is going to happen, but we don't know what. We know what will happen before it, and what will happen after it, but that slot is 'predictable unpredictability'. For example, Saturdays might have the same morning routine and bedtime routine, but between 9 and 4, anything could happen! This could be a family outing to a farm or the zoo, going swimming, or going to grandma's.

Of course, the level of unpredictability will need to be adjusted to what your child can cope with. For example, your child might need a shorter period of 'unpredictable' time, particularly if they are used to a lot of structure and routine. It might be that only activities they have done before happen in that time. You might offer your child a choice of two activities (both of which you are confident you can offer, and giving them plenty of time to process their options and decide), or you might show them the activities their brother will be choosing from, so they know what *might* happen. You might show them in advance what will happen during this 'unpredictable time', so that even though it is something different each week, they know what it will be. In these ways, we can create flexibility, but in a way that reduces anxiety for our child.

Learning to tolerate uncertainty, unknowns, and changes to routine is important. Life is unpredictable after all, and even with the best routine in the most organised family there will be times when things get thrown out the window – like when the car breaks down, or a pipe bursts. One of the reasons why I think it is important to build some flexibility into routines is that it helps our children to learn to tolerate some uncertainty in their routine. This means they will be better able to cope with unexpected changes in routine that we can't control for. The best way to do it is by starting with small times of 'unpredictability', and making them more predictable (such as offering them a choice, showing them what might happen, or telling them what will happen instead). Then, over time, you can add more 'unpredictable' times, longer 'unpredictable' times, and gradually provide less choice and warning.

Lastly, it is important to remember when we create a routine that it has to work for everyone – the child and their family. That might mean compromise on both sides. Yes, you might be sick of 'In The Night Garden' being played on repeat, but if this is something

Billy enjoys, then it is important they have at least *some* time for this (although we may need to put boundaries around it if it is getting out of hand), for example, watching it only once, or in his room. Likewise, Billy might be very set in their routine of coming back from school and watching 'In The Night Garden', but if their sister really wants to go and join the football team and the whole family needs to go to drop her off, then we need to try and help Billy manage this by letting him know what will happen (maybe that 'In The Night Garden' will be after football, or on his iPad in the car), comforting him through his distress, and keeping it consistent.

## KEY POINTS

✓ Sometimes establishing a good routine for your child means we have to have a better routine ourselves.

✓ If children don't have a routine, they will get a sense of predictability they would have got from a routine from controlling the situation themselves.

✓ Routines are easier to set up when a child is young.

✓ Routines slip over time – that's ok, it happens, just look back at what your routine was meant to be, check it still works for everyone, and then get back on it.

✓ Routines will change over time as people change and the situation changes – it is ok to revisit routines and change them.

✓ While your child developing differently may need a more detailed routine than others in your family, everyone in your family will need to be on a routine.

## IMPLEMENTING YOUR ROUTINE

Ok, so let's get the bad news out of the way first. Implementing a routine often causes distress. After all, it is change, and you may be taking away some control your child felt they had over the situation, or you are making the predictable unpredictable because you're changing what usually happens. Usually, this distress is not unbearable for the child (or their parents), and subsides as the child learns the routine and settles into it over the following weeks. Often, parents can be hesitant to impose a routine because it causes short-term distress, and of course every parent hates to cause their child to be upset. This is completely understandable. However, it often kicks the problem of teaching the child routines and boundaries further down the line, when it will usually be even harder and more distressing. Equally, trying a routine for a few days, then backing off and going back to how things were, only to try again a few weeks or months later repeats the distress of moving onto a routine over and over, and may lead to distress becoming the way your child learns to react to change as that distress makes the change to go away. If we are going to do this, we need to be willing to stick with it. That doesn't mean we have to be cold-hearted about it – we should absolutely be comforting our child, communicating with them (not just with words!), and trying to ease them into their new routine. However, we need to stick to the new routine.

That said, anything that causes your child distress means you need to stop, think, and consider getting professional advice. As I wrote in the disclaimer, I can give general advice in this book, but I can't tailor it to your child, so you need to apply common sense and your knowledge of your child when it comes to implementing it. In this case, if your child is becoming too distressed, and/or the distress isn't subsiding, *STOP*. Get some professional advice from someone who can get to know your child. They will be able to ensure that there isn't something else going on for your child which might require a different approach, and that the routine is being implemented cor-rectly for your child in a way which reduces their distress as much as possible.

So, with that in mind, where do we start? Well, first off, we need to know how to communicate this routine to your child. For example:

- If your child can't use photos or symbols yet, you might be focusing on simply following the routine, and relying on them learning through experience. However, even here, I'd be trying to find objects of reference we can use to try and help cue them in to what is going to happen. Remember to try and keep things as specific as possible – having the same plate to show them to cue them in it is time for dinner, taking the same route to see the grandparents, showing them their school bag when it is time to go to school. (Pro-tip – make sure you've got several identical copies of that plate, so that you can afford to lose/break a few, and give yourself some flexibility to wash them).

- If your child can recognise a few photos, then maybe it's time to try a chart system called 'now and next'. Here, you're still following the same daily/weekly routine. However, with a now and next chart, you can help your child see what is happening now, and what will happen next – you're reinforcing to them that the schedule they have learned from experience is being followed, and reminding them of what is to come. (See the downloadable appendix for how to make a now and next chart.)

- If your child has mastered now and next, or if they are a bit older, then a visual timetable might be right for them. This is the same sort of idea as now and next, but rather than just showing 'now' and 'next', we can show a whole list of activities for a certain period (a morning, an afternoon, a day, etc.).

- Maybe your child who's a bit older feels a visual schedule is a bit childish. Maybe they are comfortable reading and want something more grown up. That's fine – you can give them a written timetable, or mix and match with words and symbols (e.g. the word 'school' and a symbol for school). You can give them a timetable where they don't take Velcro-ed items 'off' but instead tick them off. Maybe they can tell the time, and you can start to put timings on here. Maybe a schedule on a phone or iPad (with alarms? reminders? etc.) works well for them as they feel they have a bit more ownership and control over it. Find out what sort of timetable they want and get them involved in making it!

However, remember, this isn't *just* for your child, it is for the family. Your child will feel much more included and (as they grow up) feel it is part of normal life if everyone has a timetable or schedule of some sort for their routine. That means you! It might just be a daily plan of what happens stuck to a fridge, but it will help you lead by example (and who knows, you might even find it helpful!)

The next step is following the routine. This can be particularly hard when the child doesn't have much of a routine to start with. In these cases, look hard at your child's day to see if there is *any* routine you can use as a starting point. Maybe they get up, come downstairs, have a snack, then start playing. Maybe when they come back from school they get changed then play in their room. Maybe they come down for dinner, then put the TV on. This may be routine they are mostly in control of, but it is still a bit of routine.

We can use this bit of routine in a couple of ways. First off, we could start by adding our visuals to comment on this, especially if they are new to using visuals, or using visuals to say what they are going to be doing. Then, I'd start by trying to expand the routine a little. This could be:

- Forwards. Doing something just after the routine finishes, or just before the routine finishes. For example, coming down for dinner, then doing some drawing with mum before turning the TV on.

- Backwards. Doing something before the routine starts, such as washing hands with dad, then coming down for dinner.

From here, we can gradually build up a routine for the whole day. You might be able to identify several bits of the day which have a little routine too, and you could expand each of these forwards or backwards (although, only try and change one or two bits of routine in a day at once).

Some children I meet don't have any routine, because they have learned the way to control their anxiety is to control their environment, so they know what is going to happen. If your child doesn't have much of a routine yet (at least, not one set by you), then when you add new activities, try to make them enjoyed activities (at least to start with). We want your child to learn that following your direction leads to good things, and that when you say something is going to happen, it is going to happen. Likewise, if we're asking them to do something they enjoy, they're less likely to be as resistant to doing it, even if they'd rather follow their own routine.

In time, we might have to add less enjoyable things to the routine, and use our enjoyable bits of the routines as breaks or rewards. If there are some not-enjoyed things in the routine that really need to be in there now (such as school), then you can, of course, add them in now. However, if your child has no routine at all, starting with a routine that ends in school means they are unlikely to want to start (and therefore do any of) that routine, and will likely push against it hard. I'd usually suggest ensuring there are enjoyed activities either side of a not enjoyed activity, ideally with timers. If you're building a routine leading to school, I'd also work closely with school to help ease their transition into school (for example, a soft start, starting once the other kids have settled, having an enjoyed activity in school to start off with, considering how long they will tolerate school for now and how you're going to build it up to a full day), and rather than just having a big, long task of 'school', breaking it down. Rather than 'walking to school', then 'school', could it be 'walk to the playground', 'play catch with Mr Jones', 'Go in and see Mrs Bailey and my class', then starting the school routine.

Once you say something is going to happen in the routine, you need to stick to it. This helps them learn you hold your boundaries, but also trust you that when you say something will happen, it is going to happen. If they are having a really bad day, all you might get is a brief splash of water on their hands before coming down for dinner, or a quick scribble on a piece of paper after dinner – that's fine, they've still 'done it'. Ideally, we want more, but better a small token gesture than them opting out of that bit of the routine entirely, or us triggering a major meltdown. However, on ok days, we should be expecting more than token engagement (even if it might cause a tantrum), and on good days, more still.

For other children, they might already have a bit of a routine – it's just not formalised. People know roughly what is happening, but it isn't written down anywhere, and it isn't strictly kept to. This gives us a great starting point, and is much easier to work with. Here, the first thing I'd do would be to apply some structure to this usual routine – for example, starting to use now and next, or a visual timetable, if your child is developmentally ready for it. Once they get the idea that these visuals describe what is going to happen, then we can expand. This might be by:

- Replacing one activity with another – if you do this though (especially if it was for an enjoyed activity), make sure they know when the change is, and when they'll do the old activity again.

- Shortening or lengthening a bit of it using a visual timer.

- Expanding the routine, either backwards or forwards, to add in new elements to it.

As before, it is always best to change the routine a bit at a time. If you try and change it overnight, it will likely be very difficult for your child to cope with. If, however, you can change one bit at a time (such as a bit in the morning and a bit in the afternoon), it will be far easier for your child to cope with and get used to. Once they are used to it, you can then change it again.

Lastly, we've spoken largely about *changing* routines. Of course, there are some situations where your child doesn't have a routine because the situation is completely new to them. For example, moving house, changing school, or going on holiday. These can be a good opportunity to set a completely new routine (especially if they are used to you setting the routine and trusting you to do that) so a bit of planning to ensure that routine is right first time can go a long way. However, even here, it can be helpful to have some chunks of familiar routine (like the bedtime routine, for example) as this will likely be a difficult time for your child anyway. Likewise, we want to ensure there are plenty of breaks and enjoyable things so your child can get through their new routine comfortably.

## KEY POINTS

✓ Implementing new routines often causes distress. We should absolutely try and comfort our child, communicate with them, and make the transition to a new routine easier for them if we can, but we need to stick to the routine. Inconsistently using a routine, or going back and forth between an old routine and a new one is going to cause more distress long term.

✓ After you've designed your new routine, the first step is working out how to communicate it to your child in a way that is appropriate to their developmental level – from objects of reference, right up to a schedule on their phone with reminders set up.

✓ The next step is choosing which bit of the routine to implement. Most children have *some* routine, even if it is short, and very much set by them. Ensure you've got your child used to visuals *describing* the current routine first, then try adding in a new part to the routine to expand it backwards (a task goes in before it) or forwards (a task is added at the end of the routine). For children used to following a routine set by you, start by formalising what their current routine us – communicating it in a way they understand. You can then either change one bit at a time, or add more detail to the routine/make it cover more of the day.

## SETTING CHILD FOCUSED, REASONABLE EXPECTATIONS

Earlier in this book, I spent a section talking about child development, the idea of the 'Zone of Proximal Development'. This is because we need to understand where your child is in their development in order for us to set *child focused, reasonable expectations*. By this, I mean:

1.  Child focused: This is about *your* child. Not Ellie down the road, or their big brother Andy. Your child is developing differently, and that means we can't compare them to other children, and instead need to take a much more personal approach based on their unique developmental stage.

2.  Reasonable expectations: We should always have reasonable expectations about our children. This is part of setting boundaries, helping children learn self-discipline, self-worth, and self-confidence. We may have a reasonable expectation that our typically developing 15 year old will be able to organise themselves to get ready for school and be able to walk to and from school. We don't do all the organisation for them because it is part of teaching them independence and organisational skills (and if they show up in the car and you insist on a kiss goodbye, they won't hear the end of it from their mates for

the rest of the day). This may, however, be different for a 15 year old developing differently...

Child focused, reasonable expectations are about setting reasonable expectations for *your child in particular*. For me, this is one of the hardest aspects of my job. Most people have an idea about how a 5, 9 or 15 year old 'should' act, what they 'should' be capable of, how we 'should' communicate with them (and you'll remember my feelings on the word 'should' from earlier in the book). Therefore, people are pretty good at knowing how to interact with a typical 9 year old, what they are capable of, and what to expect from them.

When we have a child who is developing differently, however, while they might look like a 5, 9, or 15 year old, in some aspects of their development they can be delayed. This leads to a mismatch between our expectations of what they are capable of, and what they are actually capable of *at the moment*. This mismatch is one of the biggest causes of distress and anxiety (and the challenging behaviour which follows) for children developing differently that I see. For example, the trap I often fall into is meeting a 9 year old child who I know full well has difficulties with communication, yet I catch myself using the language I'd use to a child with the development level of a 9 year old, rather than pitching communication to suit *their* level of development. The result? At best, the child ignores me, at worst, they become understandably frustrated and upset because I'm confusing them and expecting them to understand.

It is so easy to do too, particularly with communication. Even parents who know their child really well can slip into setting expectations based on their age, rather than their stage of development. When parents tell me a story of how Kay had a meltdown, and how they tried to prepare her, explain to her, and reason with her, the first thing I'll ask is 'and, remembering Kay's level of language development, how much of that do you think she understood?', often followed by a 'ahhhh... ok yeah maybe not a lot'. In fact, most of the parents I work with will tell you that as soon as I hear them use the word 'tell' (as in 'so then I told Kay...'), I'll immediately interrupt them and ask them to explain exactly *how* they told her, and whether it was at her level (such as by using visuals, objects of reference, routines, etc.). I catch myself in the same way in clinic. If I'm doing one-to-one therapy with a teenager with an

Intellectual Disability, and I feel they haven't quite got it, usually the problem is *my* level of language, and the fact I've *told* them something, rather than *shown* them something. This applies to much older kids too – just because someone is a teenager, doesn't mean that they have the same understanding of language as other teenagers.

Child focused, reasonable expectations apply to much more than communication. The length of timer is another common example of where our expectations of your child might not be realistic. Yes, a typically developing 8 year old might be able to wait 10 minutes, but an 8 year old with difficulties with attention and hyperactivity might not. The result might be a child who is currently unable to sit for 10 minutes who keeps having the timer reset on them, so spends an hour sitting with both them and their parents getting all the more upset at each other.

Screen time is another big one. I know a lot of young kids who play what, on the surface, look like developmentally appropriate games on a phone, computer, or tablet, and indeed, they can do most of the game pretty well. However, they haven't yet got the developmental maturity to learn when to come off because the game stopped being fun (so having a meltdown/throwing the controller across the room because they can't beat a level), or how to come off when we tell them they need to. These games are designed to keep you playing for 'just a little bit longer' (how often have you been engrossed in a game, said just five more minutes, then a while later looked at the clock and seen it is two in the morning?).

Child focused, reasonable expectations apply to a child's behaviour too. Ok, Sarah may be 5 years old, but if she is behind in areas of her development, is it fair of us to hold her to the same standards we would a 5 year old? No. We have to think about what she is capable of, and *hold her to **that** standard*. That might mean at times understanding that she's acting like she's in the terrible twos, because developmentally that might be where she is, and we need to meet her needs as we would a 2 year old. Maybe she can't share like other 5 year olds, and so when she is in a group of 5 year olds and doesn't share, it isn't fair for us to judge her compared to her peers. That doesn't mean she *is* a 2 year old, or we should always treat her like that. Indeed, there may be some areas of Sarah's development when she is at her chronological age, and here we need to have higher expectations of her. However, we need to remember what level your child has developed to in their different skills, whether they have the skills to manage the situation we've put them in, and the type of support they are going to need.

Remember too that when kids are stressed, they can (temporarily) take a few steps back in their development. They may usually be able to talk and think rationally, to remember the rules, to follow their routine. However, a child who is overwhelmed or over stimulated may not be able to do these skills, particularly if they are relatively 'new' skills that they only recently gained independence with, or still need help to do.

The reason I talk about child focused, reasonable expectations here is that we need to think about what our children can manage when we set up their routine. We could have the most detailed and organised routine in the world, but if your child isn't able to manage it, then there is no point in it. This is something we need to always be considering. Having child focused, reasonable expectations applies to every section of this book, and at all times.

Think back to that exercise where I asked you to map out where your child is up to in their development – what they can do independently, what they can do with help, and what they can't do yet. In order for us to set child focused, reasonable expectations, it is really important we know where your child is in their development. Day-to-day, if we ask your child to do something they aren't able to do yet, ask them to do something independently that they can only do with our help, or ask them to do something they aren't able to do right now because it is a shaky skill and right now they are too stressed, then we will be setting them up to fail. No parent or professional wants to do that, but it is so easy to do.

If a child is getting angry or upset at something, take a step back and think, 'What am I asking them to do right now? What is this environment needing from them right now? Are they able to do this with or without my help normally? Are they able to do this now?' If we are expecting our child to do something they can't usually manage, then we need to change our expectations.

Of course, there is a flip side to this too. We always want to be encouraging our children to keep growing and developing, and part of that may be putting them in situations or giving them tasks where they need to (with support) learn or use new skills, or learn to use them with less support. We don't want to be saying 'but he isn't able to do that' all the time, or putting everything down to not being developmentally ready – we are ambitious about what our children can do! Think back to the example of Sarah not being able to share with the other 5 year olds. Maybe if sharing can become a 'can do with help' skill, this is an opportunity for us as adults to get in there and help show Sarah that this is a sharing situation, show her what will happen, guide her through giving and receiving, and model it ourselves. If Sarah is in a place to learn, this is a great opportunity to help her develop new skills so that in the future, she'll be able to manage this situation with more independence.

There will also be *plenty* of times where your child is getting upset and your answer to the question 'are they able to do this now?' will be *yes*, they are able to do it, they just don't want to. You know they can do this because they've done it before, without your help, in this same situation, and they were fine. However, right now, you think they are having a tantrum. In this case, we might need to use some of the strategies described later in this book to work out what to do next. For example, is this a tantrum because they just don't want to do something (in which case, we will probably be sticking to our guns and riding out the tantrum) or is it saying that there is something wrong, something that is scaring them or upsetting them, in which case we may back off and try and make the situation easier for our child.

## KEY POINTS

✓ We need to set child focused, reasonable expectations. These are expectations specific to your child about what they can do, can do with help, and can't do yet. These expectations are based on their developmental level in different areas, not their chronological age.

✓ It is very easy to see a child and fall into the trap of having expectations for what they can do based on their age, rather than their developmental level.

✓ When we set up our expectations of a child based on their age rather than their developmental level, we risk setting them up to fail.

✓ Having child focused, reasonable expectations does not mean saying 'my child can't do that'. We should always be looking to help your child grow and develop – maybe they just can't do that *yet*. Having child focused, reasonable expectations means we can set your child up for success, and provide them with opportunities for growth so they can develop skills.

## VISUAL TIMERS

One of the most common stumbling blocks with routines is that a child either wants to rush through a task, or doesn't want to stop what they are doing. Because a lot of children who develop differently have difficulty telling time (and/or often judging the passage of time – e.g. knowing how long five minutes is), their schedules rarely have specific 'times' to them. As adults, we might mentally have a copy of this timetable with specific times, but the child doesn't, and if they did, they may well not understand it. Your brain has learned to work based on a series of hours and minutes – once a certain hour has passed, the next activity starts. Depending on your child's level of language and development, their brain may well work based on a series of activities – when this activity finishes the next one starts.

If our child thinks in terms of a series of activities, the result can be a child who knows 'now is something boring, next is something exciting', so does the boring thing briefly, and then expects to move on to the exciting thing – that seems perfectly rational to me. A classic example of this is 'dinner time is now, playtime is next', and so taking two bites of dinner, then saying it is playtime. At the other extreme, when what is happening now is something entertaining, and next thing isn't, they might try to make what is happening now last longer. For example 'now is iPad, next is nap time', and just staying on the iPad indefinitely because they don't want to finish it because the next thing is, well, boring!

The way we get around this is timers. Specifically, *visual* timers. A classic example of this is a sand timer. You can get these in all sorts of fun colours and different lengths of time. The child might not know how long 'five minutes' is but, over time, they can learn that when the sand timer runs out, that means time for whatever they are doing is up and it is time to move on to the next thing. This sets an end point for an activity in a way they can *see*, and so more easily grasp.

There are lots of different versions of visual timers. You can get lots of apps that have a visual countdown (note: just numbers counting down isn't enough! They are abstract symbols – we need a visual representation of time), although, be warned, I've met many savvy kids who have learned how to reset these, or back out of the app to play a game. There are lots of physics based timers, such as different sizes of sand timers, or ones which use coloured water trickling from one side to another. There are mechanical ones, which work in a similar way to wind-up egg timers, except they look more like a clock running backwards, slowly covering up more and more of the clock face with a red overlay until, when the time is up, the whole clock face is red. You can even make your own visual timers, described in the downloadable appendix.

When introducing timers, there are a few key things to remember. First, don't try and use it to stop a really high interest/much loved activity, or prolong a really low interest/hated activity – at least, to start with. If you do, there is a risk your child will start to see the timer as a bad thing. Think about the transitions between activities they can currently manage, and then use the timers to show them exactly when that transition from one activity to another will be. Once we can get them on board with the idea of timers, and use them consistently, then we can apply them to the really loved and hated activities, but not before! If we do, the chances are it will become really hated because it is always the bearer of bad news.

Next, remember to direct your child's attention to the timers. Often, I'll meet families who have got a timer and use it, but their child is so engrossed in playing on their iPad they forget to look at it, or don't even notice that parents started the timer. If the child isn't paying attention to it, **they can't see the time has changed**, and they may not have an internal 'sense' of how much time has passed. If they child isn't looking at the timer regularly, it may as well be in the drawer for all the good it will do.

We need to:

- Get our child's attention.

- Show them the timer starting.

- Give them a clear instruction. Usually parents will give a verbal instruction like '15 minutes of iPad, then tea time', which is fine, but *back it up* with visuals – such as the now and next board, the visual for tea time, to show them what will happen next, and ensure the visual timer is visual (they may not know how long 15 minutes is – they need to see time pass!).

- If your child is verbal, ask them to repeat back the instruction.

- Redirect our child's attention to the timer every now and then, particularly as the time gets closer to the end – perhaps at roughly five minutes, two minutes, and one minute. This is particularly important for screens (tablets, phones, computers, and TVs), as these tend to be particularly engaging, and even typically developing children can find them difficult to come off, or feel 'I'm sure that wasn't 15 minutes!'

Once a timer runs out, we need to stick to it. If we start saying 'ok, five more minutes' because they get upset, I can guarantee you the same thing will happen again and again, and the timer will lose any value. It also makes it more of a battle between you and your child – that's not what we want. Ideally, we want you and your child to be on the same side, and it is the timer that is the bad guy saying something has to end. As soon as they realise you can overrule the timer, it then becomes about trying to persuade you to do so. While some tantrumming is to be expected while your child gets used to it, if your child is finding this particularly distressing, as always, seek professional help to see if there are any other ways to make this transition easier for them.

## KEY POINTS

✓ Children developing differently can have difficulty judging the passage of time, or understanding our language when we say how long they have left on something. This can lead to children extending enjoyed activities or rushing through activities they don't enjoy.

✓ Visual timers can help children to transition to or from activities, particularly when having to leave something they are enjoying or having to start something they don't enjoy.

✓ Visual timers come in lots of forms, and for different lengths of time. The important thing is they visually show the passage of time (such as by seeing something move or disappear), rather than relying on a clock face or numbers changing.

✓ When introducing visual timers, use them on activities where a child has no problem starting/finishing, so that they learn what the timers mean. Using them straight away to leave enjoyed activities or start disliked activities will stop visual timers being a communication aid, and make them something they resist.

✓ Visual timers are only useful if your child regularly looks at them – remember to direct their attention to them every now and then.

✓ When a timer moves out, **you must move on**. If a child learns you can overrule the timer, they will become frustrated at you for not doing so, and the possibility of a timer not always meaning the start/end of something makes it lose all purpose.

## MODELLING BEHAVIOUR

So much of what children learn, particularly in the early years, they learn through observing and copying others, rather than being taught. For example, children learn to walk through trying to copy what all the adults are doing, not by listening to their parents give them a lecture on how to walk. So, the way we teach our kids, particularly in the early years, will not be about what we tell them, but about what is in their environment. We want to ensure they have lots of opportunities to learn the positive behaviours we want to see, and preferably don't see any of the behaviours we don't want them to learn. This means, if you want your child to learn their 'pleases' and 'thank yous',[1] we need to make sure they get to see you and others do lots of it. Likewise, if we don't want them swearing, we've got to zip it!

---

1   Fiona, a very wise Speech and Language Therapist colleague of mine, pointed out that using 'please' and 'thank you' is a terrible example here. For children struggling with learning language, it is *far far* more helpful to teach them functional words like 'drink', 'help', 'toilet', etc. 'Please' and 'thank you' are social niceties which, sure, are great to learn if you've already got language, but if they haven't got that, let's focus on words that are going to be useful to them. However, since I think this is such an important point to make, I've left this deliberate mistake in as a way to talk about it – sorry Fiona!

The process of learning through watching others do it is called modelling. We can think about this as having three basic stages – exposure, interest, and opportunity.

Exposure is us providing our kids with the chance to see us do the behaviours we want them to copy. So, it might mean making a special effort to ask our partner for 'juice' at every opportunity. However, we can help your child further if we slow the behaviour down a bit so they get more *time* to observe it, exaggerate it a bit so the steps are *clearer*. So, in this example, you might slow down your talking when you say 'juice', say it a little louder to add emphasis, and maybe add a little extra context so it is clear why you are using it: 'I want juice'. We also want to keep it simple 'Juice' or 'I want Juice' is much easier to observe and learn from than 'Simon dear, could you get me some juice please?'

However, you can make the behaviour you are doing as clear as you like in exposure, but it means nothing if they don't notice! See if your child is paying attention, and if they are not, can you get their attention before you demonstrate the skill, or wait until they are paying attention? There are a few ways we can do this. The simplest way of doing it is **calling their name**. I know it sounds really simple (...and it is), but so often we forget to check a child is engaged, or to prompt them to pay attention by just calling their name. There are lots of other things you can do too though. For example, can you make it funny, or go over the top with it (funny things are memorable, and get a big reaction!). Could your partner go over to your child and try and get her attention, then try to get her to look at you when you are about to ask for juice? For children who appear very much 'in their own world' get down to their level and copy their behaviour for a bit, as this can sometimes help them to engage (more on this later in the book). Could you turn it into a game? For example, you could ask for a hug from someone and turn it into a fun game of tickle, which your child might want to join in. Here, saying 'hug' becomes the first part of this play routine, and encourages them to use the word 'hug'.

Finally, you've got to give them opportunities to use the skill you've demonstrated – preferably as soon as they have seen it, as they are far more likely to try something they have just seen, than try it a few hours later. For example, modelling asking for more peas probably isn't going to get tried if they are full (or if they hate peas!).

Likewise, if we know they love mashed potato, and always ensure they have plenty of it on their plate, they won't have much need to ask for more. Instead, we might only give them a small amount of potato on their plate, then have someone model asking for more and getting it. This gives them a demonstration, then an opportunity and motivation to ask for more. You can also try and make the task a little easier for them, or prompt them to use the skill they've just seen. For example, if you know they are wanting more potato, saying 'more?' or 'potato?' both as a question, and as a prompt for what to say.

Lastly, remember to be consistent in when you do this. If you only do it sometimes, then there will be fewer opportunities for your child to learn. Plus, if you aren't consistent then it is harder for your child to realise *when* to do the behaviour – sometimes you do it, sometimes you don't, so how do they know when is a good time and not a good time? When we are trying to teach a new behaviour, we need to model a behaviour every time so it is nice and clear for your child.

## KEY POINTS

✓ Modelling requires exposure – you need to do the thing you are trying to get your child to learn. Make this nice and clear by slowing it down a bit, and exaggerating it a little.

✓ Modelling requires interest – your child needs to actually see it and be interested in it. Try and ensure your child is looking by calling their name, getting a partner to direct their attention, making it funny, or making it into a game.

✓ Modelling requires opportunity – your child needs to be able to copy the behaviour. Try and ensure your child has a chance to copy the behaviour right away.

✓ Be consistent – this helps your child learn, and learn when to do what they are learning.

## CREATING PERSONAL SPACE

Children developing differently have a lot to cope with: struggling to communicate their needs, an unpredictable world inhabited by people who like to change their minds and do things 'spontaneously'; overwhelming sensory input, and on top of all that, they've got to learn language, social skills, motor skills, and not to mention ten years of education at school! No wonder they sometimes get overwhelmed.

This is why it is really important that children who are developing differently have their own personal space. This doesn't need to be a whole bedroom – just a small piece of it, such as bunkbeds with a sheet draped over the lower bunk creates a nice space, a piece of furniture to divide a shared room, even a big chair they can drape a blanket over to hide in. A lot of my parents use pop up tents – they may only be thin, and might not keep noise out, but it can give a sense of safety and enclosure, and be a very helpful way to help a child stay engaged and around the rest of the family. For example a pop up tent in the corner of the living room that a child can duck in and out of might save them having to go upstairs and not coming back down because once they feel calmer they get distracted by what is in their room. It also allows them to listen to what is going on, or even be half in and half out, so they can look and see what is going on, but know they're able to get back to where they feel comfortable, safe, secure, and aren't going to have demands put upon them. Plus they are portable! I've also known children who have found wardrobes or cupboards very comforting spaces to retreat into when things get too much (although, note it is *their choice* to retreat to these places – we're not talking about turning your child into Harry Potter locked under the stairs!).

Personal space should be somewhere a child finds comforting. For some children, this might mean soft blankets, sensory lights, and cuddly toys. For others, it might be somewhere they can sit among their hundreds of toy cars and feel content knowing they are all there, and that nobody is going to take them away from them. Some children might want somewhere dark and quiet, while others might need something bright, where they can make or play as much noise as they need to without disturbing other people. Consider what it is your child finds calming and comforting and work to that. You also need to consider what is safe. Breakables may get smashed if they are angry or upset, small things may get put in mouths, and hard things may get thrown.

Children should never be forced into their personal space – otherwise it won't be a *positive* personal space. If you force a child into a personal space they won't want to stay there. Indeed, you should never *have* to force a child into a personal space. If it contains the right things for your child, they should *want* to use it. If they are not using it, it is either not right for them, or they don't need it (not all children will need it, and children will not need it all the time). We can let, encourage, or prompt your child to use their personal space, but not force it.

If their personal space becomes their only way of calming down, or is just too good to leave, they may start to spend all their time in there. If that happens, there is a risk they will miss opportunities for growth or enjoyment, and their comfort zone might start to shrink. When their comfort zone shrinks, things that were easy to cope with before become hard, and things that before were merely difficult are now impossible. However, a child in distress who takes themselves to their personal space probably shouldn't be forced to come out – they are taking themselves away to somewhere they feel safe to calm down. That is a really advanced skill, and one (along with seeking comfort from others) we want to encourage. Instead, let's try and help them find other tools for calming down, so personal space isn't their *only* way to cope. We might want to use cuddles, sensory tools, distraction, talking, singing, play, listening to music, or games just to name a few. We could encourage them to try using these skills first, or for smaller 'wobbles', so that over time they may learn they'll have other options than just their personal space. This also comes in handy when out and about and their special personal space isn't available.

Personal space is just that – personal. That means we need to be careful about entering it. If a child's personal space is small (like a pop up tent), then this might be less of an issue – parents might not fit! However, if a personal space is big, like a whole bedroom, then we may have to be more firm about entering it at times. Entering when a child is really upset, angry, or is trying to get away from an overwhelming environment may not be the best idea. If they respond positively to you coming in and want some comfort while in their personal space, great, but if they want to be left alone, let's give them that space (provided it is safe to do so, of course).

When it comes to siblings, I'd strongly recommend keeping siblings out of the personal space. Often one of the biggest causes of sibling conflict is when a child wants space alone and the only way they know how to communicate it (or communicate the strength of their desire) is to lash out. If we are clear with siblings they are not allowed in that personal space, it will hopefully help your child developing differently learn that this is where they go when they want to be alone, rather than lashing out. The idea is that your child should know that if they are in there, they are unlikely to be disturbed – this is when they get their alone time.

Likewise, it is important that siblings have their own personal space. This doesn't need to be personal space in the same way we've talked about for your child developing differently – it may just be a bedroom, or section of a bedroom divided with a sheet or room divider, and you can enter as you would for any other child. However, it is important that siblings have clear personal space because having a sibling developing differently can be hard work. For example, I've worked with children developing differently who LOVE interacting with their siblings. The trouble is, they can get over excited, over tired, frustrated when their typically developing sibling does something wrong, can't keep up, or simply has had enough and decides they want it to end. Here, having personal space for siblings, so they have somewhere they can go to where they are not disturbed, is really helpful. It also means they have somewhere they can bring friends, if their friends are unlikely to be able to understand their sibling's needs, or how to interact with them in a positive way. Finally, it means that if our typically developing child is getting one-to-one time with a parent in this personal space, they are less likely to be interrupted by a sibling developing differently.

Again, I think having very clear rules here is important. Just as typically developing siblings are not allowed into the safe space of a child developing differently, the same should apply the other way around. If a typically developing sibling *sometimes* allows their sibling developing differently into their room to play, but at other times does not, your child developing differently might not understand why they are sometimes allowed in and sometimes not. That could lead to a lot of confusion, frustration, and upset. When you are teaching this, remember to consider visuals (symbols on the door?), and re-enforce this consistently. This includes supporting your typically developing child to give the same response when their sibling tries to come in. This will usually include a visual and verbal instruction to stop (such as holding up their hand in a stop gesture and saying 'stop') and an instruction (such as 'go to mum') so they know what to do instead. If that fails, encourage your child to call you so you can take your child developing differently out of your sibling's area – we don't want them to take matters into their own hands.

I know what you're thinking: 'Gosh, I'd love one of those safe spaces so I could get away from the kids for a few minutes'. You're exactly right! You can have an adult only space as well. It is totally appropriate to say that mum and dad's room (and/or some other room in the house) is a no child zone. Not only does this mean you have your own safe haven, but it also gives you somewhere you can store anything you don't want children to get their hands on (medicines and creams, alcohol, Christmas presents, fluffy handcuffs...). This is not something you need to feel guilty about – remember all that talk about self-care? Some parents are hesitant to do this, and that's fine – you don't have to. However, if it is just because of things like that image of the kids piling in on a Sunday morning and joining you in bed to watch cartoons, there are other ways to get that (duvet day in the living room, for example). Do what works for you as a family, but remember to look after yourself.

## KEY POINTS

✓ Personal space is important for everyone – including parents and siblings. It is space to get away from people, and to feel safe.

✓ You can create personal space either by assigning a whole room, sectioning off part of a room, or creating a den/using a pop up tent.

✓ Ideally, nobody but the person should be allowed to enter their personal space. The exception to this is parents needing to enter a child's room if that is their 'personal space'.

✓ We don't want to force children into personal space (then it becomes a punishment) – we can however encourage or prompt them to use it if they are becoming upset.

✓ We don't want to force children out of their personal space either. Instead, we need to think about helping your child find other ways to cope (if they are using it to escape/calm down), and ensure the outside world is still really appealing.

## SENSORY SENSITIVITIES

Back in the previous step, we learned that:

- Children developing differently can sense the world differently.

- There are the five external senses (sight, sound, smell, touch, taste), but also internal senses, such as hunger, pain, balance, and body position.

- These senses can be hypersensitive (volume turned up too loud, so trying to get away) or hyposensitive (volume turned down, so trying to get more of it).

- Different senses can be hyper or hyposensitive. Likewise, what is hyper and hyposensitive can change over time.

- Children developing differently can take longer to 'habituate' – to get used to a sensory input.

Let's look at what that looks like in practice.

|  | Hypersensitivity | Hyposensitivity |
|---|---|---|
| Hearing | Covering ears, getting upset at slightest noise. Sudden, loud noises are very distressing. Common culprits include vacuum cleaners and hand dryers. May notice sounds others don't and find them distracting. May be calmer when listing to music, or somewhere quiet. | Seeking out lots of noise. They may play music really loud, play sounds very close to their ear. turning the TV/music/computer up all the time. Not regulating their volume of speaking to the situation, talking to self, not responding to name or needing instructions repeated. |
| Smell | Gagging at the smell of certain foods, even if some distance away. May find the smell of certain places or people hard to get used to (different people's houses, perfumes, different hospital/school cleaning materials, cars, etc.). May be unable to enter the kitchen while cooking. | Smelling anything and everything to seek out new smells – even smelling things we might think of as unpleasant (including pee and poo) or unusual (pencils, sofas, etc.). May be sticking their nose right in scent diffusers, smelling their fingers, etc., or going up to people and smelling them. |

*cont.*

|  | Hypersensitivity | Hyposensitivity |
|---|---|---|
| Vision | Looking down when out and about, liking dark places, wearing dark glasses, avoiding bright lights or really 'busy' displays, wearing caps/hats/hoods. | Fascinated by bright colourful things and flashing lights. Sitting really close to screens, getting distracted by bright, colourful displays. |
| Taste | Picky eating, eating the same foods, often very bland flavour pallet. Noticing if a recipe for something has changed, even slightly, and refusing to eat it. Gagging on certain foods. Might sniff or lick things before eating them. | Happily eats items regardless of flavour (even if they are not food sometimes).[2] For example, licking a lamppost to see what it tastes like. Likes really strong flavours, and unusual flavours. Might cover their food in strong tasting sauces. |
| Touch[3] | Very sensitive to even light touch. A brush against someone in a corridor might be really painful for them. Not being able to tolerate labels in clothes, seams in socks. Needing very soft materials. Only eating foods of a specific texture. Finding being touched uncomfortable. | Seeking out lots of new textures. May be very tactile running their fingers (or face) over everything around them – carpets, leaves, doors, bedding, fences, people, etc. Loving hugs and being very touchy feely. |
| Pain | The slightest scrape is agony. Sometimes even touch can be painful. | Having broken bones, appendicitis, or an obstructed bowel and not complaining, or complaining as much as might be expected. |
| Hunger | Goes quickly from being really hungry to being full. | Does not realise when they are hungry (so not eating for ages), or when they are full (so doesn't stop eating). |

2  Some children who develop differently experience Pica, the eating of inedible objects. This *always* needs to be checked out by a doctor (usually a Paediatrician).

3  Note that the skin has different nerves for light touch (like a brush or caress) and for deep pressure (like a hug). Children can be hypersensitive in one, but hyposensitive in another. For example, children who find light touch overwhelming can respond really well to deep pressure hugs. However, always consult an Occupational Therapist before trying any deep pressure strategies to ensure your child is safe while you do it.

| Balance | Hates anything that spins them around (swings, rollercoasters, see-saws). | Loves anything that spins them around. Falling over and difficulty standing on one leg. Always on the move, sitting or spinning. |
|---|---|---|
| Body position | Holding their body in odd positions. | Not aware of where their body is in space, so tripping over themselves, accidentally knocking things, dropping things, leaning against things, etc. |

If we are going to create an environment suited to our child, we need to think about what their sensory profile is like. Not all children who develop differently will be hyper or hyposensitive – some don't have any sensory sensitivities, while others might just have a couple. Spend some time observing your child, and trying to work out if they might be hyper or hyposensitive to anything. As always, if you are unsure, stuck, or if anything worries you or is causing a lot of difficult behaviour, consult an expert – in this case, an Occupational Therapist.

There are some great tools online that can help you to do this. I particularly like the series of sensory questionnaires on the nhsggc. org.uk/kids website, as these are specific to different age groups, go through each sensory area separately, and give you specific ideas based on your answers. However, there are lots of other sensory checklists and questionnaires out there. Best of all, the good ones are developed by Occupational Therapists, who (unlike me) are experts in this area.

Some tools will talk about being for Autistic people – that's ok. Autism is probably the neurodevelopmental disorder people are most aware of, and there has been a big push in the Autism community for greater recognition of sensory issues, meaning there are more resources. These sensory resources are fine to use for any child developing differently (as always, with common sense applied). Just make sure they consider both hyper and hyposensitivities.

Sensory checklists all follow broadly the same format – they list a number of examples of hyper or hyposensitive behaviours and ask you to tick if they apply. They might not give you an output such as 'your child is hypersensitive to sound but hyposensitive in vision', but they might help you identify certain sensory aversions or interests.

Once you've got a handle on your child's sensory profile, you can then think about their environments. For example, at home, if they are sensitive to smell, could you use odour eliminating sprays, rather than air fresheners? If they are hyposensitive to vestibular input, are they able to move about enough to help them focus? What about out and about? A child who is hyposensitive for vestibular but hypersensitive for vision might *love* the monkey bars at a play park, might not want to go if it is really bright – would a hat help them manage? Could you go to one in the shade, or when it's darker? What about indoor soft play?

Again, there are lots of great resources online to help you think about how to adapt your environment, but also strategies which might help calm children with specific sensory sensitivities. I absolutely *love* NHS Greater Glasgow and Clyde's 'KIDS' (Kids Independently Developing Skills) website (www.nhsggc.org.uk/kids), which has lots of handouts and resources on sensory issues, among many other topics. This is my go-to resource when parents ask me sensory questions. They also have sensory box ideas to help children with sensory sensitivities explore their senses and get the feedback they need.

Thinking about a child's sensory profile can also help us unpick why they are becoming distressed, or why we are seeing certain behaviours. For example, a colleague of mine worked with a child who was very sensitive to smell, and every Monday afternoon would become extremely distressed. After months of searching, the school realised that on Monday afternoons a specific part-time member of staff visited the school, and she happened to have a rather strong smelling perfume. This child could smell this from their classroom, and became really upset by it, so staff asked this teacher to come in without her perfume (to both the staff's and the child's relief).

Lastly, I want to think about how we can use sensory input to help a child do their best.

This is the Yerkes Dodson Law. Like the Zone of Proximal Development we met in the previous step, it is a simple idea with a complex name. The Yerkes Dodson Law tells us the relationship between mental arousal (psychologist speak for how much stress, sensory input, alertness, etc. someone has) and performance.

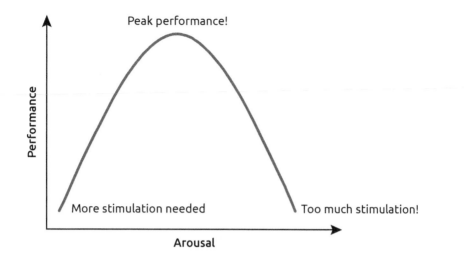

When you get into work on Monday morning, still tired from staying up too late the night before watching TV, you're not very aroused (not that way! Get your mind out of the gutter). Your brain isn't firing on all cylinders, and you need something to help wake you up – some coffee, listening to the radio, etc. before you're going to be able to do any quality work. What you're doing is giving yourself more arousal (chemically by coffee, but also through the sensory input of music), to try and move you further into the middle, closer to your peak performance.

At the other extreme, if you're too stressed, the office is noisy, and your hand is shaking because you've had too many coffees, you're not going to produce any good work. You're too aroused. You need to get into a quiet room, go for a walk, do some relaxation, or find another way to bring your arousal down and get yourself back into the middle where you can do your best. It's the same reason you turn the radio off and stop talking to people if you're driving the car and at a really tricky junction.

We can use our knowledge of a child's sensory needs to help them get to this point of peak performance. For example, a child who is under-aroused, bored, and trying to find something more interesting, might need music, fidget toys, or to doodle to be able to stay still and focus (like me listening to music while writing this book). People assume that just because a child looks distracted by something that they are not listening, but for a child who is under-aroused, it is the opposite, they may *need* that music, fidget toys, or doodling in order to focus. In fact, they can listen far better with it because it is giving them more sensory input, as it is moving them from that low arousal state to the middle, to the peak performance zone. On the other hand, a child who really has trouble focusing on anything because everything is far too distracting or overwhelming may start off too highly aroused, so need a very low arousal room, low noise, and a really calm manner to get them back down into that middle zone.

Lastly, remember that your child's level of arousal may change throughout the day. For example, I need music to write when I'm working in the mornings, but in the afternoons I find it distracting, so I write best in silence then.

## KEY POINTS

✓ We need to consider our child's sensory profile to understand how they experience their environment. There are various tools and check-lists to help you do this, but simply watching if/how your child seeks out or avoids certain stimuli can tell you a lot.

✓ Once we know how your child experiences their environment, we can work out what might need to change within it to help them work, relax, or play.

✓ Our child's sensory profile may also help us understand their behav-iour – sometimes our child's behaviour might be driven by their sen-sory sensitivities.

✓ If your child is under-aroused, they will not be able to play/work/learn at their best. In this state, they might need and seek out more arousal, such as a fidget toy, music, doodling, playing, etc.

✓ If your child is over-aroused, they will not be able to play/work/learn at their best. In this state, they might need to get away from stimuli, take a break, or do something else for a while.

## SCREENS

Screens are the bane of my professional life. Computers, laptops, phones, tablets, it seems that technology is becoming the must have toy for all children, including those who develop differently.

Now, that's not necessarily a bad thing. In the modern age, exposure to technology and learning how it works could be seen as a good thing – technology can be a great way to develop problem solving skills and learn. This can be particularly true for children developing differently where being in a classroom or being around people is really hard. Being able to learn from a YouTube video which you can rewind and replay over and over, where you can learn about what interests you at your own pace, can be a great resource. It can be a way to relax. I think most parents' idea of a good night in is a glass of wine, a comfy sofa and Netflix, and so it is for our children too (without the wine, obviously). More so for children who are developing differently – screens are predictable, engaging, safe (with parental controls), and fun. What more could you want?

The difficulty I keep coming across is *boundaries* around technology or more specifically, lack of boundaries around technology. Too often, a child gets a screen without any limits being put on it – they can access it whenever they want. If you give a child a really high interest toy like a tablet, they are going to find it really hard to come away from it. There really isn't much incentive for them to do something else, as there isn't anything else as good as what they have now! In fact, the psychological processes computer games use to keep kids and adults playing more and more are the exact same ones this book uses later on to drive positive behaviour change. They even employ psychologists to try and make people keep scrolling, playing, or clicking.

For parents, after a long day when you've not had a moment to sit down, it can be oh so tempting to think 'well, they are quiet, and I can *finally* have a few moments to myself'. Imagine that – a toy which keeps children quiet and entertained for hours at a time, and that they don't get tired of? It's a miracle!

The trouble is, a screen is not a parent, and there is no substitute for quality parent–child time. We know that young infants react differently to parents compared to a screen. This is because while a screen can be entertaining, engaging, even addictive, it is not *reciprocal*. A parent with a child can listen and react, and can change what they do to meet the child's needs – they can interact and you can have a back and forth. A parent interacting with a child can start a game of peek-a-boo, and let it evolve into a game of hide and seek by following the child's leads. A parent interacting with a child can notice when a noise happens which makes their child freeze, and can think about what might be causing that, and what might be going through a child's head. This interaction is essential for children's development. It teaches them how to interact with other people, how to communicate, how to manage emotion, what the rules are we follow, and how their behaviour will have an effect on others.

All that said, screens can be really useful. On those days when you really need a break, when you need a little time to do your self-care, screens can enable that. They can also be a tool your kids use for *their* self-care – they might be a bit of escapism, distraction, or just fun (because, you know, they're a kid – they are meant to have fun!). Screens are a valuable tool, but one that needs to be used in moderation, and with clear boundaries set.

One of the difficulties for children developing differently is that they might not be able to think of other activities they could do instead to keep themselves occupied. They might need someone else to suggest something else they could do to relax or entertain themselves. Another difficulty can be managing the transition from being on a tablet to being off it. While they may be physically away from their tablet, their brain might still be working away on the tablet and frustrated they can't access it, while other children may be more easily and quickly diverted onto something else. Finally, it often feels for parents (and for the children) that this is one of the few things that keeps their child calm, quiet and happy, and they don't want to take that away from them, so we need to find a bigger variety of engaging and enjoyable activities.

Ok, so how do we manage this? We set it up as part of our routines. We have specific times when the child has access to a screen. A common time is after coming home from school – for a lot of kids, this is the time when they are most tired, frustrated, and just need a little space (quite right too!).

Saying when they get it is the easy part. The hard bit is when we need to help them move away from it. We do this in several ways:

1.  We need a consistent time (or rather, point in the routine – remember that our children often have difficulty with telling the time) when the screen goes away.

2.  We need to give our children plenty of warning of this change. This is where your visual timers come in, as well as verbal warnings that it is ending soon.

3.  We need a high interest activity for them to move on to. Tea time is often a good one (food can be a great motivator after a long day!) as well as anything fun that involves one-to-one attention with a parent (remember, attention is often the biggest motivator for most children). If you try to go from a high interest activity to a low interest one, such as going from computer games to homework or going to school, you're in for a losing battle.

4.  When it isn't screen time, we need to put the screen away if possible: out of sight and out of mind.

5.  We need to stick to this routine quite strictly, particularly at the start. Later on, if your child is able, you might be able to use extra screen time as a reward (although do so with caution).

However, if despite all these best efforts a child is still really struggling to come away from screen time, then it may be time to consider if a screen is something your child is developmentally ready to cope with. Coming off screens isn't easy, and some kids really struggle to do this (as do some teenagers and adults!). If they don't have the skills to come off screen time, despite all our supports, then we need to take the screen away (especially phones/tablets/computers/video games; TVs are usually less problematic as they are less interactive), else we are setting them up to fail. If you do this, be aware it may feel really unfair if other people are allowed screens, or they see screens around them, so you might have to set house rules on this to minimise their exposure to seeing something they can't have but want, which is really hard for any child. This doesn't mean they can never have screens – we might be able to try again in six months or a year. However, some kids just can't cope with coming away from screens yet, and everyone is happier and calmer in the long run if they are taken away completely.

Similarly, I meet some kids who love screen time, and their issue isn't so much coming off when parents say to, but rather they get too into a game and get really frustrated when they get stuck, or the screen doesn't work/runs out of charge/etc. It can be really hard to pull yourself away from games – they are designed to make you keep playing, so we as parents may have to step in to prompt your child that screen time is finishing, if we can see they are getting increasingly frustrated and that it is going to end in tears. This means that while screens can provide parents with a bit of time to think about other things, we still need to keep an eye on our child. Equally, if they keep getting frustrated at a game, and we are always having to prompt them to come away from it before they get too upset, then it might be time to uninstall that game, until they are developmentally ready for it.

So how much is too much? That is a difficult question, and it will depend on the child. I've met parents who worry about their child being on a screen for an hour a day, and others who think six hours isn't a big deal. Ultimately, the choice will depend on your own parenting style, and what you feel is acceptable – I'm here to give you the tools, it is up to you where you think you need to use them. The most important thing isn't so much how *long* a child spends on screens, but that:

- You as parents are able to set and maintain consistent boundaries around screen time.

- Your child is able to *function* (maintain their physical and mental health, learning, friendships, etc.) with the screen time they have.

- That the child has plenty of other activities – such as time to be creative, get outside, do sports or some kind of physical activity, cook, etc. which do not get dropped in favour of screen time. It isn't their only outlet.

- That there is still *plenty* of that quality parent–child interaction – which is what we'll talk about next.

## KEY POINTS

✓ Screens are not necessarily a bad thing – they can be a great way for kids to learn, unwind, and have fun, and can allow parents some time to do other things. The issue is when a child can use them without any limits on it, or when a child has difficulty coming off them.

✓ If your child has screen time, make it part of the routine.

✓ Our kids need to have warning of screen time coming to an end.

✓ We need to provide our kids with a really engaging activity to move on to.

✓ If, despite our support, a child cannot cope with coming away from screen time, or is getting frustrated with their game/tablet/etc. every time they get it, we may need to stop giving our child screen time as they may not be developmentally ready for it.

# STEP 4: THE RIGHT INTERACTION

We should now be in a position where we've set up your child's environment to be well adapted to meet their needs (or at least, as much as we are able to and is practical – there is no such thing as perfect!). This alone will help eliminate many of the stressors and strains for both your child and your family. The next step is how we interact with your child. This can be tricky for three main reasons.

The first is that we learn how to be parents from our parents. However, what if (when you were a child) your experience of being parented by your parents wasn't ideal? Maybe there was a lot of hardship in the family? Maybe your parents had physical or mental health problems which (despite their best efforts) made it harder for them to be the parent you needed them to be? If your experience of being parented wasn't good, it will make it much harder for you to be the parent you want to be for your kids. This is a bit like asking someone to sit an exam when we only provided them with half the teaching – they can still do well in the exam, but they might need a bit of extra tuition and self-study to help them through it. There is absolutely nothing wrong with that.

Another reason parenting can be difficult is (as I've already mentioned) all the other stuff parents have to cope with. Managing work, paying the bills, and keeping the house clean are just the start. There is also your own mental and physical health, and your other kids' needs too.

Finally, children who develop differently can require a slightly different approach to typically developing children. They might need more attention, more support, and a parent who is tuned into where they are in their development, and how to respond to them. It can take more trial and error to work out what your child needs, and how we can practically meet those needs, because their needs are different to the needs of other children.

This next section is going to focus mostly on this last bit – how to interact with children who develop differently. We will touch on the other two issues, but they aren't going to be our main focus.

If you want further help and support on learning how to best interact with your child, *The Incredible Years* by Carolyn Webster-Stratton is your go-to book. I also highly recommend parenting groups based on the Solihull Approach, which has a greater emphasis on parent–child relationships and attachment (see: solihullapproachparenting.com).

Often when I mention parenting classes based around Solihull or *The Incredible Years*, parents look at me with a horrified expression. They think that I'm saying they don't know how to look after their child, that I'm saying they are bad parents because they need parenting classes. That is *not at all* what I'm saying. However, if you've got more to cope with – if parenting is more challenging for you and your child for whatever reason, then some extra training could be really helpful. There will be a lot you already intuitively know, but there will be a few crucial things that maybe you hadn't thought of, or that you could apply in a different way, that are tried and tested and could make your life a lot easier. It is a bit like going to a cooking master class. You already know how to cook, but this is going to ensure you do the basic stuff in the best way possible (like that really fast and accurate way chefs chop veggies) and teach you some more advanced recipes so you can impress your hard-to-please friends when they come round for dinner.

## KEY POINTS

✓ Getting our interaction with our children right can be tricky, sometimes because of our own baggage, our own mental or physical health, or the added challenge parenting a child developing differently brings.

✓ Parenting is hard – and parenting courses are designed to give you extra tools and to hone your existing skills. Going to a parenting course doesn't mean you are a bad parent.

## ATTENTION

All parents know that kids need attention – and lots of it. Just as a bored dog will start chewing up the chair legs, a bored parrot will start over-preening itself, and a bored cat... well, a bored cat will probably sleep until you come home and give you the death stare because you've not fed him yet, but you get the idea. All animals (including humans) need lots of attention. For our child, they may be able to be entertained through things like toys, games, or (dare I say it?) screens. However, these are not enough. Sure, they might keep a child quiet for a while, perhaps even a long while, but they are not providing enough of the right stimulation that your child needs. What your child needs most of all is attention.

By attention, I mean when you put down your phones, laptops, work, or whatever else it is that tends to keep you busy and give your child your full attention. How you give your child attention will vary by their age, ability, and interests. The most important thing about this time is that you can put distractions away, and are really *with* your child. This is the foundation of reciprocity, which I'll talk about in a later chapter.

Putting everything down and focusing on our child can be really hard to do. After a long day at work, my partner and I both just want to watch TV and do puzzle games on our phones. We're both shattered, and just want to switch off. We're both ok with that – I know it is what she needs to do, and she knows it's what I need to do. However, we both know that we need to also have time when we put our phones down, and do something together – watch the TV together (chatting and commenting on it, not just zoning out), go for a walk together, cook together. It's the same with children. If they try to talk to you but you're half on your phone, that's going to make them feel ignored and unimportant. If you are playing a game with them but your head is thinking about work, or what's for tea, they are going to realise you're not quite all there. So, what do you think they are going to do? They'll either switch off and stop trying to get your attention, or get frustrated and try to find other ways of getting it (often in ways we don't like!).

Another important thing to remember is that attention is not the same as 'keeping an eye on them'. You can keep an eye on your children while you make dinner, you can watch them play outside while you chat with your friend. Here, you're splitting your attention to keep them safe, but they're not getting your full attention.

Attention can, however, come with some challenges. In particular, because attention is so rewarding for a lot of children, it is one of the most common reasons for challenging or unwanted behaviour. That makes sense: if you're a child and you want to get some interaction with your parents, a guaranteed way to get their attention is to frustrate, embarrass, or infuriate them! Sure, it might be negative attention, but you'll have their attention completely. Likewise, managing the end of attention can be difficult because we're taking away something they love – you! However, there are things we can do to make this easier:

1. We want to help to teach your child more appropriate ways of getting your attention that we will (almost) always respond to. If your child tends to get attention in negative ways (by screaming, throwing things, etc.) but sometimes requests attention in a positive way (such as asking, tapping you, bringing you a toy), then we want to make sure we're responding with loads of attention to those more positive ways: we want them to learn these are the best and most effective ways to get our attention.

2. If your child has certain times or situations when we know they are going to do something to try to get our attention in a way which we don't like, then let's give them attention *before* they need to use those behaviours. For example, if we know that after dinner your child starts throwing things to try and get attention, then let's give them lots of attention in the time immediately after dinner so they don't need to throw things to get attention.

3. When we have our child's attention, we need to give them plenty of warning that we are going to be moving on. Think back to the section on timers for guidance on how we do this, but the key thing is the child should be aware that the attention will end. When it does end, we have to be careful to not respond to tantrums aimed at getting our attention back (although, as always, use common sense and discretion

to ensure your child is safe if they go from a tantrum to a meltdown), or else your child will learn this is how to prolong these sessions.

4.  Plan the next activity carefully. It can help to have an enjoyable activity they do next, or you could start doing an activity together which they are able to continue themselves once you leave. Remember that if we go from a really high interest activity (our attention) to a really low interest activity (such as homework), it will be much harder for them to tolerate.

5.  Try to have regular times for one-to-one attention built into your routine. This will help your child to learn that just because this one session is ending, it does not mean it is not going to come back again. They know when they will get your attention again, and that they will have the opportunity to pick up where they left off.

We need to make sure your child has enough attention throughout the day. Here, parents often (quite rightly) say 'But I give Alfie so much attention already – he can't be left alone due to developing differently'. This is true... Sort of. There is a difference between attention and supervision. All children need supervision, and children developing differently often need more of it. You might be trying to keep an eye on them while you cook dinner, play with their younger brother, or clean the house. Maybe they will be sitting at the dinner table with everyone else... But that's not attention. Attention is when we are really *with* our children, undistracted, and able to give them our full attention. How often are you able to do this? Do you think they need more? Is when this happens consistent? Does it always last for a decent length of time? Are you able to give it without too many distractions or disruptions? The best interaction is when your child knows they are the undivided focus of your attention, and they get quality time with you.

While most children love attention, sometimes too much attention can be overwhelming. A child with good language and insight may be able to tell you to go away (or to 'F*** off' if they are a teenager), a lot of our kids might not be able to do that yet. Instead, they might express that on their face, with their body language, or with their actions. One of the advantages of getting up close with children, face-to-face, is that we are more likely to see these warning signs and know when to back off. Attention does need to be balanced with personal space, and children who are able to realise and tell us either with their words or actions that 'things are getting too much, get away from me else I'll not be able to manage' have a really valuable skill. This does not mean we shouldn't offer attention. Rather, we need to think about *when* we offer it, and *how* we offer it. Is this a good time for your child, or are they just home from school, tired, grouchy, and needing to play with their favourite toy for 30 minutes before they are going to be receptive? Are you using the skills for play and interaction discussed later in this step, or are you going in with your own agenda of what you want to do? If your child wants to be by themselves and needs that time, forcing attention on them isn't going to help.[1]

Of course, you might say 'but I'll never be able to give my child enough of my undivided attention!' and that's fair – you already do so much for your child and there are only so many hours in the day. My aim here isn't to berate you for not spending every moment of your day with your child. Quite the opposite. I want you to have plenty of time for your other children and yourself too. But consider whether you're spending your time how you want – are you supervising or paying attention? Would you like to give more time to one child (or yourself), and if so, how could you do this?

It can be really hard to give your child (what feels like) yet more attention, particularly when there is so much else going on. However, my advice is that while it can be hard to start with, once it gets going, giving your child quality attention can produce huge benefits for everyone. Even 10–15 minutes of quality time can make a big difference. Often, your child will be happier and less disruptive, and

---

1   I do also work with some children who often appear to need constant attention, and get really distressed if they don't get it, or if a parent shows any attention to anyone else. Often, this comes from a place of anxiety – wanting to know their parent is always available to them – and they often show separation anxiety when being taken to school/nursery. We'll talk about anxiety later in the book, but all this other stuff is still important to have in place (for example, having routines so your child can learn that when you go, you will be back at a predictable time). However, as always, if you are worried at the level of distress your child is showing, seek professional advice.

you'll both feel like you have a better relationship with each other. Because of that, there will be less 'snatched five minutes here and there' (which eat up time because they are so frequent, but aren't as effective) so you might find you actually have more time to spare. Clubs and groups are a great way to generate this time for one-to-one attention. If Sam has after-school clubs on some days and Emily on others, then you've got a golden opportunity to have quality time with each child. Likewise, arranging a 'special day' with each of your children can be a wonderful way to get an extended bit of time with them doing something they really want to do and which feels special, provided all children get this equally over a period of a few months, so none are left out.

Of course, attention is important for ALL children. Quite commonly, I'll see siblings of children who develop differently start to act out during my work because their parents are having to spend extra time with their sibling, and they are understandably jealous. Equally, having a sibling developing differently can be a lot to cope with, and they'll need quality one-to-one time with their parents to help them manage this, so we need to ensure EVERY child gets some quality attention.

## KEY POINTS

✓ Kids need attention – and plenty of it. If they don't get it, they will find ways to get it.

✓ There is a big difference between supervision or giving your child a bit of your attention, and giving them your full, undivided attention, without distraction.

✓ If our child is getting our attention in ways we'd rather they didn't: a) make sure you are responding whenever they seek your attention in appropriate ways, b) give them attention at times they are likely to seek it, c) give warning about when attention will finish, d) have a high interest activity for them to move on to, and e) make times for one-to-one attention part of a routine.

✓ Sometimes kids can need space – they might not always want attention when we were planning on giving it.

✓ Focus on quality time, consistent time, for at least 10–15 minutes at a time. This applies for all your children, not just your children developing differently.

## PLAY

Grown-ups suck at playing. Really, we do. We start our lives being (quite literally) naturals at playing. It's almost like we are born knowing how to play... However, years of education, conformity, meeting targets and demands, and generally learning how to be an 'adult' train a lot of that out of us. If I gave you a bit of playdough, would you make something boring like a cube, or a ball? Would you play with it a bit, then place it down, all in one neat piece on the table to make sure it doesn't get into the carpet? Now give a bit of playdough to a child and see what they do with it!

It could be a person, a dog, a sofa, a sword, a baby, dinner. It doesn't matter that this particular dog is bright purple with orange spots – it's a special dog! Maybe they aren't yet able to make models, so are exploring how it feels to smoosh it between their fingers, what it smells and tastes like, what happens when they throw it, when they rub it against the table, how it breaks apart and then comes back together. Can you imagine what it must be like for a child when they explore playdough with this curiosity – as a whole sensory experience? And that's just playdough!

Our children *will* play, one way or another. It is how they learn. It might not *look* like play to you, it might not even be typical for their age and stage, but play is how many animals discover the world, including us.

You can describe play development in lots of ways. For example, you can look at the content of play. Children start with sensory play. In really early stages, this is about finding out how their body works and how to move around. Then, it becomes about exploring how things taste, feel, and smell, what they look like and what noises they make. Great toys here are things like noise makers, water play, bubbles, ball pits, light up and flashy toys, and anything else which enlivens your child's senses!

Next is cause and effect play. This is play where a child is working out 'if I do this, that will happen'. Pop up toys are a great example of this – children learn if they turn the handle enough they get a jack-in-the-box jumping up and giving them a scare. They learn that if they place the car at the top of the track, it will race down in a really satisfying way.

Finally, you have imaginative play. This is when a child starts to be able to 'pretend'. A child who has reached this imaginative play stage is able to 'pretend' that they are making dinner in the cookery corner. They know they aren't cooking, but they are able to act *as if* they are. A child who hasn't yet reached this stage might still play in cookery corner, but they are more interested in collecting the vegetables, in tipping them all out and putting them away, getting the pretend microwave to make that 'ping' sound, or simply copying what others do.

You can also look at play socially. Children start off playing by themselves – babies are able to occupy themselves for a time by working out how their bodies work, or being mesmerised by coloured lights or sounds. When this becomes more recognisable as play, they will often be quite happy to play by themselves for a bit, although they'll usually still love adults entertaining and engaging with them.

Gradually, as your child becomes more mobile and communicative, they will start watching others playing. They will start to learn to tolerate others playing alongside them, often on the same thing. This is parallel play – playing next to each other, rather than *with* each other. This phase is something some people associate with Autism, but *all* children go through this phase of parallel play.

However, around 3–4 years old, a child starts to become more able to include others in their play, however briefly. Over time, this evolves into cooperative play with someone, and even being able to share joint imaginative play.

Play is clearly really important. This is a major way your child learns about the world, creativity, social interaction, and communication, and builds their self-esteem. It is also a great way to bond with your child, and give our children our undivided attention. However, as I mentioned, adults generally suck at playing. Luckily, Webster-Stratton's book *The Incredible Years* includes an excellent guide on how to play well with your child. Unsurprisingly, for such an important topic, it is the first step of her book.

That said, there are a few general rules that I'd like to make here which, if remembered, can really help play go well.

First, remember who is the expert at playing here – the child. Let them lead the play, and show you *how* to play. That means, if your child is lining up cars, building a particularly wobbly tower that is about to fall, or is playing the wrong sounds for their story book that comes with sound effects, *don't correct it*. You're the student here – not the teacher. Instead, join in! Share in the precision of lining up the cars. Share in the shock when the tower falls. Share in the hilarity of seeing Peppa Pig go 'Beep Beep' instead of 'oink oink'. Often, adults see play almost as a task: 'We're reading a book? Ok, so let's read, turn the pages in the right order and press the right buttons at the right time'. That's fine for you as an adult, but your child might just want to play some funny sounds and watch some pictures – who cares about page four anyway, it is boring as it just has a picture of a lorry on it! If they are getting stuck, you can offer help or hints, but let them experience the success of *solving* the problem. It is far more rewarding than carrying out *your* solution. For example, guide them to the right area of the shape sorter, rather than putting the shape in the hole yourself.

Children who develop differently often play repetitively. They will often do the same thing over and over, ask for the same story over and over, or watch the same thing over and over. Often parents panic, and think that this is 'bad' because it is a sign of their difficulties and so should be discouraged. Wrong. *Most* children go through a stage of repetitive play – it's quite normal. Yes, children who develop differently may stay at this stage of play for longer, perhaps indefinitely. Others may develop beyond this stage but keep coming back to it as a preferred form of play. Both of these are ok. Repetitive play can be soothing, calming, and entertaining. It can also cause distress, and if repetitive play is starting to cause problems for either your child or you, or they are not moving on from this stage, then it's worth seeking professional help. While you might find this repetitive play boring, it is an opportunity to join in and interact with our child. However, remember that they are the expert – you're along for the ride and to learn.

Likewise, your child will guide you in *what* to play. If they don't want to play with the kitchen set, then there is no point trying to force it. If they don't want to play with the cars on the car mat but instead line them up on the windowsill, that's fine too. You might look around and see other children doing what looks like more advanced play than your child. However, your child is developing differently, and that may mean their play develops differently. We want to provide them with opportunities – we want them to be able to see you playing with the kitchen set and using the cars on the mat, but if they aren't responding, don't force it. It is more important that you're there and you are both playing together than that you're playing 'the right way'. Ultimately, the relationship you build with your child through play might be what helps encourage them to try out those odd new ways of playing you're doing.

Be a talkative teacher's pet – give lots of praise and encouragement for their play, particularly if they are doing something new, creative, or persisting with something challenging to do. See the section on praise for tips on how to do this.

Comment, don't question. This is probably the biggest piece of advice I can give you about playing well with your child. It is really important to comment on or describe what is happening in your child's play, rather than asking loads of questions. Early in my clinical training, we had to role play a piece of 'play' with a child – one of us would pretend to be the child, and the other the adult. I was amazed how many questions I found myself asking – I was asking this 'child' far more questions than I'd ask an adult ('What's that? What's happening next? Is that the blue one?'). It was really hard to resist – it was like it was hard wired into me. When I was the child in this situation, it made it feel like my play was either 'right' or 'wrong'. I felt like I and my play were always being examined or interrogated, and that there was a lot of pressure on me. However, when the 'parent' was *commentating* on my play, it was completely different – it felt encouraging, engaging, that I had much more attention, and in a more positive way.

Comments are also helpful in encouraging our child's language. It provides a chance for our children to copy our language and join in, rather than feel tested. For example, if you are commenting on something (even just pointing and saying one word), they can use language easily and appropriately by simply repeating your comment. However, if they have to answer a question, then they have to work out what the answer is, which words to use and in what order to say them.

Comments also show you are interested and engaged with what your child is doing. Take 'what's that?' – if you are paying attention to your child's play you should already know what that is! Comments also mean we *follow* their play rather than direct it. When we start asking questions, we tend to push our kids into a certain direction – we are asking them to elaborate or do more of a certain bit of their play, which might not be the bit they want to focus on. But if we just comment, we're being less directive. For example, you might be interested in the car and where it is going and asking all these questions about the car, so your child feels they need to play and make up a story about the car. However, they might actually be more interested in something else on the play mat which they aren't playing with because you just seem so fascinated by this car!

It can be hard to do, but avoiding questions and focusing on commentating on your child's play is really valuable. Here are the two ways I try to stop myself asking questions and instead make comments:

1. Answer my own question:

   - 'What is that?' becomes 'that's the truck'.

   - 'What's happening next?' becomes 'you're driving the truck to the garage'.

   - 'Is that the blue one?' becomes 'that's the blue one'.

   - 'Where are you running off to?' becomes 'you're running!'

   - 'Do you like that?' becomes 'ooh, you like that!'

   - 'Where is that car hiding?' becomes 'the car is hidden'.

2. Try and be the child's voice:

   - Rather than asking questions about the plane, going 'neeeaaaaawwwww'.

   - Rather than asking your child what they are excitedly pointing at, saying 'ooh, it's a dog! You love dogs'.

## KEY POINTS

✓ Your child knows more about playing than you do. Follow their lead!

✓ Children can be thought of as going through three stages of play – sensory, cause and effect, and imaginative.

✓ Play can also be social. Play will often start off solitary, but can develop into parallel play, then cooperative play.

✓ All children go through a stage of doing repetitive play, and children developing differently can spend longer at this stage. That is ok, it is still play.

✓ **Don't:** Correct play, ask lots of questions, do it for them, try and get them to play with something they aren't interested in, direct their play.

✓ **Do:** make comments, join in, follow their lead, offer hints or nudges in the right direction if they are stuck, copy them, praise them.

✓ It is good to think about what the next stage of play for your child might be, and introduce these toys by modelling how you can play with them. However, if they aren't interested, don't push it.

## PLAY TO LEARN

In the previous section, I talked about how to engage in *child* led play. This is where we start, as it helps to build your relationship with your child (which you will rely on later when you're laying down instructions or rules) and will also encourage learning. However, *in addition*, when they are developmentally ready, it is important to have some more *adult* led play. This is because when we take more of a lead in play, we can use it as a way to teach skills.

Adult led play is particularly important for children developing differently. Play is where children learn new skills, such as:

- sharing

- waiting

- communicating

- co-operating

- managing frustration

- negotiation

- following rules.

Typically developing kids all develop at roughly the same points, so it means that when one child is ready to start learning a new skill (such as sharing), there will be another child around also ready to learn that skill, so they learn how to share by playing with each other. Our child, however, may be ready to learn this skill later on, and might not have any child their age who is at the same level who they can learn with. The other kids have already got that skill, so expect other kids to know how to share, and may not be very accommodating. Here, we may need to take that play role.

Your child may also take longer to learn these skills, and so need us to take a more systematic approach. We might specifically target a skill they are starting to show signs of being able to do, and give them lots of opportunities in play to practice and develop this skill fully, that they might not get through playing with peers.

When we start to do adult led play, we need to go back to the idea of the Zone of Proximal Development (what your child can do, can do with help, and can't do yet). In play, our first priority should always be for both you and your child to have fun together – that alone is a success. However, a *bonus* aim might be to practice a developed skill, or grow a developing skill.

For example, maybe your child struggles with taking turns. If they can't manage taking turns, sharing is likely to be even trickier, so let's not do a sharing game with them yet, as this will result in everyone getting frustrated and angry, and you and your child being less keen on interacting with each other. Instead, let's do a game that involves some simple turn taking. This doesn't have to be a formal turn-based game like a board game, or saying 'it's my turn now, then it will be your turn'. You can get turn taking from rolling a ball back and forth between you both, or by you picking up the car at the end of the track to give it back to your child. Think about what interests them: adult led play should still be *play*, it should not be a lesson in disguise, and we should not be forcing a child. Instead, if they don't want to do something, we need to think about *why?* Is the play engaging enough?

Are they developmentally ready for it? Are they in the right frame of mind for it? Are they bored of it? **Is it fun?**

Often in adult led play, people try to add some 'structure' to the play. Usually, this means we have a set of complex ideas and rules for how things should be, and we want to impose them. That doesn't sound very appealing for a child, does it? (Remember, we suck at playing!) Now consider that a child developing differently might not be able to understand or remember your rules. Often, we don't even tell kids what our rules or expectations are and just assume they know the correct way to do things. So, let's keep the rules to a minimum, and ensure our play is really rewarding. Let's think about whether your child is ready for explicit verbal rules (e.g. 'you do this when I do that') or whether they need to discover the cause and effect of their interaction with you (whenever they do something, you do something that is big, exciting, fun, attention grabbing, etc.).

What does this look like in practice? Well, lots of children are really motivated by bubbles, so how about we get out a bubble wand and say 'ready, steady... Go!' then blow some bubbles. This is a really rewarding activity for a lot of children, so they are likely to want more. After a few more repetitions of you saying 'ready steady go' and blowing the bubbles, you stop after 'ready steady', and look at the child expectantly. What we're looking for is some kind of gesture (point, flap, reach), some eye contact, vocalisation, or saying 'go' (depending on the level the child is working at) before we blow the bubbles. This is rewarding, and it hasn't *required* us to use language to explain the game. Instead, we are rewarding behaviours (not just language/saying the word 'go') that are making a request. They might not be perfect (we might rather they *ask* rather than say 'go', for example), but we are rewarding the *act* of requesting and, as the child gets better and better at this then we can ask for better and better requesting – we raise the bar for what they have to do to get the bubbles.

We can apply this to other play too. For example, we can use painting together with potato stamps to make requests. We might say 'can I try that one please?', hold out your hand, *gently* pulling on it to see if they will let you have it or if they want to keep it (don't snatch!), and reward them ('thank you! That's very kind', lots of praise, hugs, clapping, etc.) when they give on request. We can then use it and give it back so they can see giving you something doesn't mean it's gone forever. If they really like watching a balloon soaring around the room, we can teach patience by blowing up a balloon and counting down from five (so they have five seconds or so of waiting) before we release it, then slowly making the countdown longer and longer. As they get older, we might be able to do things like getting them to help us read words in a book ('Jamie, what's this word? Pur, pur-ple?'), ask them to add up the dice in a board game for us ('hmm, I'm not sure what I rolled there Ellie – can you help me?'), or take turns ('is it my turn now Simon?'). With all of these, we are engaging your child with a rewarding activity and plenty of attention, but also giving them opportunities to practice and develop skills (and often skills which they have just seen us do – even better!).

Finally, it is really important we encourage play with others once a child is able to manage this. I use 'with' loosely here. I've already spoken about how children develop through different stages of play. A playdate with a child at the same developmental stage (or a much older child who can accommodate our child's play needs) can be helpful in providing opportunities for your child to develop their play skills. If they are still at the stage where they can watch other children play but can't join in or tolerate others joining in, that playdate might mostly be watching the other child play. This is fine! It is still a useful learning experience, and is in no way a failure – just make sure the other child is at the same point so they aren't trying to join in with your child when they aren't ready for that. Likewise, if they are at the parallel play stage, they may be learning to tolerate another child's noises and play preferences while they are in close proximity. There may be arguments and tantrums which need to be carefully managed so that the experience is overall a positive one. Typically developing children may need only light supervision at this point, but children developing differently might need an adult there to keep the peace, to structure the play, or prompt one or other child to do something a bit different to avoid conflict. It might be that with an adult playing and refereeing the play, your child is able to tolerate the other child playing 'with' them, when they would struggle to tolerate the child alone.

Sometimes it can be helpful to introduce some structure to the play. This tends to be when a child has developed more language and cognitive skills, but might still need help with their social skills. A good example of this is LEGO® Therapy. This is an intervention used for

Autistic children, where they take on different 'roles' (such as architect, builder, brick finder, etc.) that have to work together. This is a piece of play that the adults have structured in order to make the social roles more defined, to aid the development of social skills. Here, the adults are not just commentating on the play, but designing it. Any kind of game with rules, such as board games, sports, or innumerable family games are ones where we are imposing a structure to play. If your child is developmentally ready, these can be a great way to build skills in winning and losing, co-operation, communication, and social skills. However, if you have a child who cannot cope with following others' plans (yet), winning and losing (yet), taking turns (yet), or following someone else's rules (yet), then do not force the issue. Forcing it will just result in tears all around because they don't have enough of these skills to develop them further with these games. We need to work at their level – give them opportunities to practise skills they have and are starting to acquire. Take a step back, work out what they can do, and do that more before moving onto the next skill.

## KEY POINTS

✓ Children developing differently may benefit from some adult led play (in addition to lots of child led play), as they may have less opportunity to learn skills with peers through play.

✓ Remember to consider what your child can do, can do with help, and can't do yet before you try and help your child develop a skill through play. Either practise a skill they can do, or try and help them become more independent with a skill they can do with help.

✓ Adult led play needs to be fun! Even then, sometimes children won't want to play your game and want to do something else. That is ok.

✓ Don't overcomplicate play with lots of language and rules. Do make it really rewarding, engaging, and exciting.

✓ Encouraging play with peers is also important. These peers need to be at the same developmental level, or old enough to adapt to your child's level. You may need to closely supervise this to ensure it is positive and avoid arguments.

## LISTENING TO YOUR CHILD

Parents listen to their child (they might not always agree with what they hear, or do what the kids are asking, but they listen). However, for parents of children developing differently, that can be much harder. Typically developing children quite quickly learn to *tell* you what they want you to know. They may be able to use language, understand subtext, implied meaning, and context. They can remember what you said, and keep it in mind in the future. Children developing differently can struggle with one or more of these skills.

Take a moment to think about a typically developing child you know. Look at how much that child communicates in one day, not just to their parents, but to everyone else. You'll likely see a child communicating almost constantly to those around them (with the exception perhaps of teenagers who lock themselves in their room, but even then, they are often on the phone or computer communicating with friends). They won't just be communicating verbally, but also using things like tone of voice, gesture, their actions, facial expressions, text, and other written communication to communicate. The child is in a constant dialogue with the world around them – they are part of it, enmeshed in it.

Children developing differently can have far fewer ways of communicating. For some children, their only way to communicate is through their behaviour. Others may have some language, but they might also use objects, symbols, and gestures to help them communicate, and some of these will have very specific and personal meanings. Sometimes that language might be used in a straightforward way, but other times, a child's language can also have specific meanings. For example, a child screaming 'it's too loud' could mean that the environment is too loud, or it could be a phrase they have learned that quickly and effectively communicates to those around them 'this is too much, I'm really distressed'.

Other children can use language ably, but might not be able to use language effectively when they are really upset or distressed (remember twisting your ankle on the streets of Paris a few chapters ago?). It's quite normal, but can be more common when working with children who find communication harder anyway, and are more prone to feeling intense emotions.

Of course, at the opposite end, you have children who aren't able to use language, but who do understand at least some language – sometimes a lot. Just as we can't assume that a child who *uses* language well *understands* language well, we can't assume that a child without language does not understand language. These kids in particular often get incredibly frustrated that they can't communicate their thoughts, wants, and needs, and that people underestimate what they are able to do.

This means that when it comes to children developing differently, we need to listen really carefully not just to what our child says with words, but also what they say with objects, symbols, and most importantly their behaviour. Similarly, we need to be careful, as while their meaning may seem obvious, sometimes what they are communicating might mean something different to what you'd expect.

Because children developing differently can often communicate more in ways other than spoken language, and may sometimes have different meanings to what you might expect, it can sometimes be helpful to create a 'child to English' dictionary – what the child says or does, and what this means – and incorporate this into their Communication Passport. This might have some actual translated phrases especially if certain phrases have unique meanings (such as 'McDonalds' meaning 'I want chips'). It might list lots of behaviours and what they mean. Sometimes these might be quite obvious (at least to you), but by writing these down, it can help remind us that our kids are going to communicate with their behaviour, and remind us of some of their most important behaviours we need to look out for. Lastly, it might also tell us about which symbols or objects your child uses, and their meaning (for example, if your child grabs a certain bowl, that this means they are ready for breakfast). A lot of these will be things you've picked up intuitively. Here is an example of what I'm talking about:

| What your child says or does | What your child is communicating |
| --- | --- |
| Shouts (upset/distressed) and screams. Hits things around. | Escape: No, get away from me, or get me out of here. |
| Stands near something and looks at it. | Requesting, please, more, give me, etc. |
| Singing loudly and throws things towards people. | Where are you? I want attention! |

*cont.*

| What your child says or does | What your child is communicating |
| --- | --- |
| Grabs blanket and sits down with it. | I'm tired and I need a break. |
| Turns away from you. Pushes your hand away. | I've had enough, I need some space. |
| Puts shoes on after breakfast. | I'm expecting to go to school now. |
| Brings you symbol of a swing. | I want to go to the park. |
| Hands you their plate. | I'm hungry – it's dinner time. |

Some children have very clear communication so do not need this. Equally, your child might communicate in ways where you're not quite sure what they mean, so quite rightly you decide to leave it off, rather than make assumptions about what your child is communicating. However, if your child communicates in ways which might not be obvious, or that require us to pay extra attention to listen to, it can be helpful to draw up your own table of exactly what your child means by the things they do. Our child is communicating with us, so let's make sure we're *all* listening!

This isn't just to remind you of what to look out for (in fact, you're probably the person who needs this the least). However, your child needs to communicate with lots of other people: family members, teachers, and (importantly) their doctors. While an experienced teacher or doctor might be able to get a rough idea of how your child communicates from experience, a good one will want to learn from you how to communicate best with *your* child, and would love a quick cheat-sheet handed to them. I also love it when parents bring examples of what objects, pictures, symbols, visual schedules, or social stories they use, as it helps me think about how I can use and adapt my own to their child. We might even have our own communication tools we can use, such as a social story about seeing the doctor, emotion faces, or pain scales.

## KEY POINTS

✓ We need to listen to our children.

✓ Our child may communicate in different ways to most children. They may have difficulties using verbal language, so we need to 'listen' to their behaviour.

✓ Children (and adults) may not be able to communicate as well when they are angry, upset, or scared.

✓ It can be helpful to create a table, a 'child to English' dictionary, to help everyone understand your child, and to remind you of what your child might be trying to say, and make this part of their communication passport.

## RECIPROCITY

The best part about being a parent (or working with a child) isn't watching them, or looking at photos of them, it is interacting with them! When you give your child your full attention, you can be in the moment with them, having a natural to and fro interaction. It is like a dance between you and your child. Your child acts, so you respond, and they respond in turn. This could be with words, or (particularly for children developing differently) with actions.

In this dance, we try to get in tune with our child, to understand what they are thinking and feeling, what their motivations are, and to share these together. This takes interaction with a child beyond a simple exchange of words, or a simple action–reaction pattern of behaviour, to a level of emotional understanding and connection. Reciprocity requires us to have some 'headspace'. We need to make some room in our minds so that when we are in that dance with our child, we are completely there 'with' them. This means we notice their communication in all its forms, and think about their thoughts, feelings, and motivations.

However, maybe we've had a rubbish day. Maybe we're running late, we've got a headache, bills to pay, and our partner is going to be late from work. Maybe we have our own physical or mental health issues. We can have reciprocity with our child with all these things, but they make it harder to carve out room in our head for our child. So, while we are paying attention to our child and physically next to them, if there isn't space in our head, we might not really be there *with* them. When this happens, we won't respond as well to our child. They might be giving us cues to say 'look at this!', 'let's do that', or 'do that again', but we're caught up in our own stuff and don't notice and do something completely different. We're not in sync – while they're trying to waltz with us, we're in the corner poppin' and lockin'.

Parenting requires us to have that mental space for our child, and good self-care helps us to deal with life, get some reciprocity and help from others, and (frankly) sort our own stuff out. That helps make all the stuff going on in our head more manageable, so when we want to carve out some headspace for our child, we've got room to do it. Being an adult is hard work, and being a parent is even harder, so you might not be able to have that headspace for your child every time. However, if you're regularly finding it hard to really be present with your child and in their world, then we need to think about how full our own heads are, and whether we need some time to sort ourselves out (rather than beat ourselves up for not responding as we'd like).

Establishing reciprocity with a child developing differently can be hard. Other parents have it easy – their child might be learning language quite quickly, so they can have this dance to a large part (although not completely) with words. However just because a child is developing differently doesn't mean we can't get reciprocity, it just means we need to be thinking about interacting with your child at their level.

If your child is delayed in their language development, we may need to pay closer attention to behaviour: their face, gestures, and actions. We might also have to interact with our child in a way we'd expect of someone much younger. That is ok. We cannot force your child to develop faster. Therefore, we need to be led by their level of development. For the youngest children, it might simply be lying next to them and mimicking their noises and expressions. Some kids might want you to play with them and their toys, or watch and comment on their play. For older kids, it might mean might talking or playing a board game, reading them a story, or doing arts and crafts together.

Across all ages, being with our child means getting up close and personal. Get face-to-face with your child, even if this means getting on the floor with them, or running around with them (not, as I sometimes do in clinic, sit and hope they come back so you don't have to move!). That face-to-face contact helps your child know that you are interested in them, but it will also help them learn how to pick up what another person is looking at or interested in, and how they can direct your attention to different things. It can even help them see how to form words! It is also really useful for you too. You can check on how they are feeling (is this too much and do I need to back off? Are they bored? Do they need the toilet?) and what they are interested in (where are they looking? What distracted them? Why did they suddenly look happy/sad/angry?) which might help you work out how to keep their attention and your interaction going.

Getting reciprocity with children with delayed or impaired social understanding or motivation can be harder, but is by no means impossible. Some children seem more interested in objects than people, make less eye contact, and may make fewer attempts (or even give us fewer openings) to engage. This can be really hard for parents who desperately want that interaction with their child. This can lead parents to feel rejected by their own child and feel inadequate, or to push their child to interact with them because they are so desperate for that interaction. This has the unintended consequence of making it *less* likely their child will interact, because it's gone from being what should be a pleasurable experience to something they are perhaps trying to avoid because it is constantly being sought from them. We don't want to be the dance partner that is nagging and then forcefully pulling our partner onto the dance floor – all that will happen is the dance partner won't dance and will spend their time trying to get back to the bar and out of sight. Instead, we want them to see it as something rewarding to do. That means providing lots of opportunities to interact, and taking a softly softly approach. It also means accepting that a child developing differently might not want to interact as much, or give us as much back as we might want or expect. This isn't about you as parents; it's about your child developing differently and needing different things.

For example, a child might be really fascinated by toy cars and lining them up, and not interested in playing with the cuddly toy you've got. Rather than trying to force them to play with something else, we could try and join in lining up the cars. They don't like that? We could make our own line of cars, or we could pick the cars out of the box to hand to them. If they are lying down to look at the nice neat line, we could go to the other side and imitate them. We might name the colours of the cars, or use a car they have not lined up to roll off the table and catch. We might use the car to drive over our (or their) arm while we make 'neeeeeeaaawwww' noises. Or we might get something else we think they like to play with, such as playdough, and start to play with it next to them, or try to make a car out of playdough to add to their lineup. If your child seems receptive, we can try moving one car out of line, while being very tuned into their cues to see if this is accepted/enjoyed/wanted and could be the start of a fun game, or whether it is causing frustration or anxiety (in which case we need to stop it). Throughout, we're trying to be curious – to understand how they are playing and why, to experience it for ourselves by copying them and their play, and where we are allowed, to join in. By trying to understand their play, seeing how they respond to your interaction, and the fact you're always watching to see how what you say or do changes your child's behaviour, you're open to that reciprocal dance with your child – you've kept them in mind and, where they have responded to you (even if that was to move your playdough car out the way, or to indicate you need to leave them be), you've responded to their actions. Yes, the dance might be short and jerky, but it is still there.

Throughout, we are not forcing your child to join in with us. While we might make attempts to join in with what they are doing, we are not taking over or stopping them from doing what they want to do, and we need to be alert for signs they want us to back off. However, we are giving them lots of opportunities to join in and learn the dance. As soon as they do, we want to be rewarding it with praise, play (if they want it), smiles, etc. This interaction may only be a look, or taking the car from our hands, but it is still a bit of interaction. We are 'dancing' in front of our child, showing them it is fun, and as soon as they join in even for a moment, we are helping them learn the moves. However, we're not forcing them onto the dance floor, and we're not forcing them to stay. When they do decide they've had enough, or they don't want to join you, try not to take it personally – it is not your fault or theirs.

Children can have difficulties paying attention at the best of times, and a lot of children developing differently have more difficulty keeping their attention on track. This can mean that interactions seem really brief, or broken off unexpectedly. For verbal children, it might be jumping from topic to topic. It might be a child who seems to flit from one activity, one interaction, to another. It can feel like you just started to get some engagement, to build some reciprocity, and they're off again. The chances are this will start to feel really draining; however, it also shows you're trying to follow them, and that the reciprocity you are having has resulted in empathy – you're feeling tired on their behalf! For these children who have difficulty controlling their attention, who want the interaction but keep getting distracted, they may respond well to gentle guidance to help them stay with you. This might be using their name, or trying to keep the interaction fresh and exciting by not staying on any piece of play or chat too long, and moving on. Here, you're still flitting, but you're in control of it, so you can come back to things more easily and not go off track too much. You can also try and keep them on one thing for a little longer each time, to build up their ability to refocus on the task at hand.

Attention can also be related to sensory issues. We discussed earlier how some children have real difficulty focusing if they don't have something to play with or fidget with, while others have difficulty focusing their attention if there is too much going on in their environment to distract them. It can take time to work out what is driving your child's difficulties in staying engaged with you, but anxiety and sensory issues are good places to start.

Throughout this chapter, what I hope I've made clear is that reciprocal interaction is something that both parties have to want to do, and is not something we can force. We have to meet your child at their level, and with their wants and needs, rather than imposing what we think our children want and should be able to do. We need to be offering lots and lots of opportunities for interaction at their level, and not get disheartened if they aren't always in the mood, or they are not as interested in interacting – the important thing is we are giving them plenty of opportunities for it, and trying to make it fun, meeting them at whatever level they are at.

## KEY POINTS

✓ Reciprocity is a dance with our children. It is about listening to your child and responding to them, it is about being in tune with their thoughts, feelings, and motivations, and most of all, interacting with our children.

✓ For genuine reciprocity, we need some head space to hold our children in mind. This is hard to do if we are distracted, have a lot on our plate, or are dealing with our own issues or emotions. This is where good self-care helps.

✓ We have to be at our child's level – this may mean relying on play, behaviour, gesture, etc. rather than language.

✓ Some children may be less socially motivated. We don't want to force interaction here. Rather, we want to give lots of opportunities to interact on their terms and with their interests, but accept that our child may have had their fill, not be in the mood, or not be ready yet.

✓ Some children can have difficulty keeping their attention on task. We may need to help keep them focused by using their name, keeping the interaction fresh, or not staying on one piece of play too long. Remember too that sensory issues can affect attention.

## USING LANGUAGE

I've said it before, and I'll say it again – for many of the kids I see, spoken language is not their 'first language'. However, we live in a world dominated by language, so parents naturally want to encourage this as much as possible. That's great! But we've got to ensure we're meeting your child at their developmental level. To use language to communicate, a child needs to want to interact, be able to pay attention to their conversation partner, have learned a range of words they could use (often through play), and have developed an understanding of what the words actually mean. This is all before we even get to the physical act of trying to use sounds and shape them into words.

That might sound like a lot, and a bit daunting, but don't worry, there are lots of things we can do to encourage our child's language development.

**Use fewer words and shorter sentences.** This means your child will have fewer words to work out, making it easier for them to understand what you've said, and work out the words' meanings. A lot of children developing differently have difficulty paying attention, or don't have as much working memory (the amount of stuff they can think about at once). In this case, if we give them too much information at once they might only remember the first or last bit of what you told them. For example, if I tell a child to 'get your bag, put your shoes on, and get your lunchbox', they might only remember the first bit (that they need to find their bag) or the last bit (get their lunchbox).

**Use the same words regularly** (i.e. use 'drink' consistently, rather than saying one of 'drink', 'juice', 'squash', 'water', etc.). This means it will be easier for them to learn the meaning of the word, and to learn how to say the word.

**Leave them time to listen, think, and respond.** You've been using language for years – they're still learning, so they'll need more time to work out what it means. However, we as adults have an awful habit of filling silences by rephrasing what we just said, thinking the person hasn't understood. When we do this, our kids have something new to figure out, so have to go back to square one! With young kids, I always advise parents to count to ten before rephrasing. This might be less for older kids with a better grasp of language, but even with teenagers, if I know they have or have had difficulties with language, I'll leave some extra time between sentences.

**Say what you want your child to do.** Words like 'don't', 'stop', 'can't' and 'not' can be really tricky to grasp. They are small words, and they are easily missed, but they completely change the meaning of what follows. For example, telling a child 'don't run away'. If our child doesn't understand the word 'don't', didn't hear it, didn't understand it, or didn't pay attention to it, all they might hear is 'run away', when in fact we mean the opposite. This is why it is so important we use *positive language* – we always say what we want our child to do (e.g. 'walk'), not what we don't want them to do (e.g. 'don't run').

**Consider the environment.** A noisy environment with lots of kids and adults will make it harder for your child to 'tune in' to us (to filter us out from the crowd), and make it harder to relate the speech sounds they hear to the mechanics of how you are saying it. Not to mention they may find it harder to not get distracted!

These strategies will help your child to learn language, and it will also help them play and stay engaged for longer, because you're communicating at their level. It will also give you a bit of thinking time, so you can work out how you want to phrase something in the best way possible.

We've talked a lot about the Zone of Proximal Development (what your child can do, can do with help, and can't do yet). Using that idea, we want to try and match our communication to what your child can do, and what they can do with support. A child will typically:

- start communicating with gesture

- move on to single words

- put words into meaningful pairs 'go car'

- put words into short three or four word phrases ('go Grandma now').

So, matching that, if we have a child communicating mostly with gesture, we want to use gesture (what they can do) and a few single words (what we're hoping they'll be able to do soon). If a child is communicating with some single words, we should use plenty of single words, but we can also throw a few two word phrases into the mix. We want to be communicating at their level, and supporting them to move to the next level when they are ready.

Often, if a child is developing single words, we tend to expose them to lots of nouns ('name' or 'label' words). For example, we might point to a dog and say 'dog', we might show them a banana and say 'banana' to indicate what they are having for lunch. This is fine for single words, but it makes it harder when your child is trying to put two words together if all they have are nouns. When your child has a few single words (likely nouns), we might try to give them a few verbs too (doing words such as running, swimming, flying, drawing, sleeping, etc.). For example, if your child starts running, we might say 'running'. If a child is building with blocks, we might say 'building'. That way, when they are ready to start putting two words together, they can say 'mum building'.

As we talked about in the section on play, we want to be using lots of comments when talking with our child, and not asking them questions all the time. We want to narrate our child's life, not question their actions. It will make your child feel we are paying far more attention to them, and will feel a lot more encouraging and a lot less pressured.

That said, sometimes we need to ask your child questions. After all, one of the best ways to help your children feel in control is to give them a choice, and knowing how to ask questions helps with learning. However, if we're going to ask your child a question, we can try and make that question easier. Choice questions are the easiest ('do you want x or y'), followed by 'yes/no' questions, so try to stick to these initially. Then, in ascending difficulty, are 'what', 'where', 'who', 'when', and 'why' questions. When and why can be particularly tricky as they involve abstract concepts (such as time or others' motivations). Finally, 'how' questions are the trickiest – leave these until last!

Next, as I talked about in modelling behaviour, we need to ensure we are giving your child plenty of opportunities to practise their skills – in this case, communication. It is very easy when we have a child who is struggling with language to anticipate their wishes and act accordingly. We may know when they are likely to be thirsty to give them a drink. We may know they don't like eggs, so rather than giving them a choice between eggs and beans we just give them beans. We might be so busy labelling their environment around them that they don't get a chance to comment on what is happening themselves. We need to always make sure we are meeting your child needs, but equally **we need to give them a chance to tell us about what they want and need**.

This can be really hard. As a parent, particularly of a child developing differently, you feel that the world is hard enough for them and you just want to solve problems before they occur for your child. However, sometimes we need to step back a little, wait for them to respond, and give them the opportunity to practise their language. So, rather than ensuring they always have a cup of water available so they never need to ask, let the cup run out so they have a reason to ask.[2] Rather than choosing the TV programme you know your child will prefer, show them two options and get them to point. We still

2   Common sense alert – do not dehydrate your child! Just allow them to be thirsty so they have a reason to ask.

want to make sure we are meeting our child's needs, we just want to give them something to communicate about.

## KEY POINTS

✓ Reduce your language: use fewer words, use the same words regularly, and give your child plenty of time to think (count to ten before you say the next thing).

✓ Remember the Zone of Proximal Development – kids will go from using gesture to single words to word pairs to short phases. Make sure you are communicating at their level, and dropping in some communication at the level above to encourage them to develop that next skill.

✓ Avoid giving your child *only* nouns (naming words). Make sure you're adding in some verbs (doing words) to pair with those nouns.

✓ If you are asking questions, give simple choices (x or y), then yes/no questions. You can then move on to what, where, and who. When and why are harder still, and how questions are really hard, so save them for last.

✓ You need to give your child a reason to communicate! If you anticipate all their needs, they won't have as much need or opportunity to communicate.

## FEELINGS TALKS

There is a stereotype that the British aren't very good at talking about their feelings and, while it won't be true of everyone, I think there is some truth in it. We just don't like opening up. However, emotional intelligence is a really important skill, and that starts by talking about feelings with our children.

Now, to be clear, I'm not saying you should pour your heart out to your child about how your boss at work is a two faced [insert your expletive of choice here] who can't tell his head from a hole in the ground. We are not putting our emotions 'onto' our children – we are not asking them to help us manage our emotions, we are not looking for them to comfort us and make things ok (that's our job!), or to make them feel guilty. However, that doesn't mean we can't talk about how we are feeling.

For example, let's say your child has just been really helpful and it makes you happy – share that happiness! Say 'Emma, you're so helpful! It makes me really happy when you do that'. If they are sad that the trip to the zoo is called off due to rain, say 'I know you're feeling sad we can't go to the zoo, Will, I'm feeling sad about it too'. Even if they do something which makes you angry, it is ok to say (calmly!) 'Beth, it makes me feel angry when you talk like that to your brother'.

What you're doing in all these examples is *labelling* how you are feeling, and talking about *what* made you feel that way. Also, note that all these phrases use the word 'it' not 'you'. 'It' (i.e. their actions or the situation) makes me angry, happy, or sad, never 'you', the child. The last thing we want your child to take away is that they themselves make people sad or angry. However, we do want them to understand that their actions do have an effect on others' emotions. This is a critically important distinction to make. We must also be careful when talking about negative feelings that we are talking calmly, and that we aren't overdoing it – this isn't about us blaming our kids' actions to make us feel better, it is about helping them understand their actions have effects on others' emotions. Likewise, if we only ever talk about actions which make us feel sad or angry, what message is that going to send to our child? We want to outweigh any negative labelling of feelings with far more labelling of positive feelings!

Just as important, we can help label emotions in our children. If we see they are upset, we can label that emotion in them. Depending on their level, we might tell them how they feel ('you're upset Danny'), comment on how they feel ('you look upset Danny'), ask them how they are feeling ('are you upset, Danny?'), or ask them why they are upset ('are you upset because we aren't going to the zoo?'). Here, we are helping our child to recognise, articulate, and understand their feelings. By asking questions, we are also giving them the chance to open up and talk to us about what is wrong (helping with containment – see next section).

Helping a child to label emotions in themselves is really important. You can point it out in other people, but that requires a child to imagine how other people are feeling, which is a really advanced skill, and can be particularly hard for our kids. So, we need to double down on the other way kids learn about emotions – by people labelling those emotions in *them*. Until that time, it is just a lovely/uncomfortable/horrible/nice (depending on the emotion) feeling which they can feel, but have no way to communicate other than with their face, body language, and actions. We can't talk about emotions until we can label them.

It also starts to model empathy. By labelling emotions in our child, we are sharing their experience – we are understanding their perspective. This is the foundation of empathy and, if a child experiences this, they are more likely to try it out.

Of course, the children we work with might have difficulties with either their language skills or their socio-emotional skills, which makes all of this harder. However, there is still plenty we can do.

First, just because a child doesn't have language doesn't mean that we can't do some labelling. A child might not be using spoken language, but that doesn't mean they don't understand some of it. Therefore, we can still use simple words to describe emotions (happy, sad, angry, as a basic three to start with). We might augment this with some photos or symbols of a happy, sad, and angry face. Remember that for a lot of children developing differently, spoken language is not their 'first language' – their first language is visual, so while it might feel odd to us, showing them pictures might be more empathetic to them than any spoken language. There are plenty of 'packs' of feelings cards available to buy, as well as many free images you can use. It also starts to build up a shared language for them to communicate how they are feeling, rather than you having to guess. Yes, introducing new visuals when a child is a bit upset or angry is never the best time to do it, but better than when they are *really* upset or angry.

If a child has some use and understanding of language, then we can start to use spoken language to talk about emotions. However, even then, children may have difficulty understanding the emotions we are talking about. It's tricky to link the word not only to how they are feeling now, but to how they have felt in the past, and how others might feel. So, while we may be able to use spoken language, it might take a lot longer for them to understand the emotions we are talking about, and we might need to narrow the range of emotions we use.

Better to talk about a small pool of three to six emotions which they can learn well, than try to teach them 12 which they are struggling to really understand. Again, visuals can be helpful to augment what we're using language for. However for older children, I might also encourage them to use other media to express how they feel – music, images from Google or, if they are creative, their own art or drawing.

If a child is quite good at using language but really struggling to understand emotions, I might try opening up a discussion (when they are calm) with them about different events they have experienced, and trying to categorise them into (sometimes literal) emotion 'buckets' – 'happy', 'sad', 'angry'. I might then take one emotion 'bucket', and try and help the child to put them in order of how strongly they felt the emotion. I like this as it provides a bit more of a structured framework for a child to talk about emotions, and opens up lots of opportunities for discussion. However, it does require a reasonable level of verbal ability, attention, and cognitive ability, which might only be achieved by older children.

## KEY POINTS

✓ We can label the effect our child's *behaviour* has on us. We can say their *behaviour* (rather than the child themselves) makes us happy, sad, angry, etc. We want to label far more positive emotions (times they make us happy) than times their behaviours make us sad or angry.

✓ It is important to help your child label their own emotions. This needs to be pitched at their communication level, so it might be all visual, or it might be using words.

✓ Feelings are hard things to talk about, and if your child is feeling very happy, sad, or angry, they might not be in the right place to label or think about those emotions. Try for 'mild' versions of these emotions at first.

✓ Start with just a few emotions (like happy, sad, and angry), and focus on learning these few first, then expanding later on.

# STEP 5: THE RIGHT RESPONSE

One of our most important jobs as parents is to raise children who go on to become responsible adults. This is just as true for children developing differently as children developing typically. However, this can be harder for some children developing differently, and for some children we might need to adjust what we think of as 'responsible'. For me, the core of what makes a responsible adult is about being responsible for your own behaviour. What a lot of people think of as 'responsible' (things like managing money, chores, looking after others) is important too. However, you can't get to these more complex, more abstract parts of responsibility if you can't be responsible for your own behaviour.

This is where the right response comes in. This is about how we react to a child's behaviour. It might be a positive behaviour we want to encourage, a negative one we want to reduce, or helping them manage their own difficult emotions in a responsible way.

I often tell parents that, while you might be able to control a 3 year old's behaviour simply by picking them up and taking them somewhere else, the day will come (and sooner than you think) when you cannot physically control their behaviour. What then? It's a bit like driving a car with your child at the wheel. We can talk to them all we like, but ultimately, they are in the driving seat of their behaviour. That means our job then is to train them how to drive the car – that's a big job so we'd best start now!

If we teach our kids to drive their car early, and we teach them well, we can for the most part sit back and be chauffeur driven while sipping bubbly in the back seat. However, if we don't teach our children how to drive, if we teach them how to drive badly, or if we are bad at teaching them to drive, then we'll be a bit like my dad when I first drove him after I passed my driving test: strapped in tight, clinging with both hands to the handle above the door, with a look of terror on his face screaming 'Hit the brakes! THE BRAKES!'

This section, then, is about teaching our children to drive the car of their behaviour.

We need to approach this with caution. As parents, we have a huge amount of power over our child, and even more so for a child developing differently. There are absolutely behaviours that are not ok – such as those that cause themselves or others harm, distress, or to be put at risk, or that might mean your child is excluded from activities they enjoy. Part of our job as parents is to help our child live in a society which has rules, so we need to teach those rules. If we don't, we are setting them up to fail – we're asking them to sit their driving test without ever having a lesson. However, our child might also have behaviours which are unusual or idiosyncratic, but are just part of who they are! So what if Andrea enjoys singing and flapping her hands in the supermarket? It might be uncomfortable for us going around with them with everyone looking, but they aren't hurting anyone. So what if Michael doesn't like making eye contact or going to parties? As long as he is happy with his social relationships, then it isn't a problem for him, and it needn't be a problem for us.

Your child's idea of fun, of play, of expressing themselves may be different to ours, and we need to respect them for who they are. We can't train them to be like every other child, or to be less 'different', but we do need to teach them how to be a part of an increasingly diverse society. To overstretch a metaphor, we absolutely need to teach our child the rules of the road, but we don't get to choose what kind of car they drive.

## KEY POINTS

✓ We can't control our children's behaviour (at least, not for long). All we can do is influence it – teach *them* how to manage their behaviour.

✓ We need to help your child learn how to be part of society, and there are some behaviours which are not ok, such as those that cause themselves or others harm, distress or to be put at risk. However, we also need to respect who they are, what they do and don't enjoy, and how they express themselves.

## CONTAINMENT

Emotions are scary things, particularly if you are a child. Emotions make us do crazy things. They make us shout and scream, run in fear, call up that ex at two in the morning, or get carried away and take things too far. They can feel like getting swept away, like you're out of control, and incredibly uncomfortable. Of course, emotions can be wonderful too – without excitement, joy, contentment, elation, and others, life would be pretty dull. We cannot have happiness without sadness – you've got to have one to have the other.

Emotions can also be protective. Fear keeps us from doing stupid things (at least, some of the time). Sadness tries to tell us not to do something again, or to change the situation. Anger tells us to fight to defend ourselves. However, while emotions are a useful and essential part of being human, they are also a part we need to know how to manage.

A large part of how we learn how to manage our emotions comes from our attachment relationships. For example, a newborn baby knows nothing about managing emotions. Its emotions tell it to feed and to be held, and it relies on us to manage these emotions for them, to make them ok. Sometimes we manage these emotions by meeting that need (holding them or feeding them), but other times, babies don't know why they are upset, and we have to try and make it all ok despite there being nothing we can change about the situation. With our actions, our tone of voice, and by holding our child, we try to soothe them. We try to make those emotions ok to experience, and in doing so, we provide them with containment.

As a child becomes older and better able to walk and talk, containment might change too. The terrible twos are full of children facing the dual challenge of knowing what they want to say but struggling to communicate it, or realising that they have some control over their own destiny (they are realising they are at the controls of that metaphorical car), but that they can't always get what they want (you can yank control of the car back... for now). Now, when we provide containment, we might start to use more language. Along with our hugs, body language, and other actions, we might say how we think they are feeling, and show we know why the situation is so hard for them.

As children grow up, they slowly learn how to contain and manage their own emotions, and they'll rely on these skills a lot. Remember how, when I introduced attachment in step 2, we talked about how we internalised some of what our parents did to help us manage our emotions – things like hugging ourselves, telling ourselves it will be ok, just as our parents did? That is us trying to contain our emotions, the same way our parents tried to contain our emotions.

So what exactly is containment? Containment makes emotions 'safe'. It does not get rid of them, or stop them happening. However, it makes the emotions less scary. A child experiencing containment may still be upset at the loss of a prized toy, but being contained means they are not scared of the feeling of sadness. They feel that being sad is ok, it is manageable, and they feel comforted and empathised with. We are not trying to stop the child expressing their emotions, quite the opposite, we are trying to create a safe space for them to express and work through their emotions without feeling out of control. We do this through reciprocity – that dance of interaction between us and the child where we act and react with our child, keeping them and their emotions in mind, and sharing experiences – in this case, difficult emotions.

The way I think about containment is like this: a child hands over a ball of big, scary, un-comprehendible, and unmanageable emotions to a parent. In my imagination, it looks like a big tangled ball of multi-coloured string, constantly writhing and casting shadows all around it. The parent then holds that ball of emotions either for or with the child. The parent shines a light on that ball of emotions to remove the shadows, labels it, and slowly starts to untangle it. As they do so, the big ball of string slows down, and becomes smaller, with colours more evenly sorted and less tangled. Eventually, it is small and slow enough that the child is able to take it back and manage it by themselves.

How can we achieve this? The most important first step is reciprocity – 'being with' your child. To experience their pain, fear, or sorrow with them. To empathise rather than sympathise. When we do this, we start to hold part of that big ball of emotions. That doesn't mean we should be bursting into balls of tears ourselves. Remember, we want to show these emotions are manageable, and that we are not overwhelmed by them. But we can still show some emotion. It is completely appropriate to cry with your child at the loss of a grandparent, provided you are able to manage your emotions as well as theirs. It is fine to be disappointed with your child that their favourite ride at Alton Towers is closed after they had been looking forward to it for months, and show your disappointment in your face, tone, and body language, as well as your words. When we do this, we show we are 'in sync' with our child, sharing the same emotional space.

Once we've got that shared emotional space, we can start to manage this big ball of emotions. Remember, the objective here isn't to make the emotions go away (that is a fool's errand – you cannot stop emotions), just to make them manageable. Part of that might be providing physical comfort in the form of hugs, soothing words, stroking, being a shoulder to cry on, etc. We might tell them that it is going to be ok, and that it is going to be all right. Importantly, we stay calm and contained ourselves – we show we can manage this ball of emotions of theirs.

We might start to shine a light on the emotions by labelling them, and how we think they came about. This serves two purposes. First, it shows that we are trying to understand what they are feeling and why, and gives a child a chance to correct us if we're out – we ensure we are as synced as we think we are. Second, it starts to make these emotions more understandable. We can help a child see the reason for their emotions, and teach them ways to communicate their emotions by giving them a language to do this. It also helps us to normalise emotions: simply by labelling, empathising, and understanding how emotions came about, it will help our kids to understand that how they are feeling is normal, and that other people feel the way they do.

Sometimes, it can be tempting to jump in and try and 'fix' an emotion. There are occasions where this is completely appropriate. For example, if a child is crying because they dropped their toy, it isn't a big deal to go get it. However, there are times when a child isn't looking for you to fix an emotion, or fixing an emotion isn't possible. Instead they are looking for you to give them some comfort and containment. For example, maybe Sarah is being mean to Zoey at school. Yes, you might want to have a word with the teacher, but in that moment, the chances are Zoey is looking for containment, rather than a plan of what you're going to do tomorrow.

It is also important that we are not asking our children to contain our emotions. If we have a lot of our own stuff to deal with, it can be easy to accidently start to pass some of these emotions onto them. We start talking about how 'Sarah is being mean, just like your Auntie Anne is being to mummy', or 'yes I know you're really stressed Andy, but so am I!' Here, we aren't really empathising with our child's emotions and experiences; rather, we're adding our own emotions and worries for your child to take on. The result is we have a child trying to deal with not just their own emotions, but some big grown-up worries that they cannot manage.

This is not to say that our children should only ever see us being happy and smiley. That isn't realistic, and will give them an unrealistic view of adult life. However, we want them to see us experiencing these emotions in a safe, contained way – that we can manage them. It is the difference between 'Daddy is f**king mad Xander, because his idiot boss gave Harry bloody Harper another f**king promotion over me', and 'Daddy is feeling really angry at the moment Xander, but I'll be ok soon. Can you give me five minutes and then we can go and play?' Of course, this is far easier said than done in the heat of the moment, however the point stands. In the first example, while dad's anger is directed at someone else, Xander is feeling the full force of that raw emotion. In the second, dad is still angry, but he is modelling for Xander that a) emotions pass, b) emotions aren't scary and things will be ok, and c) a self-management strategy – getting five minutes to yourself.

Other times, while we might know our child is upset and needs our containment, if we've got so much going on, it is hard to carve out the headspace to keep our child's thoughts and feelings in mind – to get that reciprocity that we need for containment. A child might come to us and overtly say 'Dad I'm upset', but if we've not got that headspace, it is very easy for us to respond and say 'oh, what's wrong?' 'that's awful, but it will be ok Alice, things will get better', without any kind of thinking – we're almost on automatic pilot. We're not in tune with our dance partner here, and it is unlikely to help your child feel better.

If we get containment right, we will help our children be more aware of their emotions, and better able to learn strategies to manage these as they grow up. In doing so, we'll have shown them how empathy works, and how to comfort someone in need. These characteristics will stand them in good stead for making good decisions about their own behaviour in the future rather than being swept away by their emotions, and for treating others well.

Of course, children developing differently can find this harder. We know many neurodevelopmental disorders put children at higher risk of anxiety, low mood, and anger management difficulties. This why containment is so important; however, we may need to modify our approach slightly.

For children without much language, we may need to use only a little or no language, containing them mostly with our actions, and possibly some visual supports. It might be that your child has much greater difficulty understanding and identifying their own emotions, so might deny feeling happy, sad, or angry when to outsiders that seems quite clearly how they are feeling. Finally, some children tend to be more distant, and do not like interacting as much, or find physical touch difficult.

We can handle this by modifying our approach to containment to your child's needs, as we have for other parts of their development. For example, we might consider how much (if any) language we use with our child, how complex that language is, and put greater weight on non-verbal communication. We might have to consider developmentally what our child is ready for, and we may find that the main thing we can do for them right now is help them identify their emotions, rather than trying to explain how they came about. We might also need to think about how what your child may find containing and comforting may differ from our expectations. For example, how close they want you to be, how much eye contact to make, what touch (if any) they will find comforting, or if a particular object might help them feel contained.

The main exception to this is when a child has a meltdown. A meltdown isn't a tantrum. In a tantrum, the child is (mostly) in control, although this might descend into less contained sadness and crying. In a meltdown, a child has (as the parents I work with tend to say) 'completely lost it'. They are completely uncontained, overwhelmed by their emotions, and completely controlled by them. We'll cover meltdowns in more depth later, but the key message is that prevention is better than cure. In a meltdown, your child will struggle to be contained, and we may end up inadvertently throwing fuel on the fire. It is better either to catch it before it gets to a meltdown when you can provide containment, or provide some containment once the meltdown is finished – a period often of tiredness and tearfulness. In the middle of a meltdown, the priority needs to be keeping everyone safe, and giving a child space to work through it.

## KEY POINTS

✓ Containment is when we help your child feel 'safe' with their emotions. This is not trying to change or get rid of emotions, but making them manageable and understandable – making it ok to feel a certain way.

✓ For containment, we need to have reciprocity with our child – to hold their emotional state, thoughts, and feelings in mind.

✓ We can provide containment for your child by empathising, labelling their emotions, describing how the emotions came about, and offering comfort.

✓ We can model containing and managing our own emotions, but we need to make sure we are not putting our emotions on your child for them to manage.

✓ We need to adapt how we contain your child based on their language ability, emotional understanding, and what they find comforting and containing.

✓ Meltdowns are when a child has become overwhelmed by their emotions. A child in a meltdown is unlikely to be able to be 'contained', and you need to focus on keeping you and your child safe.

## REWARDS

The core of how we train behaviour is through rewards. Consider this: Bill teaches piano by rewarding you every time you hit the right notes with praise. A good series of notes and he gives you a sweet, and after a really great session he gives you a discount on his fee.

Ben shouts at you whenever you hit a wrong note, calls you an idiot, and after a really bad session he charges you double for making him endure your playing. Who are you going to choose?

Science bears this out too. Long term, rewarding good behaviour is far more effective at creating lasting behaviour change than punishment for 'bad' behaviour.[1] It turns out, in fact, you don't even need to reward every time for a behaviour. While rewards are helpful, if you reward every time, it starts to lose some of its effectiveness.

Rewards apply to everyone. Have you ever had that experience where your boss randomly comes up to you and tells you you did a really good job on some project, or with a customer? No? Me neither. But imagine if they did! How would that make you feel? I think I, like a lot of people, would feel really valued by that, and really motivated to do the same again.

What about if every day after work your boss thanked you for your hard work. Every day, as you walk past her desk on your way out, they said 'thanks for your work today Jane'. Would you value it as much? Would it motivate you as much? I think not.

When you look at the research, it is really striking how much more rewarding irregular, unpredictable rewards are compared to more predictable ones. It's the same logic behind how the fruit machines or one-armed-bandits work at casinos. Nobody is going to play a slot machine that pays out 50p for every £1 you put in on each pull of the handle. However, a slot machine that pays out £5 one time in 10, at £1 a go, will keep some people playing all day. You walk away with half your money either way, but the slot machine

---

1    I *hate* the term 'Bad behaviour'. When I use it, I've put inverted commas around the 'bad' bit. There are three reasons for this:

> 1 All kids push boundaries (it's how they know where the boundaries are!), and no child has perfect behaviour. This is *natural* rather than 'bad' behaviour.
> 2 As we will see, all behaviour serves a function and communicates something to us, so it doesn't make sense to label it good or bad. Instead, it is either effective or ineffective at communicating.
> 3 Finally, I worry that people stop labelling the behaviour as 'bad' and start labelling the child as 'bad'.

In this book, I'll mostly use the term 'undesirable' behaviour. This isn't great either – it is *our* interpretation of the behaviour as 'undesirable', rather than our child's. However, it is the best term I could find that didn't require a small essay to explain!

that only sometimes pays out is far more addictive. Video and mobile phone games use this to their advantage all the time. How many times have you or your child said 'I'll just get to this next level/goal/reward/etc.', only to get a small reward and want to keep going? They get you hooked not because they pay out every time, but because they *sometimes* pay out and you just don't know when.

There is one other big advantage to irregular rewards. If a child expects to be rewarded *every* time they do a behaviour, then when you stop rewarding that behaviour, two things will happen. First, they'll do the behaviour a lot more for a short time. This is called an extinction burst – basically the child going 'why isn't this working anymore!?' (like me when my computer freezes and I keep trying to hit the escape key again and again and again and nothing happens when I know it should). However, soon the child will stop doing the behaviour, as they aren't being rewarded for it anymore.

If, however, the child learns early on that the rewards are not every time, but only sometimes, then there is some built in anticipation (like the gambler at the slot machine not knowing if they'll get £5 or nothing). The child knows they might not be rewarded for the behaviour, but it is still worth it for the *chance* of a reward. Over time, we can make the frequency of the reward less and less, until rather than doing the behaviour for a reward, it is done simply through habit.

So how do we apply this to our children? Well, the first thing we can say is that you don't need to use language or a formal reward system to give rewards. You can, and these can be effective, but they are bells and whistles. You don't need to get your 4 year old to sit down and explain how you're going to reward them randomly if they use a knife and fork to eat their dinner – you can just do it!

However, unlike gamblers in a casino, your child might not know right away which behaviours they are getting rewarded for. So, at the start we might need to reward almost every time a behaviour occurs so they can work out what it is they are being rewarded for. We can also use language (if your child is able to use/understand it) or visuals to make it clear what they are being rewarded for.

The other big clue for a child as to what they are being rewarded for is *when* they get rewarded. It is much easier to tell if you're being rewarded for a behaviour if that reward comes as soon as you do the behaviour. If you reward a child hours later, even if you are able to explain to them what they are being rewarded for (or explain at the time that they will be rewarded later), it will have *much* less effect on them than if they get that reward right away.

When we apply this to our children, we need to remember that they aren't going to get it perfect right away. That's ok – *we don't reward perfection*. Instead, we focus on rewarding 'good' or 'better'. This will encourage your child to keep developing in that direction. For example, let's say you want your child to tidy their room. Only rewarding them if it is perfect is just going to demotivate them because a child or teenager's view of 'tidy' will be very different from yours, and it will be a lot to ask of them and just feel too daunting. Instead, let's reward them if they have at least made a bit of an attempt at tidying, even if it isn't very good – we want them to keep attempting, so that is what we want to reward. Once they are *regularly* making attempts, we might start to focus on rewarding the *better* attempts. As time goes on, we slowly require the room to be tidier and tidier to get the reward. To get the reward, it doesn't have to be the best they've ever done!

Just as we don't need to reward perfection, we don't require a child to be able to do something independently before we can reward it. We can use lots of ways to help make a task easier for our kids, and reward them completing the slightly easier version of the task (see the section on 'How to teach skills' in step 6).

It is really important that when we are giving rewards we are rewarding specific behaviours, not a *lack* of behaviours. For example, let's say your child has a habit of fighting with their little brother (not that *I* would do such a thing…). You can't give a reward for 'not fighting'.[2] Instead you can reward *replacement* behaviours – behaviours they can do instead of the behaviour we don't want (and ideally, can't do at the same time as the behaviour we don't want). Let's say Chris and Kyle regularly fight. Can we find something else that they can do instead? Maybe we could reward them for playing Mario Kart, for playing *nicely* together, for playing quietly in their rooms, for helping

---

2   Ok, technically, yes, you physically can – you could say 'well done Chris for not fighting' as you give the reward. But a) this is a rather back handed reward because you've linked it with a criticism so it probably won't be very effective, and b) you've just put the idea of fighting in their head.

dad make dinner – all these things are behaviours *other* than fighting that we can reward. When we do so, these behaviours become more likely to happen in the future, which in turn makes fighting less likely.

You might think that all this about rewards sounds great for young kids, but won't work on teenagers. Wrong! One of my favourite lecturers during training, Ion Wyness and the team, had a whole class of (tired, coffee fuelled, late 20s to early 30s) trainee Clinical Psychologists hanging off his every word for two days straight using this. He arranged us into groups, and each group got a piece of paper to place stickers on. He never told us what we'd get stickers for, but as soon as someone asked or answered a question and got a sticker, *everyone* was clambering to engage in the teaching. On day two he brought out a grab bag (a tote bag with a dozen cheap toys worth about 50p–£1, things like a set of four crayons, a mini slinky, etc.) and we all went mad trying to win one. If these strategies work on tired doctoral students, they will work on anyone. Ok, you might need to tailor your rewards to your child, and think about how you deliver them, but the process of intermittent rewards reinforcing behaviour is hard-wired into our brains.

A lot of parents get really fired up by the idea of rewards, and go out and buy branded reward charts. Reward charts can be a really good way of building up to bigger rewards, but usually only with older kids. They should also only be used when we have *one specific behaviour* we are trying to see more of. While some of these branded reward charts are... ok... a lot are actually awful and will not work. Don't get me wrong, reward charts can be really effective. But there are some rules you need to follow that a lot of the branded or commercial ones don't:

1. Reward charts require a level of verbal ability *and* abstract understanding. Reward charts typically work by gaining tokens (a sticker on a chart, a marble in a jar, a tick in a box) for certain behaviours, and when you have enough, you get a reward. Lots of kids can get the idea, but in practice struggle to relate how gathering *this one token now* will help them get the bigger reward later, or understand how many tokens they will need or how long that will take. This means the token itself isn't rewarding because it's not linked to the big reward

strongly enough, so the reward chart never gets off the ground. A lot of reward charts are targeted at children too young to get the idea, so are doomed to failure.

2.  Reward charts are best when they are co-constructed – where child and parent agree what the rewards will be, how many tokens are needed, and best of all *make it together*. This helps a child feel ownership of this – it is something they helped to make and *will get them rewards*, not something that is imposed on them.

3.  Rewards are never lost. Undesirable behaviour, no matter how 'bad', can never remove past successes. If you worked really hard at school all week, got five rewards, and needed five to go swimming at the weekend, then, exhausted, last thing on Friday you have a tantrum when going to bed and lose all of your rewards, how motivated will you be to get those rewards back? Not at all.

4.  Rewards should not be time bound. This is for similar reasons to point 3. If you need to get five tokens by Saturday to go swimming, and you realise last thing on a Friday you're not going to make it, then why try for the rest of the day? Instead, we might say that (while swimming has to happen at the week-end), it will be the weekend after the tokens are earned. So yes, maybe you don't get enough this week, but you only have one more to earn and you get to go swimming next week.

5.  Reward charts should never record failures or undesirable behaviour. It won't discourage undesirable behaviour, only make a child less likely to want to engage in the reward chart at all.

6.  Rewards need to be meaningful *to your child*. Money is usually the first reward parents think of, but it is usually the least effective, particularly for our kids who might find understand-ing the value of money hard. What is far more rewarding is **one-to-one attention** (going swimming with mum, going to the park with dad, etc.), **control** (getting to choose what to have for dinner, getting to choose a film for movie night),

and **activities** (doing things *with* family). There are always exceptions to this, and children with difficulties with socialising or sensory issues may only want attention under certain conditions, or find some activities you or I might think of as rewarding actually really stressful. You know your child best. Try and think about the sorts of things *they* might like and that you can offer. Better yet, have a conversation with your child about rewards they would like. Often the best rewards cost very little.

7.  Be clear what children can earn rewards for. There are times when we just want to reward a child in the moment because they did a behaviour that we really want to encourage, so we might use praise and rewards then without any kind of reward chart. Reward charts are best when we are looking for one *specific* behaviour. 'Being good' is a really poorly worded behaviour to stick on the reward chart as the behaviour you want to see more of. Who decides if 'good' is good enough? What does 'being good' look like? What will happen with 'being good' as a target behaviour is that parents are going to get over ambitious in what they want, and the child is going to get frustrated because they think they have been good but someone else disagrees. We need behaviours that are objective, and people can't disagree about. For example, finishing their plate of food, coming off the computer at the first time of asking, being ready for school by 8:15 am. These can't be disputed, whereas 'eating enough of your food', 'coming off your computer nicely', or 'being ready in time for school' can be. Doing this also means that you never risk moving the goalposts (i.e. 'how early does mum want to get to school today?') and you can't be blamed for being unfair about what you do and don't count. Instead, you can try and help your child meet the rules you agreed on (i.e. 'come on Ian, only 15 seconds left before 8:15 – you can do it!) – you get to be on *their side*, rather than the bad guy.

For further reading on rewards, I highly recommend *The Incredible Years*, which goes into the nuts and bolts of this a lot more.

## KEY POINTS

✓ Rewards are far more effective than punishments.

✓ The best way to use rewards is intermittently. Don't give a reward *every* time, start by giving the reward most of the time, then gradually reward less frequently as it becomes habit.

✓ You don't need to use language to explain why you are rewarding your child (although it can help). Just reward the behaviour you want more of as soon as you see it.

✓ We want 'good' or 'better' – not perfect. Once they have developed the first stage of a skill or behaviour we might reward that less frequently, but if they do it a little better/for longer/more, then we reward that more frequently.

✓ We can still reward our kids if we need to help them do something.

✓ Reward specific behaviours you want to see.

✓ Don't reward 'absence' of behaviours, such as rewarding 'not fighting'. Instead, reward replacement behaviours that they can't do at the same time as the behaviour you want to reduce.

✓ Rewards work on kids and adults of all ages!

✓ Don't go out and buy a reward chart. There are a lot of problems with these, and they only work for certain kids in specific situations. If you think one could be useful for you and your child, make it together instead!

## PRAISE

Praise is just another reward. However, it is free, easy to use, and when used well, can be just as (or more) effective than any reward for a lot of children. Toys, games, and screens are great, but faced with a choice of unlimited toys, or life without a parent, I know what kids would (eventually) choose.

Praise is built on (and helps to grow) our relationship with our child. Joe Bloggs on the street praising your child (while creepy) probably won't mean that much to them. However, when someone they love and respect praises them it means the world.

As with rewards, there are some similar rules to follow to ensure praise is effective:

1.  Be specific. Don't just say 'good job', say *what* you are praising them for. If they did their homework when asked, say 'Great job getting your homework done'.

2.  Don't give backhanded compliments. It might sound obvious, but don't pair a compliment with criticism – it becomes much less effective, such as: 'thank you for doing your homework – I usually have to ask you ten times!'

3.  Be immediate. Don't wait until five minutes after they did something. Praise it right away!

4.  Keep your language simple. Remember, for a lot of our kids, spoken language is not their first language – they learn and communicate best by seeing and doing. So, if you are going to praise with language, think carefully about the words you use to ensure they are easy for your child to understand.

5.  Use body language. Words help us target exactly what we are praising them for, but a lot of the enthusiasm of our praise comes from our face, our body language, our gestures. Sometimes, you don't even need words. Eye contact (if comfortable for them), a big smile, hugs, and a big thumbs up go a long way.

6.  Make it meaningful. If our kids think differently, then they might find some forms of praise more meaningful than others. For example, a young Autistic child who is really into Thomas the Tank Engine may *love* being told they are 'a really useful engine'. A teenager with an Intellectual Disability who wants to be doing things every other teenager is doing might love it when you say they are being really grown up, or acting like a teenager.

Most children love praise. There will be times where they are mad at us, or really stressed, and we need to use our containment skills instead. However, generally, most kids will love getting praise and find it really rewarding. There are, however, a small group of children who seem to react against praise. There seems to be a few different possible reasons for this:

- They might not like people drawing attention to them.

- They might have a negative view of themselves and not want to hear anything contrary to that.

- They might feel it adds pressure – that next time it has to be just as good if not better.

- They might think it is a demand to do something again.

If your child is consistently reacting negatively to praise, even when calm, it is worth getting professional advice to work out what that is about, and the best response to it. However, while waiting to be seen, you can try *indirect* praise. Two good ways to do this are:

- Talk about a child's successes to someone else while your child is in earshot. For example, telling your partner 'Didn't Sarah do well with her homework today – she came in and did it right away, and worked really hard on it too' while Sarah can overhear.

- Praise the work, not the child. For example, 'This is a great piece of homework. It is really neat, and ready to go in the school bag before I've even served dinner'. Importantly, we don't address this to Sarah, we just say it to ourselves, else she may think we are praising her, rather than the work.

However, if your child is still reacting negatively to these, wait until you're seen by a professional.

## KEY POINTS

✓ Praise is a really effective reward.

✓ Be specific with your praise – tell them exactly what you are praising.

✓ Don't pair praise with criticism.

✓ Give praise right away.

✓ Keep your language simple.

✓ Use your body language and facial expressions.

✓ Make your praise meaningful to your child.

✓ Some children react negatively to praise, even when calm. If that is the case, get professional guidance.

## CALMNESS

'Keep calm and carry on'.

Easier said than done sometimes, isn't it? I can't tell you the number of times I've seen a child in clinic who is bouncing off the walls, then when the hour is up, waving goodbye with a smile pinned rigidly to my face, closing the door, and collapsing onto my chair, exhausted from trying to keep calm. I grit my teeth and smile, but I can feel my stomach tensing as I try and keep it together, and practise what I preach. Keeping calm can be hard for me in an hour of clinic, so it must be harder for you managing it every day.

Some kids (particularly those developing differently) are hard work! I'm constantly in awe and amazed by the patience, kindness, and resilience of the parents I meet. However, I know it isn't easy, and that, sometimes, our kids can really push our buttons. This is why self-care is *so important*. It is taking time out for ourselves that gives us the strength to keep calm when sometimes we just want to scream. If we aren't looking after ourselves, giving ourselves some time out, and spending some time with people we can offload to, we simply won't be able to keep up our cool, calm, and collected parenting.

This is important because, well... how often does losing your temper with a child and shouting, screaming, turning red in the face, jumping up and down and generally causing a bigger scene than your child work? Usually not very often. Don't get me wrong, it probably works the first few times, when your child gets the 'shock factor' and thinks 'oh s**t, I've really crossed a line here'. However, if this happens too much, it starts to have less and less effect as your child gets used to it. That, of course, assumes your child gets the shock factor in the first place – a lot of our kids developing differently might not realise the effect their behaviour is having on you. If so, then the best case scenario is that your child doesn't react. The worst case is that your distress and shouting makes them distressed, shouty, and angry. I've also had kids who find this *hilarious* and start laughing at daddy having a tantrum at the school gates.

What happens when your child starts shouting, climbing, being destructive, or doing something else that pushes our buttons, is we start to feel embarrassed, frustrated, and angry, and perhaps raise our voice. Mostly likely they either don't react to it, get more upset, or realise they are getting a reaction. Either way, as their behaviour (and perhaps their distress), either carries on or gets worse, so we get even more embarrassed, frustrated, or angry, and so the cycle continues.

It is *our job* to break that cycle – they can't do this, so we have to. This is why keeping calm is so important. Our kids are look-ing to us to make their big, scary, unmanageable emotions ok – to contain them. We can't do that if we aren't able to manage our own, which is why we need to take time out for ourselves, so that when we have all these emotions bubbling up inside us, we *are* able to manage them. We don't need to make them go away. It is absolutely fine to feel embarrassed, frustrated, angry, etc. – that's called being human, I'd be worried if you didn't feel that way sometimes! What is important is how we *react* to those emotions, and our children. Can we recognise how we feel, take a deep breath, and go back to our values as parents and decide how we want to react, rather than let our emotions in the moment decide our actions?

## KEY POINTS

✓ All kids have behaviours which can be challenging, exhausting, unpredictable, embarrassing, or otherwise difficult. Kids developing differently are likely to have more of these behaviours.

✓ It is ok to get stressed, upset, or angry with our child's behaviour – these emotions are natural to have. However if we show these emo-tions or react to them, we will often make the situation worse as you and your child's behaviour will start to feed off each other.

✓ Practise self-care so you can try and keep calm when your child's behaviour is pushing your buttons.

## REWARDING THE GOOD, IGNORING THE 'BAD'

A few sections ago, I talked about the power of irregular rewards, and how these are so much more motivating than regular rewards. We can use this to our advantage – we can reward our kids pretty regularly at first (so they get the idea) then scale back to only irregular rewards. This is a great way of teaching the behaviour we want to see, and encouraging it to happen more often. This should always be our primary way of shaping our child's behaviour.

Often in parenting groups, I'll prattle on about the value and power of rewards, and then some plucky parent will ask about what to do with 'bad' behaviour. I get where this comes from, but I think it makes some faulty assumptions. In the introduction to this step, I talked about how we cannot control our children's behaviour. We can offer guidance, say what we want them to do, shout, scream, punish, or send out smoke signals, but ultimately they are in control of their actions, not us.

If we make a big deal out of undesirable behaviour, we might discourage your child from doing it, but it's unlikely to be particularly effective long term. For some children, this could even be rewarding, and encourage the behaviour to happen more often. It is far easier and more effective to focus most of our efforts on teaching our children a library of good, positive, pro-social behaviours, and rewarding these, so that children learn that this is a good thing to do, and that good things happen when you do good things. This builds internal motivation to do these positive behaviours, and it is usually quite hard to do a 'good' behaviour at the same time as an undesirable behaviour. Therefore, **if we can motivate your child do to these 'good' behaviours, they are unlikely to do the undesirable behaviours**.

So what do we do when these undesirable behaviours naturally occur? After all, kids will be kids: they will mess about, wind you up, do things they know aren't right, and push boundaries.

One of the first strategies I tell parents about is to reward the good behaviour, and ignore the 'bad' behaviour. If your child has two behaviours they could do, one which is rewarding, and one which isn't, then it is a pretty straightforward choice. If we react strongly to an undesirable behaviour, and our kids learn that this winds us up, gets a big reaction, gets our attention, or is a way for *them* to control *our* behaviour, then that is going to be *highly* rewarding for them.

One of the best ways we can avoid this happening is to ignore the undesirable behaviour.

For example, Jamie is playing with his paints on the kitchen table with dad. He is painting away, and dad is making lots of fantastic comments like 'look at that big house!', 'that looks like me – he has my blue eyes', and 'you are good at painting'. Jamie is enjoying how much praise and attention he is getting, and starts to get a little hyper. Dad, perhaps not realising this, keeps going. Eventually, in his over excitement, Jamie decides to (clearly deliberately) pour the entire pot of paint all over the table.

Dad could react in one of two ways. He could (like I suspect most parents would want to) shout and scream. 'Why did you do that?! We were playing so nicely and you go and do this. WE DON'T PUT PAINT ON THE TABLE JAMIE'. Dad starts frantically mopping up the paint before it stains the table. Maybe Jamie starts crying, and suddenly loses any interest in continuing with his 'good' behaviour: painting. Or maybe he thinks it is all quite amusing and does it again. Either way, Jamie now knows that if he wants to annoy dad, putting paint on the table is a way to do it. Yes, it might get him into trouble, but it is still a way of influencing dad's behaviour, or to annoy dad if dad has annoyed him earlier.

The second way dad could react is to immediately stop giving any praise. He sits there with Jamie, without pulling a face, and calmly in a firm (but not angry) voice says 'paint goes on the paper'. Jamie notices that suddenly all that praise has stopped, dad isn't engaging in the play anymore, and all that attention he was enjoying has disappeared. He might try it again, tipping up a different pot of paint, to see if he gets the big reaction he was expecting from dad this time. Dad keeps his cool and just looks at Jamie (without showing anger or amusement). Maybe dad grabs some paper towels and asks Jamie to help mop up and gives him lots of praise for doing this. Maybe Jamie starts mopping up, or tries painting again. Both of these are 'good' behaviours, and immediately dad starts rewarding this behaviour again. We always want to couple 'ignoring' with *redirecting our child to a more appropriate behaviour*, and *praising for engaging in that behaviour*. In this situation, Jamie learns the sorts of things he can do with paint and paper, and that pouring the paint on the table isn't particularly rewarding as dad doesn't react, and it stops their fun interaction. It also makes really clear what other behaviours he can do that are going to lead to rewards and lots of positive, fun interaction, and which behaviours cause all that to stop.

The most important thing here is that dad is ignoring *the behaviour not the child*. We *never* ignore the child. We stay in the room, and prompt a positive behaviour. We stay available for attention and giving praise if a more positive behaviour occurs. If we ignore the child, they may not be safe, they won't know what they could do instead, there is no motivation for them to resume the positive behaviours we want to see. However, we don't react to the behaviour, other than a simple calm reminder of the behaviour we want to see (remember, we always want to say what we want our kids to do, not what we don't want them to do). As soon as we have a more positive behaviour (it doesn't have to be perfect, just a step in the right direction), then we make sure we reward or praise that behaviour.

Of course, all this assumes that we are *already* giving your child lots of attention and doing lots of praising. This technique is unlikely to work if Jamie is playing unsupervised with his paints in the kitchen while we are doing the laundry. You can't 'stop' praise and attention if you weren't giving it in the first place.

Likewise, we never ignore behaviour if it isn't safe to do so. For example, we don't ignore a child running ahead along the pavement because if we do, the child could get hit by a car. We don't ignore one child hitting another because a child is going to get hurt. Common sense and, importantly, safety always comes first.

There also are instances when this ignoring approach won't work. This approach of rewarding the good and ignoring the 'bad' works on the principle that we are trying to make good behaviour more rewarding than undesirable behaviour, and making that distinction really clear. However, even if we do lots of praise for the good behaviour, if there is something inherently rewarding about the undesirable behaviour, then this approach may be less effective. This could be:

- The behaviour is guaranteed to get them something tangible, such as a chocolate bar or a toy. In the 30 seconds it takes them to grab and demolish a chocolate bar, they may not be too fussed about your sudden drop in attention when they are all focused on the chocolatey goodness.

- The behaviour gets them out of something, or avoids something they really don't like. Yes, pouring your bag of crisps all over the car and rubbing them into the seats might stop you and mum singing along with the music but, if it stops you having to go into a loud and noisy supermarket, it may well be worth it.

- The behaviour feels good. It might be that splashing water out of the bathtub and hearing/seeing the splash and slosh of water running over the bath is more entertaining than mum's praise.

So, how do we know if the reward the good and ignore the 'bad' technique is the right one? Well, if this is a behaviour that is happening directly in front of you, when you are interacting with a child, and it is safe to do so, then it is usually the first thing to try, especially if you can see them looking at you anticipating a big reaction from you. However, if not, or if the behaviour keeps on going without the child seeming remotely bothered by the sudden drop in attention, then we need to do some detective work first, to work out what the behaviour is about. This is where the next step, The Right Understanding, comes into play.

## KEY POINTS

✓ Our aim is, as much as possible, to encourage our children to show positive 'good' behaviours.

✓ We want to avoid undesirable behaviours being rewarding. Sometimes, our reactions to these behaviours can be rewarding, even if we don't mean them to be.

✓ When behaviours we don't want occur in front of us, and we've been interacting with a child, try ignoring the undesirable behaviour. It means we stop praise and all the fun interaction. We remind our child of the behaviour we want to see, and as soon as they do a positive behaviour, we reward this with lots of praise.

✓ We ignore *behaviours*, **never the child**. We stay in the room, available for attention and to give praise if we see some positive behaviours.

✓ In some situations it is not safe to ignore the behaviour – such as a child running out ahead of you. **Safety comes first**.

✓ This technique won't work when a behaviour we don't want to see is more rewarding or fun than the other behaviours we do want to see.

## LOGICAL CONSEQUENCES

At some point, most parents ask me about punishment, and if/how they should punish their child for their behaviour. The truth is, punishments don't work. We covered this earlier in how children learn – rewards are so much more effective than punishments. However, at the same time, we live in a world with consequences. I cannot go down to Tesco and steal all of their Ben and Jerry's cookie dough ice cream, no matter how much I might want to, because I know if I do, there will be consequences. This is where logical consequences come in.

Logical consequences aren't punishments. Punishments usually have a sense of 'justice', 'making them pay', 'shaming' the child or 'taking away something they really love'. Punishments say the problem is with our child, and they usually have the aim of making the child fear the punishment so they avoid doing the behaviour again. As such, they are often not proportionate, and often don't follow logically from the behaviour, and are not effective.

Logical consequences are different. Logical consequences aim to demonstrate that 'if you do that, this will happen' – that in life, actions have consequences, whether that is people not wanting to play with you because you hit someone, not having enough money because you spent it all on Pokémon cards, or that if you throw your phone it will probably break. In life, people have to take responsibility for their behaviour. With logical consequences, **we are locating the problem in a child's behaviour, not the child themselves**. By this, I mean that we are making really clear it is the behaviour that is the problem, but we still love the child and believe they can make better decisions about their behaviour. We are also trying to teach your child about cause and effect (that if they do something, this will happen) so they can learn about how to live in the world. Where possible, we are also trying to demonstrate a positive behaviour, such as removing yourself from the situation, saying sorry, or fixing a mistake. Let's look at some examples:

- A child gets angry and throws a video game controller against the TV. A logical consequence here is that the TV is turned off and the video game taken away for the rest of the day, as they aren't able to play nicely with this game right now. This consequence is directly related to the behaviour, and (depending on their developmental stage) it is proportionate. It is also logical as if they carry on like this they will break it and not be able to play with it again, so we are mimicking real life consequences. We are also trying to show what you need to do when you start to get frustrated with a video game – you need to turn it off and do something else. We may also need to help them find something else to distract them – your child might not be able to think of this themselves because they are too focused on the video game. In doing so, we are trying to help your child manage the consequences of their actions and find better ways of acting.

- A child hits another child in the living room while they were playing a building game because the other child had a brick they wanted. A logical consequence might be (depending on their developmental stage) to apologise, and separate them from the child they hit (leaving the bricks behind) for a time. This is proportionate, and it mirrors real life where you are expected to say sorry, and where if you cannot be nice around others you cannot be around others, and that might mean you miss out on things you enjoy. It is also demonstrating what the child could do if they are getting frustrated with the other child (take themselves away from the situation), and to apologise if you hurt someone.

- A child draws all over your carpet with felt tips. A logical consequence here is for the pens to be taken away for a set time, and (if able/safe – beware of chemicals!) for them to help you clear it up with warm soapy water and a sponge.

Logical consequences are something that we should be using much less frequently than rewarding the good, ignoring the 'bad', which in turn we should be using less frequently than praise and rewards (the main way we want to help our child learn positive behaviours). Logical consequences are what we use when we've done everything else and given every opportunity, or when a behaviour happens which is so unacceptable or dangerous as to require an immediate logical consequence.[3] For example, you might use an immediate logical consequence of 'you need to hold my hand for the rest of this walk' right away if a child who is usually able to walk close to you safely starts running off near a main road.

Again, *The Incredible Years* has more about logical consequences and is well worth a read. However, there are some issues that often come up with logical consequences when applied to our children developing differently:

1. They must be developmentally appropriate. If a teenager got upset at their video game and broke the TV, it might be proportionate to halve their pocket money until they have paid for a portion of the cost of replacing the TV. However, we wouldn't do that to an 8 year old – it wouldn't be developmentally appropriate. However, a teenager developing differently could be developmentally much younger. If they struggle to understand the value of money, or struggle to relate something they did weeks ago to why they don't have as much money now, then this isn't appropriate and will not be helpful or meaningful. We need to treat our children based on their developmental age, else it is not fair.

2. Our children must understand what the rules are and, in particular what the right behaviour is. It is not fair to have a logical consequence for a behaviour if a child doesn't know any better, so, we need to really think about our communication and behaviour strategies. In particular have our behaviour, praise, and rewards made it *really clear* what behaviour we want to see, that we want to see it *now*? Let's take the example of the child drawing on the carpet, and you make your child

---

3    Also, it goes without saying that logical consequences should *never* be applied to behaviours that are unusual, but part of who your child is, and that aren't harmful/dangerous/unlawful. For example, hand flapping, lining up their toys, watching a video over and over.

clear up the marks with you. If your child doesn't understand that they aren't meant to draw on the carpet in the first place, they might not understand that this is meant as a logical consequence. They may see this as just the cost of playing with the felt tips. We therefore need to be thinking about how we encourage your child to draw on paper (such as by redirecting them to draw on the paper as soon as we see them getting close to drawing on the carpet, and giving them lots of praise for doing so) before we start applying this logical consequence.

3.  Making sure we are not setting them up to fail. If we have a child who we *know* can't share their building blocks, but we set up a playdate and expect them to do just that, we can predict your child is going to struggle and may hit out, as in the above example. It would be unfair of us to have logical consequences for this child in that situation – we know they can't manage that yet, so we shouldn't put them in a situation that requires them to share (at least, not without help). The same applies to the logical consequences themselves. If your child isn't able to tolerate or understand that some things they see they cannot have, then asking them to play with their cars when they can see the blocks they really want is not fair. We know they won't be able to follow that consequence, and may lead them into escalating distress to the point of meltdown, so we need a different consequence. For example, going with you to the next room where the blocks are out of sight and where you can distract them with something else.

4.  Can we do the logical consequence right away? It is likely going to be hard for our kids to associate taking their seatbelt off in the car with not being allowed to go see Granny two days later. Even if your child has or understands language, having a delayed consequence will result in less learning in the moment, and difficulty understanding why they are facing the consequence later on. If we can't do a consequence quickly, it isn't fair.

5.  If we are inconsistent with how we give consequences, it won't make sense. If one parent allows a behaviour but the other

parent doesn't, or if a behaviour gets lots of different consequences depending on who sees the behaviour and the mood they are in, or if consequences aren't enforced, we won't be helping your child to learn (the whole point of consequences). Instead we'll just confuse them, leading them to face even more consequences because our message hasn't been clear.

So, before we give out any logical consequences, we need to go through a mental checklist:

- ☐ Do they *know* what behaviour we want to see? Are you sure?

- ☐ Are they *able* to do that behaviour? How do you know? Have they done that behaviour in this situation before?

- ☐ Have we reminded them what behaviour we want to see?

- ☐ Have we communicated that effectively? Are we sure they have listened and understood? How do you know?

- ☐ Have we done lots of rewards and praise? Have we been calm and containing?

- ☐ Are we sure we understand what the behaviour is about? (Check out step 6: The Right Understanding).

- ☐ Do we know what our logical consequence would be? Is it really a logical consequence or are we drifting into punishment?

- ☐ Can we do it straight away?

- ☐ Are we being consistent? Is this something we have given logical consequences for before?

- ☐ Can we be consistent about this in the future? We need to follow through with what we say not just now, but also every time in the future.

If the answer to all of these is yes, and you've got a logical consequence in mind, then the chances are you are ok to do it.

Out of the five issues that I highlighted with logical consequences, often the most difficult thing is consistency. Sometimes, when a child pushes back hard (crying, hitting, screaming, making a scene) and promises they will not do the unacceptable behaviour again, then it is natural as parents to want to remove the consequence, or end it early (which, if done, will only make the consequence less effective, and the behaviour more likely to happen again). Or, sometimes, the difficulty is that we might not always give the same logical consequence every time that behaviour occurs. Even if *you* are being consistent, is your co-parent? Are their teachers? If we only sometimes apply logical consequences for a behaviour, then it is not giving children a clear message, and will only confuse them, and that isn't fair.[4]

When we are not consistent with logical consequences, it will make boundaries less clear for children, and suggest to them that they may be able to avoid consequences if they try hard enough. Therefore, it is vital that, if we say we are going to do something, we do it every time. This requires good communication between parents, and with teachers.

## KEY POINTS

✓ Logical consequences are not punishments. We don't use punishments.

✓ Logical consequences follow naturally from the *behaviour* that is not acceptable. They are proportionate, mirror what happens in real life, and try and demonstrate a more positive behaviour.

✓ Logical consequences need to be *developmentally* appropriate for our child.

✓ Our children need to understand what the rules are, and what the right behaviour is.

✓ We need to make sure we are not setting them up to fail – that this is a behaviour they can usually do, and a situation they can cope with.

✓ We need to apply logical consequences right away.

✓ We need to be consistent with our logical consequences to ensure we are giving a clear message. That includes co-parents and teachers.

---

4   The exception to this is when a child has such an extreme reaction to a logical consequence being imposed that they are putting themselves or others in danger (such as absconding, self-harm, etc.). If this happens, stop and seek professional help before trying to apply consequences for that behaviour.

## CONSISTENCY

Our children need consistency. A big part of that comes from routines, which we've already talked about. The other part of it, however, comes from the people in the environment. We need to have consistent responses to our children's behaviour, the good and the 'bad'. Our children (regardless of their language ability) learn so much from how others react to their behaviour, and our actions will speak louder than our words.

We've already discussed how we can use unpredictable rewards to encourage behaviours we want to see (just as casinos do with adults). Here's the tricky bit though: we can follow the advice in this chapter perfectly; however, if other people aren't following it, *it will not work.* Let me give you an example:

Yasmin has learned that a good way to get attention is by screaming. Her parents are working hard on rewarding the good and ignoring the 'bad', and so don't react to her when she screams, but give her lots of praise and attention at other times to encourage her to get attention different ways. At school, however, it is harder to do this. When Yasmin screams, it is really disruptive to the class, so after a minute or two the pupil support assistant ends up taking Yasmin out, which means she gets some one-to-one attention from the pupil support assistant.

Here, Yasmin is getting those irregular unpredictable rewards – sometimes she is getting rewarded for screaming (by getting attention from the PSA), while at other times (at home) she is not. This is going to be *really* reinforcing and make it much more likely to happen. Over time, Yasmin may realise that this only works at school, and so the behaviour may reduce at home. However, this is by no means certain, and may take a long time. More importantly, even if it does reduce, this behaviour is still in Yasmin's toolbox of behaviours she can use when she wants attention, so if she isn't getting attention at home and *really* wants it, she may well go back to screaming again. What has happened is the opposite of what her parents were trying to do – we've taught Yasmin that screaming will get you attention, but only sometimes, so if it doesn't work first time, you better try again (only for longer and louder).

Consistency is such a hard thing to do at times, and it is where the families I work with and I often struggle. We might say we aren't going to react to spitting. We swear we never will. Yet after a hard day, or when you're driving the car and they get spit in your ear, or when it gets on your food, it is *really* hard not to react. As soon as we do react, that spitting is going to get worse. Maybe we're trying to put our kid to bed, and we swear we aren't going to respond to them wailing that they want another bedtime story. We aren't we aren't we aren't we aren't. But then it gets to 2 am and we just want to go to sleep so we give them a story, and your child learns they just have to keep going until 2am and eventually they'll get their story.

The importance of consistency goes beyond trying to help our children learn more positive behaviours. It is also crucial in keeping our kids feeling safe, calm, and contained.

Firstly, for some of our kids they learn more from our and other's behaviour than they do from our language. Therefore, if they have two people (mum and dad, dad and grandparent, mum and teacher) behaving in different ways, it is going to get really confusing. Going back to Yasmin and her screaming, having parents not reacting to screaming but her teachers at school reacting to it gives an inconsistent message. The result is that Yasmin may well feel more anxious or confused, as the behaviour is working in one setting but not another. We therefore may see her behaviour becoming worse because she is stressed and confused.

For a lot of our kids, people behaving differently to each other can be incredibly stressful. Because they often struggle to imagine what might happen in the future, they use their knowledge that people will react a certain way to help them with this. For example, if they know that when they ask an adult to go to the toilet they will be told that is ok, but then someone, say a supply teacher, says 'no, wait until the end of class', that could cause a lot of confusion and distress – why have things changed? What are they meant to do now? Could other people act this way? For more verbal kids, it might be that if mum says 'you will not have to do PE today, and here is a note to explain to Mrs Smith why you can't do PE', but then Mrs Smith still makes your child change and do bits of PE... well that's not what mum said would happen. Suddenly, our child's expectations for what will happen today have been turned on their head, and it has become a lot less predictable and secure. They might not know what is expected of them, or what to do, so become incredibly stressed.

Consistency is also important in keeping boundaries. All children will test boundaries – it's what kids do to learn about what is and isn't ok. As a child, I still remember Mum saying 'no' to something, and then going to find Dad in the hope he would say 'yes' (rather than the more usual, 'what did your Mum say?'). This was me trying to work around the rules and boundaries that my parents were trying to set. If they weren't consistent, or if it wasn't clear what was or wasn't allowed, I was able to play them off against each other to try and shift the blame (I was such an angelic child, can you tell?).

Consistency is also really important for our kids emotionally. Our kids can find it harder to understand other people, to relate and to be comforted by other people. If we react in an inconsistent way when they come to us for help with big scary emotions (such as getting angry with them, getting really upset ourselves, or ignoring them when they are upset), it makes it harder for our kids to come to us for comfort and reassurance. After all, would you want to go to a friend for comfort if sometimes they instead got angry at you, talked about their problems, or just ignored your problem and talked about something else? Quite quickly you'd stop going to that friend for comfort and advice. However, for our kids, we are often *the* person to go to for help with emotions, so we need to ensure we are able to provide that warm, comforting, containing response consistently (or, as much as we can – you are human after all).

The point is, consistency isn't just about *your* response or *my* response, it is about *all the responses the child receives*, regardless of who is about or where they are.

Of course, I can say consistency is really important, but that is easier said than done. Family life is often busy, with parents having to do 101 things at once, so it can be hard to remember to behave a certain way. Schools will always want to do their best for the children in their care, but it can be really hard to do when you have 30 kids in a class and one teacher and (if you're lucky) a support teacher. When parents have separated, it can be difficult to get this consistency in approach, especially if the parents are not on good terms. It is great that so many grandparents are getting involved in childcare, but again, this is another person who may have different ideas about parenting, and who needs to get 'on script'.

One of the best ways to get this consistency (and the reason why

I say 'on script') is to have a communication passport for our kids. Our kids are complex, and their needs, their difficulties (and their strengths) may not be clear to people. However, having one folder which provides a one-stop-shop for all this information can help new people get up to speed, and ensure everyone has a shared understanding of our child, and how to respond to them. As a starting point, I often suggest the following sections:

- Key info: Name, address, medication, contact numbers, allergies, diagnoses, important people, etc.

- About me: Likes and dislikes, food preferences, sensory preferences.

- Strengths and difficulties: What am I good at, and what I find challenging.

- How I communicate/how to communicate with me (including a translation if some of the child's communication is unusual or not obvious).

- A RAG (Red, Amber, Green): What I look like when I'm in a good place and how to keep me there, what I look like when things are going wrong and how to help, and what I look like when having a meltdown and how to keep me safe (more on this later).

- Routines: Daily routines (including bedtime routine) described so everyone knows how to follow them.

- Specific behaviours and how to respond to them.

The best communication passports are constructed together as a team with all those involved with a child (including the child if able!) and ideally led by parents. Doing it as a team ensures everyone is aware of the same information, what they have to do, and why it is important. Crucially, if done well, it means people don't feel 'dictated to', but instead listened to (this can be particularly helpful when there is a difficult relationship between home and school, or between parents). In particular, there may be genuine difficulties applying bits of the communication passport in certain contexts, which can be flagged up. For example, if something isn't possible at school, at respite, or at dad's house, then people can say an alternative (either for that setting, or for all settings) to be put in. Likewise, if new people come in who perhaps don't understand your child and have their own ideas about how to work with them, having a document that everyone has agreed to and that is being used consistently sends a clear message that *this* is how we are going to work with your child. It says that if you want to be around my child, this is how you're going to do it – anything else is going to stress them and make it harder for them to learn and progress.

If you want to see some great example of communication passports, check out www.mycommpass.com. This website has a great selection of example communication passports, each tailored to the child's specific needs. Have a look and think about using this framework to make one for your child.

Of course, this will need to be reviewed regularly as your child grows up and the environment around them changes. The result, hopefully, is that everyone is able to respond in a consistent, planned way.

## KEY POINTS

✓ Children (especially children developing differently) need consistency.

✓ Consistency comes from routine, and from everyone in that child's environment reacting in predictable ways. This means not just one person always acting the same way, but everyone involved in that child's care (co-parents, teachers, step-parents, grandparents, etc.) acting in the same way.

✓ Inconsistency in our behaviour can create confusion, anxiety, and is one of the main reasons why our attempts to shape our child's behaviour don't work, or aren't effective.

✓ Creating a communication passport with the important adults in your child's life can help ensure everyone is acting in the same way, and identify where responses might need to be changed.

# STEP 6: THE RIGHT UNDERSTANDING

The focus in this step is on strategies to try and unpick behaviour – work out why it is happening, and how we can best respond to it. You could in theory jump right in and give this a go, without doing any of the earlier work we've talked about. However, while that might sound like less work, I promise you it will end up being a lot more. If we've done steps 1–5 well, the chances are you'll need what is in here a lot less often. You can almost think of this as a step on 'troubleshooting' – trying to work out what has gone wrong, or where we need to do more. It is a whole lot easier if steps 1–5 are already in place, as there will be far fewer things that could be wrong!

The first half of this section aims to train you to be detectives in understanding behaviour. I've said before, *all behaviour is communication*, and sometimes we need to take a really careful look at behaviour to decode it. Therefore, I'm going to give you a few tools to help you do this, and key questions to ask yourself.

Generally, there are three instances when we might need the tools in this step:

1. To check that a behaviour is communicating what we think it is communicating. This is particularly important before we start 'ignoring the "bad"' or using logical consequences.

2. When we have no idea what a behaviour is about. Some behaviours you'll look at and wonder 'why on earth are they doing that?' (By the way, you're not alone in this – I'm pretty sure this thought crosses my mind at least once a day at work – and not just about the kids!)

3. When what we're doing to try and change behaviour isn't working. Our behaviour change strategies take time to work – they don't happen overnight, and quite often what we do will make behaviours worse before they get better. However, if after a few weeks of *consistently* changing our approach, we're not seeing any change, we *need to re-check* that this behaviour is communicating what we think it is communicating. If our understanding of the behaviour is wrong, our strategies will be wrong, and we'll get no improvement.

The second half of this section is looking at when things get too much – anxiety (which can be a driver for a lot of our child's behaviour) and meltdowns. I'm going to give you some pointers on how to help our kids overcome their fears, and how we can manage meltdowns safely. However, both of these issues usually require us to have done the detective work first so we know exactly what they are about and how to tackle them effectively. So, with that in mind, decide which parent is going to play Sherlock and who is going to be Watson, and grab your deer stalker hat and magnifying glass – it's time to play detective!

## KEY POINTS

✓ All behaviour is communication. However, sometimes we need extra tools to be able to decode it.

✓ We use these tools to check our understanding, figure out what is going on, or when how we are responding to a behaviour isn't working.

## KEY QUESTIONS TO ASK YOURSELF

So, there is a behaviour you want to understand. The first thing we need to do is describe it. It seems obvious, doesn't it? But when you start to get into it, it can actually be quite tricky. You might also find that while you and your child's teacher might both talk about 'hitting another child', that actually the behaviours *look* quite different. Therefore, writing it down and asking yourself a few key questions is where we need to start to get a shared understanding and define the scope of the behaviour.

## What is the 'key' behaviour?

First off, what is the 'key' behaviour? This is usually the first thing you think of when you think about a behaviour. Things like 'screaming', 'taking his seatbelt off', 'snatching things from her brother'. This is just to give us a simple name we can all use.

Be careful though, often people want to cram lots of behaviours under the one name. If these behaviours always (or almost always) occur together that is fine. For example, if Jane always 'screams' and 'hits her head', you can lump those together as one behaviour. However, if she sometimes screams without hitting her head, or sometimes hits her head without screaming, then we will probably be better separating these out as two different behaviours.

## When and where does the behaviour happen (and not happen)?

When does a behaviour happen? At this stage, we don't need to be too formal about it. We could say 'at home after school', 'before meal times', 'in the living room during the day', 'on the way to school'. There could be multiple times when this happens – that's fine too. We're just looking for a few sentences at most – if you find yourself describing in detail lots of different situations, that's great, but hold that thought and save it for later. Right now, we just want broad brush strokes.

If this behaviour occurs at the times you've just described, then does it not occur at any other times or settings? Where does this behaviour *not* occur? Some behaviours might never happen at home, at school, or in the car. Some might never happen during the night, or during the day, for example.

Our child is using their behaviour to communicate, but it is highly unlikely they want to communicate the same message to everyone in every situation all the time. We need to think about the context (time, location, people, etc.) in which the behaviour happens to decode the message. By thinking about where a behaviour does and does not happen, it helps us narrow down what your child is trying to communicate. If a child is not doing a behaviour in some situations, then presumably that behaviour isn't needed or isn't effective in communicating in that situation. Likewise, is there something about the situations that the behaviour does occur in that they have in common, or where your child might want to communicate a similar message? We don't have to answer these yet, but they are good things to think about.

## Frequency, intensity, and duration (or 'how often, how much and for how long?')

The aim of these three questions is to help us measure change in behaviour in different contexts, and track how it changes over time.

First, frequency – how often does the behaviour occur? This could be measured in how many times a behaviour happens in an hour, a day, a week, or a month. You want to choose a time scale you'll be able to see some real change with. If you have something that happens ten times a day, recording that as 70 times a week or 0–1 times per hour isn't going to be particularly useful. Likewise, if you've got something that occurs about once every two weeks, you can't really describe that in terms of hours or days.

Intensity – how 'strong' is the behaviour? If we're talking about screaming, we might think about how loud or 'pained' the scream seems. If we're talking about hitting, we talk about 'how hard' they hit. We usually measure this on a 0–10 scale: 0 means a behaviour isn't actually happening; 1–3 might be a hit which might clearly be a hit, but not particularly strong – a light hit; 4–6 is a hit you might expect from a typically developing child if they are really annoyed or upset; 7–9 might describe hitting that has become really extreme, much more so than you'd ever usually see from a child their age; a 10 is 'world ending' (such as inconsolable distress), or is likely causing serious damage to either a person or property (such as hitting to the point you want them checked out at A&E). It is a good idea to write out rough descriptors of what a few different numbers actually *look like*, so others get an idea of what you mean when you say 'yesterday Rona's screaming was an 8'. You don't have to do this for every number, but it is good to have a few marker points.

Duration – how long does it last? Does the behaviour last mere seconds, or does it go on and on for hours? There will always be some variability, but giving an 'average' time is really helpful in defining the behaviour.

## What makes the behaviour better or worse?

When a behaviour does happen, is there anything that makes the behaviour better? In other words, is there anything that makes the behaviour less intense, shortens the length of a behaviour, or makes it less frequent? Or, conversely, is there anything that makes it more intense, longer, or more frequent? Some things to think about might be school holidays, people, locations, food, day of the week, and time of day. Importantly, is there *anything you or other people do* which seems to make the behaviours better or worse?

Remember, our job is to try and decode behaviour so, just like working out where a behaviour does and does not happen, working out what makes them better or worse might give us a clue as to what the behaviour is trying to communicate. For example, if white noise seems to help, is there something about what they can hear in the environment that could be causing the behaviour? If hugging them makes things worse, are they needing space, or wanting to get out of a situation or away from people?

When I do this with parents, a lot of them will tell me that when their child does a behaviour, they do 'something' (maybe hugs, maybe talking to them, maybe trying to fix the iPad, etc.) to try and make the situation better. They keep trying the same thing (sometimes for years) but it doesn't usually make the behaviour better. When I point this out to parents, they tend to respond 'but I feel like I need to do something'. That makes complete sense, and I agree we need to do something to help our child. Likewise, we should never give up the first time we try something and it doesn't work – some things take time to work, or only work under certain circumstances. However, if it's not worked the first 100 times you've done it, it probably isn't going to work the 101st time. As hard as it may be, let's try and stand back and think about what is going on, and about if there is anything *different* we can try, or even try (if safe) not doing anything. Our kids are developing differently, so sometimes we might need a different approach to the one that other parents might use, or that we might think 'should' work. If we don't, if we keep trying what we think should work but isn't, we're going to get stuck very quickly.

## When did the behaviour first happen, what was going on, and what happened?

Behaviours don't come out of nowhere (although sometimes it feels like it). Often, the first time a behaviour ever happens, it happened because your child had something to communicate and this new behaviour turned out to be effective at getting that message across. If it worked, they will keep going back to that behaviour over and over. Therefore, if we know what was going on when the behaviour first happened, it might give us a big clue as to what it was communicating. Sounds simple enough, but requires a decent memory and a bit of guess work if it has been a longstanding behaviour, so we have to take it with a pinch of salt.

So, when did the behaviour start? What was going on around that time? At the time of writing, it is a sunny weekend a few weeks into lockdown during the COVID-19 crisis. I've had several phone calls with my kids' parents over the last few weeks, and, of course, they have had a raft of new behaviours, or reoccurrence of old behaviours. Curiously, they all started a few weeks ago, when lockdown started. I'm really proud that almost all my parents were pretty clear that they knew what triggered the behaviour: all the change in routine and anxiety associated with lockdown. From there we were able to work out what to do to help. This is a more obvious example, and often the changes are subtle things we might not realise, such as a change of food brand, a change at school (such as a favoured playmate going off sick), a new shift pattern for mum – or (the one that fills all parents with dread) puberty!

If we know what was going on when the behaviour started, we've got an important piece of information – what might have triggered the behaviour. However, if we think about *what happened next* (what did they do, what did we or other people do) that first time the behaviour happened, we might also get a clue as to what that behaviour tried to communicate. Remember, this behaviour wouldn't be repeated if it wasn't effective at getting the child what they wanted, so that first time, there must have been something that made it effective for your child to keep communicating this way. Maybe it was a scream in a supermarket so we left, gave them a chocolate bar, or stopped and gave them big hugs and lots of attention. Each of these different responses that we might have done back then might give us a clue as to what your child uses screaming to communicate now. If we left the supermarket, could screaming be a way to get out of situations? If it got them a chocolate bar, could it mean 'I want something'?

## What is the lifecycle of the behaviour?

Back at the start, we identified a 'key' behaviour. This is usually the behaviour that we focus on because it is usually the most disruptive or distressing to us, and therefore the most effective communication method for our child. However, most of the time, we see a pattern of behaviours leading up to this. These are often smaller, less noticeable behaviours which if not responded to, lead to the bigger behaviours we find challenging. For example, a child might start with saying 'mummy' (1). If this isn't responded to, they start throwing things (2). If still they haven't got their message through, then they start screaming (3). If that still doesn't work, they start hitting themselves (4), then other people. Here, we've got at least four 'precursor' behaviours in the build-up to the key behaviour – hitting other people. Likewise, there might be behaviours that come after our 'key' behaviour if your child still isn't getting their message across, and so not getting what they are looking for.

It is really important to get this information. If this is a predictable pattern, and if we can work out what the behaviour is trying to communicate, then we can respond to our child much earlier because we are able to look out for these behaviours (i.e. listen to our child), and respond accordingly, without them having to resort to bigger behaviours to get their message across. This means we can meet your child's needs faster, and we can avoid behaviours that often they and/or other people find distressing or difficult. They may be hard to spot at first, and need us to try to stop and think (often when we are stressed because we've got our child's key behaviour to deal with). That's not easy. However, it is well worth the effort if we can find these earlier behaviours.

## Could it be physical?

Before we attribute behaviour to any other possible cause, we need to ask ourselves whether there could be a physical cause for the behaviour. By this, I mean pain, toileting problems, seizures, etc. For children who have enough language (and understanding) you can flat out ask them, that is great. However, if you have a child who is non-verbal, who has limited language, or who might be able to use words but sometimes uses words with different meanings, then we need to be more careful. A few red flags for me are:

- hitting their head, particularly hitting the side of their head around the ear or eyes

- a history of seizures, absences, or 'funny spells'

- a history of toothache or dental issues

- a history of constipation/difficulty pooing

- a behaviour that is new but has quickly become very frequent, occurring most days, or in 'spells'.

However, this list is *not* exhaustive. As a parent, if you think a behaviour *could* be due to pain, get them checked out by your GP or Community Paediatrician before you do anything else.

The reason we *always* need to rule out a possible physical cause for a behaviour before going any further is that all the strategies in this book won't do anything if the underlying issue is about their physical health. Worse, while we are trying to solve the wrong problem, the underlying physical health issue could be getting worse. In most of the kids I see, there isn't a physical cause to their behaviour, and you don't need to take your child to your GP every time there is a new behaviour we need to unpick. However, we always need to keep this question in our mind, and if we are *at all* unsure if the behaviour could be related to physical health, we need to get them checked out.

## KEY POINTS

✓ When trying to understand a behaviour, we need to map out:

- What is the key behaviour we want to understand?

- When and where does the behaviour occur and not occur?

- How often does it happen, how much does it happen, and how long does it happen for?

- What makes the behaviour better or worse?

- When did the behaviour first happen, what was going on then, and what happened after?

- What is the lifecycle of the behaviour – what leads up to the key behaviour?

✓ Most importantly, before we try and tackle any new behaviour, we need to rule out any possible physical health issues that could be causing the behaviour, such as pain.

## THE FIVE KEY FUNCTIONS

So, I've said that all behaviour is communication. All behaviour is trying to tell us something. However, behaviour also has a function. For example the child screaming at the supermarket checkout may be communicating, 'I want a chocolate bar'. However, this behaviour also has a function – to get that chocolate bar!

There are five key functions which I always run through in my head whenever I'm trying to unpick a behaviour.

**Tangible** – This is when a child wants something like food, a toy, a game, etc. They want something 'tangible' that they don't have or they want more of.

**Attention** – All kids want *and need* attention. There is nothing wrong with kids wanting attention, and our kids often need a lot more of this than others. Behaviour is a great way to get attention, even if it is negative attention (such as being told off, or stressing mum out to the point she starts shouting).

**Escape or avoidance** – Get me out of here! This is when a child is trying to get out of a supermarket or noisy place, trying to avoid doing homework, trying to avoid eating their broccoli. Escape is a child trying to either stop something undesirable happening in the first place, or stopping something undesirable continuing to happen to them.

**Sensory** – People do things that feel good. Eating, drinking, sex, music, long soaks in the bath, fluffy blankets on sofas – all of these are sensory things we enjoy. For our kids, their sensory things might be a bit more unusual, such as rubbing their faces on a carpet, twirling around and around, or looking at flashing lights. We've also got to remember that our kids can process sensory information differently, so may not (for example) realise they are full, but still enjoy the taste of food, leading to constant eating. Pain can also be a sensory behaviour, and sometimes doing things that are painful can feel good, either due to the body's reactions to injury (natural pain killers), or distraction from a different pain.

**Repetition** – While traditionally people tend to think of the four functions above, I also include the extra function of 'repetition'. These are behaviours which happen not because the behaviour communicates or gets the child anything, but that the behaviour is part of a predictable sequence, and it is that predictability and constancy that the child likes. For example, a child developing differently who was hungry one night and was given a biscuit at 8 pm now always expects a biscuit at 8 pm, even if they are not hungry. The behaviour of asking for a biscuit (either verbally, or with physical behaviour) now isn't about getting a biscuit (they might not even eat it, or eat it despite not being hungry), it is about following a regular routine.

It is often hard on the surface to work out what is driving a behaviour. Often, behaviours can (and do) have multiple functions (you didn't think they would only have one did you? That would be too easy!). However, there are tools we can use to help us do this that I'll cover in the next couple of sections. If you find it hard to work out what the function of a behaviour is, don't worry. *It is hard.* There are many times I'm scratching my head alongside parents trying to work out the function of a behaviour. We try and make it as scientific as we can, and this certainly makes it easier and more accurate, but there is an element of 'art' to it too. Experience helps, and having a really good understanding of your child and their past behaviours is essential. If you find you're struggling to work out a behaviour, that is ok. You can always ask for help from your child's healthcare team, teachers, and family members.

## KEY POINTS

✓ All behaviour is communication, but all behaviour also serves a function: we don't do anything without a reason!

✓ Behaviour usually has at least one of the following five functions:

- tangible – the child gets something

- attention

- escape – the child gets away from or avoids something

- sensory – it feels good

- repetition – it is part of a predictable routine or sequence they enjoy.

✓ Behaviours can have more than one function.

## STAR CHARTS AND FREQUENCY CHARTS

STAR charts (originally developed by Zarkowska and Clements[1])are my bread and butter at work, and something I use on a daily basis (or rather, I get parents to use them on a daily basis). STAR charts are *not* reward charts filled with stickers or coloured in stars, which is what most people jump to when I start talking about STAR charts. Instead, STAR charts are sheets we fill in to record behaviours, which helps us to look for patterns and therefore predict behaviours. STAR stands for Setting, Trigger, Action, and Response.

**Setting** – Where did it happen? What time of day? What day of the week? Who was around? What was happening around them? What

---

1    Zarkowska, E. and Clements, J. (1994) *Problem Behaviour and People with Severe Learning Disabilities*. Boston, MA: Springer.

was he/she doing? What was the environment like – noisy, busy, any smells, hot or cold, etc.? Did they sleep ok that night? Were they hungry or in pain? Were they out of routine? Were they getting ready to do something?

**Trigger** – Is there anything which *might* have triggered the behaviour? Things like being told off, being told 'no', being scared of something, etc. You don't have to be 100% sure a trigger is a trigger – sometimes parents will tell me a behaviour comes 'out of the blue' which is code for 'we can't see an obvious trigger'. That's ok. We can however think about what was happening just before a behaviour, to see if we can get some ideas as to what it might have been. Similarly, sometimes what triggers a child one day, they can cope with the next – if they are in a better place (further from the edge of their window of tolerance) they may be able to manage a trigger they might not cope with if they are already stressed.

**Action** – Describe what you see. What did they *actually do*? Where did they do it? How much did they do it? How intense was it? How long did they do it for? Did they look upset/angry/happy/etc.? Did they say anything? Did they do the behaviour towards anyone (e.g. hitting themselves or hitting their brother)? Did the behaviours escalate from one to another before they got to the 'key' behaviour?

**Response** – What did other people say or do? How did they say/do it? What did they say or do next? Were people upset/angry/happy? Did they make the behaviour better/worse? How long did people respond to the behaviour for? What was your child doing while people were managing the behaviour and the consequences of the behaviour (e.g. while mum clears up the cup of water they spilled, what is the child doing?). How did it end?

I've stuck an example STAR chart in the appendix, which is available to download from https://library.jkp.com/redeem using the code YJXGEFU, but you can easily make your own too. Some people fill these in by having one event per page. Other people will fill in an event, then draw a line across the page under the lowest point (so it is clear what text relates to what event).

There is one big rule when filling in STAR charts: **you need to be objective**. By that, I mean you need to describe what you *actually see*.

We cannot know how your child is actually feeling, or what they are actually thinking (even if they tell us). All we know for sure is their behaviour (which, for verbal kids, includes what they say). It is fine to write 'Toby was crying, screaming, etc., pointing towards his car – appeared upset'. However, saying simply 'Toby was upset – wanted his car' is a big no-no. This latter example has jumped from behaviour to *interpretation* of the behaviour. We want to get lots of examples of a behaviour before we try and interpret it, so we need to try and stop ourselves jumping to conclusions. For example, maybe Toby was upset because the car was broken? Or because it had fallen and hit him on the head? Therefore, we always need to only include the behaviours we see – leave the interpretation until later.

Often people can feel quite daunted by STAR charts when they realise how much writing is involved. And yes, I'm not going to lie, they are a lot of work. However, we can make it easier. You might find after a few of these that you keep writing the same things. If that is happening, you can develop your own shorthand. For example 'LR' for living room, 'HS 5' for 'hit self with intensity 5', and people's initials rather than using names. Another pro-tip is not to do them *right away*. You certainly don't want to be waiting too long (make sure they are done the same day as the behaviour), but they are best filled out when you yourself are feeling calm and have five minutes to actually *think*, rather than always trying to fill it out on the fly.

What do I mean by 'intensity 5'? Well, this is where those key questions at the start of this step come into play. If we've done our prep work, we'll know what behaviour we are investigating, and we will have done things like mapping out our intensity scale, so we have a scale for measuring our child's behaviours that we can use for our STAR chart.

The other thing to be aware of is drift. Drift is where we start out intending to look at one behaviour, but over time, we start looking at more and more and more behaviours. It can really muddy the waters if we start including too many behaviours, and you'll end up filling in thousands of STAR charts without getting any answers. For STAR charts, we need to just focus on *one* behaviour that we have carefully defined (using the 'key questions to ask yourself') to keep you recording *only* that behaviour and the behaviours which lead up to it. If you really want, you can use STAR charts to look at more than one behaviour at a time, but I don't advise it. If you do, keep these STAR charts separate as it makes it harder to spot patterns, which is what this is all about.

The main aim of STAR charts is to help us identify patterns in our child's behaviour. Often by simply filling these in parents start to realise what a behaviour might be about, and can then take steps to address it. It is also really helpful to fill these in or review them with someone else who knows your child well, when you've got plenty of time to think and read together (and a glass of wine doesn't hurt). Is there something common about the setting that makes a behaviour more likely? Can you identify one or more triggers which are likely to start a behaviour happening? And importantly, what does the behaviour achieve – how does it change other peoples' behaviour? What happens to your child? What causes the behaviour to end?

If you're struggling, or have a behaviour you can't get to the bottom of, don't throw away the charts in frustration, but do seek professional help. The chances are, they will want to see these charts, and they may save you having to do a lot of re-recording! If you've filled in 20 or 30 instances of a specific behaviour and you're not getting anywhere, you can probably stop – that should be more than enough to see a pattern if we are correctly focusing on just one behaviour.

While I mostly use STAR charts, I sometimes also use frequency charts to gather information on when a specific behaviour happens. For example, if we think Oliver bites himself in phases, or spells, we might use a frequency chart to see:

1. Does Oliver *actually* go through periods of biting himself more, or is it just our imagination?

2. Is there a pattern to when Oliver bites himself?

3. Does something we are doing (changing Oliver's environment or our response to the behaviour) change how often Oliver hits himself?

A simple frequency chart (like the one in the downloadable appendix) will have set regular time 'bins', into which we keep a tally of how many behaviours occur in that time period. These bins could break the day down into chunks of 15 minutes, an hour, a day, etc., depending on how frequent the behaviour is.

Just like with STAR charts, it is really important to make sure you write down and agree *exactly* what the behaviour looks like. Something like a frequency chart will often have to be done at home *and* at school, so it is important to ensure everyone is on board and understands how to complete it. Equally, remember that if you try and record more than one behaviour on the same chart, it is going to make it hard to see a pattern, so best to only record one behaviour.

Lastly, if we are using frequency charts to see if a change we've made has been effective, then it is important we give it some time. Sometimes, it takes a while for a change to take effect, and we might even see a behaviour become more frequent for a short time before it reduces. Equally, we need to ensure we are only changing one thing at a time, else we won't know what made the difference!

## KEY POINTS

✓ STAR charts are a way of understanding the function of a behaviour.

✓ STAR stands for Setting, Trigger, Action, Response.

✓ Try and fill in STAR charts soon after the event, but better to do it a bit later that same day when you have time to do it properly, rather than in a rush.

✓ It can help to review STAR charts with a partner or friends to try and see patterns to understand what makes the behaviours more likely, what starts them off, and what the behaviour is trying to achieve.

✓ Frequency charts record how often a behaviour happens.

✓ You can use frequency charts to check how often a behaviour actually happens, to try and identify patterns in when it happens, or to see if a change we have made is making a difference.

✓ For both STAR and frequency charts, only focus on one, well defined behaviour at a time, and make sure you've carefully defined that behaviour using the 'Key questions to ask yourself' section.

## DEVELOP SKILLS, DON'T PUNISH IGNORANCE

Once we have a good idea as to the function of a behaviour, we are much more likely to be able to better respond to that behaviour, and possibly change it. We can do this in four ways:

1.  We can respond before the behaviour happens.

2.  We can respond immediately.

3.  We can teach other behaviours which meet that need.

4.  We can make unhelpful behaviours less effective.

### Responding before the behaviour happens

If we are able to work out in which situations a behaviour is likely to occur, and we know what the function of that behaviour is, we can respond before the child needs to do a behaviour. For example, if Paula screams and shouts because she is thirsty, then if we can make water available to her when we know she is likely to get thirsty, then she has no need to scream and shout.

This can get tricky when responding to the behaviour before it happens means avoiding things. For example, going to the park. If we know that Mary's behaviour happens because she wants to get away from the park or avoid going there in the first place, then one answer is to just not go to the park. However, there are two problems with this.

The first is the effect on the rest of the family. If Mary's siblings want to go to the park, is it fair that they don't get to go? There may be ways around this – if Mary is ok with *some* parks, or her siblings can go with one parent or their friends. However, if not, then you as parents need to weigh up the costs and benefits to Mary *and* her siblings to decide if you'll go anyway, and what you can do to make it easier for everyone to manage.

The second factor is whether this is something that Mary needs to learn to deal with? If it is just one park she really doesn't like, that is probably not going to be an issue for her long term – it's not going to stop her living her life. However, if she doesn't like going to any park because she might see a dog, then that is likely going to have a huge long-term impact on her life, and restrict what she can do.

Therefore, we might choose not to avoid this situation, but try and tackle the fear (see the 'Facing fears' section).

## Responding immediately

If we know what a behaviour is trying to communicate, then as soon as we see these early signs of it, we can respond right away, which will make it more likely they'll use that way to communicate in the future. That's great if the early behaviour is a positive one that we want to encourage – such as pulling on your sleeve to ask for help. Responding quickly will make them more likely to use that again in the future.

But what if this behaviour is (even in this early stage) not ok – such as hitting? Or what if it is because they want something we don't want to give them/we need to set boundaries. For example, if they don't want to go to school. In these situations, we need to make a choice – *fast*.

If we respond right away, we are making it more likely those early behaviours will be used to meet that need. This, depending on what those behaviours are, may not be a great outcome. However, it may be *a lot* better than waiting until a child has progressed to even more undesirable behaviours, or even a full meltdown, and *then* giving them what they want. We might change our minds and 'give in' because their behaviour has become too dangerous not to give your child what they are asking for, or because you are mentally, emotionally, or physically exhausted and can't resist it – that is ok, you're human! However, when we 'give in' to these more extreme behaviours rather than the early ones, we are making it more likely your child will use these more extreme behaviours again in the future, and will use them sooner.

So, when you see the start of a behaviour that isn't positive, take a moment to think about how you are going to respond to it. If you think you don't have the headspace to manage this behaviour, or if you know it is going to become too difficult or dangerous to manage, then let's cut our losses and give them what they want now, rather than waiting for things to escalate. This way, we're only reinforcing these lower level behaviours, not the bigger more difficult ones.

## Teach other behaviours to meet that need

This is *it*. This is what we should *always* be aiming for. This is what can make such a huge difference to our child's lives. *I cannot emphasise the importance of teaching other behaviours to meet the need enough.* Going back to the metaphor of our kids driving a car, this is where our kids actually learn to drive!

There are lots of different skills we can teach that can replace a behaviour. One of the most common skills we can look at is communication. Your child may be using their behaviour to communicate, and **we absolutely want that communication, but it is the way they are communicating (for example, by scratching you) that isn't ok.** If we can teach other, better ways for your child to communicate that need or to meet that need, then everyone is happy. Not just that, but we will have developed our child's skillset.

This is one of the many reasons why Speech and Language Therapists are so important. They can ensure that your child has the best tools that they currently are able to use to communicate, which is especially important for children who are non-verbal, or use signs, photos, symbols, or gestures to aid their communication. For example, if scratching is how your child tells you they want to go home, and this is a want we're happy to do, then ensuring your child has a symbol, gesture, or sign to communicate that will likely be really helpful. If we can give your child the tools to better communicate their needs and wants, and we encourage them to use these tools by prompting and responding right away when they use them, it will soon become apparent to the child that these new tools are far better at getting their needs and wants met than their old behaviours were.

Of course, there are lots of other skills we can teach. If a behaviour is about difficulty with waiting, we could look to build skills or tolerance for waiting. If they are getting upset because the iPad ran out of battery, can we teach them how to realise when this is going to happen and plug it in? If they are getting upset at their sibling, can we teach them to come to mum or dad for help? If they are getting frustrated at having to share or take turns, can we teach them how to manage? Some of these are quite complex, but all can be taught *if the child is ready.*

There is no one size fits all for learning skills. The skills that *need* learning will depend on the situation, and the skills the child *can* learn will depend on their level of development and existing skills. However, because your child is currently finding ways to get that need met, we know they are motivated to get that need met – if we can show them a faster, more reliable way to get that need met, your child should be pretty motivated to learn it and use it! In the next section, I'll go over some advice on strategies we can use to help train skills.

## Make unhelpful behaviours less effective

This is often what people jump to first. 'My child is hitting me and I want him to stop' is something I hear regularly. One simple way to deal with this would be to identify what it is your child gets from this behaviour (let's say parents' attention) and stop our child's behaviour (let's say, hitting) from having the desired effect – in this case by ignoring the hitting. The chances are this will get worse before it gets better (the 'extinction burst' I talked about a while back – our child going 'why isn't this working? I must need to try harder'), but long term, if stuck to, it will be effective in stopping the hitting.

While this might *appear* sensible, it doesn't address the *function* of the behaviour. This is a *big problem* because:

1.  Your child is likely to persist with this behaviour for much longer, as **they don't know what to do instead** to get their needs met: we're taking away their best (and maybe their only) tool for getting your attention, which is something they *really want and need*. So, they are going to try really hard to make that tool of hitting work again.

2.  The *need* that behaviour served isn't going to go away. Ok, your child may have learned that hitting you doesn't get your attention, but they still need your attention! How are they meant to get it now? They will probably start trying new behaviours (quite possibly equally or more undesirable behaviours) to try and get your attention until they find a new behaviour that works. Perhaps they will start spitting? Screaming? Running away? If we focus on stopping the behaviour without meeting the underlying function (their wants and needs), then we will end up playing whack-a-mole with these behaviours because

as soon as we stop one behaviour, our child will try and find a different way of meeting their wants and needs.

3.  We end up ignoring our child's communication. They are telling us something – the last thing we want to do is ignore what they are saying. We *want* to give them our attention, we just would like them to find better ways to ask for it, or perhaps to wait until we can give it. Even for other needs, where we might not be able to fix the problem or make it better, we should still be responding as compassionate, understanding parents, even if we must maintain rules and boundaries our kids don't agree with. **We always want to listen to our kids, and our kids often communicate with their behaviour**.

For these reasons, **I never focus just on making behaviours less effective**. It is something I might use, but only ever *in combination* with teaching new behaviours, eliminating the need for the behaviours, and/or responding quickly to the lower level behaviours to avoid the more intense or extreme behaviours. For example, in this case, we might focus on responding quickly when your child says 'mummy' or 'daddy', as this will teach them that this is a really effective way to get our attention. If your child usually starts pulling you hard by the arm before they progress to hitting, we might ensure we always respond to that behaviour to stop it escalating. We might also try and identify when your child is likely to want more attention, and give it to them at those times so they don't need to ask. As well as all of these, I might suggest that if your child starts hitting, we don't respond to it, but that is only ever one piece of the puzzle, and should never be used alone.

## KEY POINTS

✓ When we understand a behaviour, we can:

-   Respond before a behaviour begins – avoiding the need for our kids to use this behaviour.

-   Respond right away, as soon as a behaviour starts.

-   Teach other behaviours which meet their needs. This is what we always want to be aiming for first and foremost.

- Unlearn behaviours by making the behaviour less effective at meeting the need your child is trying to communicate. However, this should only ever be used in combination with other strategies (in particular, teaching other behaviours) to encourage your child to find better ways of having that need met.

## HOW TO TEACH SKILLS

Already in this book, I've covered how when a behaviour is rewarded or is effective at getting a desired outcome, it is more likely to happen. Similarly, if a behaviour stops being effective or isn't rewarded, it is less likely to happen again. However, this is only one part of helping our child develop skills – we've also got to think about the teaching we can use alongside these rewards to help them develop new skills. I've already covered one of these, modelling, in step 3.

## Shaping

Shaping is a pretty simple idea. Basically, we are rewarding behaviours that are getting *close to* what we are looking for. It is a bit like when you've hidden a surprise for your child and you play the game of 'getting colder/getting warmer'. Here, if a child is 'getting warmer' (i.e. their behaviour is closer to what you're looking for) you reward it. Remember when earlier we talked about how we didn't wait for behaviour to be perfect to reward it? Same idea. We want to reward *better*, even if it is only slightly better.

My favourite example of this comes from one of my lecturers, Ion Wyness again. He told us how he trained his teenagers to hoover the living room correctly. Initially, the praise was just for doing *any* hoovering at all. Over time, praise was reserved for when they did just a little bit more than a cursory whizz through the middle. Then to when they got into the corners. It took a few months, but eventually, these teenagers were doing an immaculate job!

You could equally use it to help our kids learn how to, for example, bathe themselves. Initially, we might have to do most of it, but when they grab a sponge, we can give them lots of praise. Once they are regularly grabbing the sponge, most of our praise might be reserved for when they use it to rub on themselves. Then we might give most praise when they do it all over their body, and so on, until they are washing themselves.

## Forward chaining

Forward chaining is another pretty simple idea. We break down a complex skill into steps. We get the child to do the first step (helping them a bit if needed), but once done, we do the rest of the steps ourselves – your child only has to do the first bit. Once they can do the first step themselves without a problem, then we might get them to do the first *and* second step before we take over. Then the first, second, and third step, and so on, until they are doing the whole thing.

A practical example? Teaching a child to make toast. The first thing we get them to do might be getting a slice of bread out of the bag. We do the rest. Then, once they can get the bag and get a slice of bread out, we get them to put it in the toaster before we take over.

## Backward chaining

This is my favourite to use. With forward chaining, *we the parents* get the 'little win' of *finishing* a task. That sense of accomplishment. Except, for us, making a slice of toast isn't much of a win. When we take over with forwards chaining, it can also be a bit demoralising for the child. They might also lose interest as there is nothing else for them to do, or they might not like that someone has taken over. Backward chaining, on the other hand, eliminates these problems.

Imagine learning to play a piece of music, or do a level of a game. You have to practise and practise and practise. Each time you practise, you start at the beginning, and you do pretty well at the first bit, but then you hit a tricky bit, mess up, and have to go right back to the start. It gets really frustrating. You start rushing through the first bit that you know so well to get to the tricky bit, which then means you are more likely to mess up the first bit. Eventually you give up. You never got that feeling of completing the piece of music or the game, and each time you messed up, being sent back to the start almost felt like a punishment. Backward chaining stops that happening.

With backward chaining, we do everything for the child up until the last step, then they get to do that last bit and get the reward of finishing the task. To use the slice of toast example, we do everything up *until* cutting the slice in half. Your child does that (with our help at the start if needed), and gets the extra reward of being able to say *they* made the slice of toast, *they* did it! Once they can do that reliably, we get them to finish buttering the slice too, before cutting it themselves and finishing the task. And so, we progress backwards until they can take the bread out and make toast themselves. For an older or more independent child, we might want to help them organise themselves for the school day. You might start by checking their timetable, taking out any books they don't need from their bag, then putting in all the books they need for the next day – then ask your child to check the right books are in their bag for tomorrow. The next step might be for them to realise you've missed one or two, and put them in themselves, then re-check. As you build backwards, you might only need to empty the bag, and then they re-fill it. They may start to be able to empty the bag too, and eventually, hopefully all you need to do is 'start' the sequence by saying it is time to get their bag ready.

## Hand-over-hand learning

This is simply guiding your child through the actions by putting our hand over theirs and using their hands to complete the job. Again, taking the slice of toast example, we might hold our child's hand (or arm) in ours, and guide them over to the bread and help them take it out. Then we manoeuvre it into the toaster. This type of learning means your child can focus on the actions, rather than on thinking about what we've told them or are telling them (even better for those kids with limited language, as they learn best by seeing and doing!).

## Scaffolding and errorless learning

Scaffolding is yet another of those fancy words psychologists use for a simple idea: providing our kids with just enough support to ensure they can do the task. We can do this by managing a part of the task for the child so they can focus on another part of the task, or by reducing the difficulty of the task. We do this all the time: A mum holding a child's hand as they start to walk so they can focus on co-ordinating their feet, rather than doing that AND trying to keep their balance. A teacher who gives their student a few opening sentences to choose from to help them write a paragraph. A dad who pre-weighs the ingredients for a baking project so the child can focus on following the recipe.

By using scaffolding, we can promote *errorless learning*. People talk about learning from their mistakes, and they are right, that is a great way to learn. However, we learn better by getting things right first time. Let me give you an example.

My partner has grandparents near Liverpool. We usually try and drive down to visit a couple of times a year. The first time we drove she told me that her grandparents live on Hook Road (don't try and look it up – I changed the names), but that she always confuses it with London Road (which is next to it) – she'd even wrongly addressed letters a couple of times! Every time we go down, she puts the address in the sat-nav. She knows she always gets it wrong, and so each time she'll think it is Hook Road, second guess herself as she knows she always gets it wrong, and enters London Road. We've made at least half a dozen trips and she's only *once* got it right!

My partner is not alone in this. We all do it (I just prefer to make her mistakes public, rather than my own). **When we make a mistake, there is a risk we learn the mistake, not the correction.** So, the best thing we can do is avoid making errors in the first place. This is particularly true for our kids, as it is harder to remember whether what you did last time was right or wrong – it is much easier if the only thing you remember was doing it right.

Thinking back to the Zone of Proximal Development: the idea that there are things your child can do, can do with help, and can't do. We want to try and keep your child just on that line between can do and can do with help. We don't want them to fail, because we are aiming for errorless learning. We can use scaffolding to adjust the difficulty level, and use things like shaping, forward and backward chaining to break tasks down into manageable chunks. We are trying to ensure your child has enough of a challenge that they are going to learn something, but not too much that they are going to make a mistake. When a child is able to do something reliably without help, we start thinking about the next link in the chain – teaching the next skill.

## KEY POINTS

✓ We can combine praise and rewards with specific techniques for teaching new skills.

✓ We can teach skills by shaping: rewarding and praising behaviours that get *closer to* the behaviour we are looking for.

✓ We can teach skills by forward chaining: your child (with our help if needed) does the first step, then we take over and finish the task so they can see the other steps and how to do them. Once the first step is mastered, they might do the first two steps.

✓ We can teach skills by backward chaining: we do all except the last step, then get your child to (with our help if needed) do the last step. Once mastered, they might do the second-to-last and the last step too, and so on.

✓ We can teach skills using hand-over-hand learning. This is when we guide our child's body through the actions so they can learn by actually doing the skill, rather than just watching or being told with words.

✓ We can use scaffolding to adjust the difficulty of a task. This is when we take over parts of a task so your child can just focus on the bit they are learning, and learn one bit at a time.

✓ We want to aim for errorless learning. This means using the above techniques to try (as much as possible) to ensure your child gets things right first time, without making mistakes, so they don't accidently learn the mistake rather than the correct way to do things.

## EXPANDING COMFORT ZONES

Some of the most common difficulties I see in children emerge after something has happened which has taken the pressure off. Most recently, it has been not going to school or going outside due to COVID-19, but other times it can be not going to school due to school holidays, a very wet winter meaning they aren't going out as much, or going through a hard time (for example, stress or illness) so people (quite rightly) have reduced demands and expectations on the child. When this happens for a while, the number of things your child is able to cope with reduces. Things they were able to do without worry are now causing them anxiety, and things that were anxiety provoking to start with are now simply too much. This applies to us as much as our children – if we don't do something for a while, it becomes harder to go back to.

I think of comfort zones as being a bit like a bubble. Imagine having a bubble wand, and trying to blow a really big bubble. You have to keep blowing into the bubble to make it bigger. If you stop blowing, the bubble starts to shrink as air escapes from the hole. In exactly the same way, if we aren't pushing our child's comfort zone just a little bit, that comfort zone will start to shrink.

We also need to be gentle when we expand our child's comfort zone. If you blow a short sharp breath into the bubble, it will burst and you'll have to start back at square one. In the same way, if you overwhelm your child, you'll create fear and set them back several steps. Instead, we need to blow gently and consistently into our bubble. We need to help your child push their comfort zone in little ways on a regular basis. This doesn't need to be something new each time – it could simply be doing something that is a *little* uncomfortable. If a child doesn't like going to the corner shop but can manage it, then let's go there to pick up some milk. If they don't like being around lots of kids but can usually manage, let's walk home via the park. We don't want to do something big, unmanageable, or really scary (these are meant to be little nudges, not shoves), and we aren't looking to make their whole day about being out of their comfort zone. Most of all, we want to make *sure* it is something they will be able to manage. However if we nudge our child's comfort zone just a little bit, most days, in small achievable ways, our child's comfort zone will expand.

You need to judge this on a day-to-day basis. Some days, you just know they are going to have a bad day. That's fine – our kids have more than most to deal with, so let's give them a break. However, most days, it is helpful to be trying to do something to push them out of their comfort zone just a little.

Just like blowing a big bubble, you need to know when to stop – the bubble is as big as it's going to get. In the same way, you might decide things are getting too much for them, so you aren't looking to expand your child's comfort zone any further now – that's fine, but we'll still need to keep doing the things *near the edges* of that comfort zone to stop it shrinking. If you decide you need to go even further and actually let that comfort zone shrink, you can do that, but be aware it will be more work to get it back where it was than it will be to maintain it now. Equally, be extremely careful of letting that comfort zone get too small (such as not going out of the house), as it becomes very difficult to make larger again if it is really small.

Expanding your comfort zone is also good for you too. Have you ever come back to work after a long period off and felt a bit uneasy? Or maybe not driven or ridden a bike for a long time, then feel a bit nervous, a bit like you're re-learning how to drive or ride? That's natural. All our comfort zones will shrink if we aren't pushing them out a little. So, we need to practise what we preach and as much as we are looking to expand our child's comfort zone, we also need to try and expand ours a little.

## KEY POINTS

✓ Comfort zones will start to shrink if we are not regularly pushing them out just a little bit. Things that we (or our children) were able to do may become anxiety provoking if we don't do it for a long time then come back to it.

✓ We need to be gentle when expanding our children's comfort zones. This should always be something your child can manage. A little unease for a short time is ok, but we are not looking to cause them anxiety or distress, and we don't want to make their lives all about being out of their comfort zone.

✓ Consistently doing something that pushes your child (and ourselves) to near the edge of our comfort zone will help keep it stable, or grow it.

## MANAGING ANXIETY

Right back at the start of the book I said that if we got the child's environment right, we wouldn't need much in terms of anxiety management strategies. That is true, but there are times when we can't control the environment, or where even with the best environment in the world your child is still struggling, and so some strategies may be useful. You'll probably also notice a lot of overlap between what I'm suggesting here and the self-care stuff I talked about in step 1. That's because a lot of self-care is about keeping us in our window of tolerance.

What I've got here are some *general* strategies for managing anxiety – they aren't too tailored or specific, and are meant as things to try to help if your child is a little bit anxious about something and you're looking for things to help them. This is not meant as a substitute for professional advice, and if your child is really anxious, get professional help. Similarly, everyone feels anxious sometimes, and it is impossible to eliminate completely. Instead, the aim of these and other anxiety management strategies is to bring anxiety down to a manageable level.

## Exercise

I know that sometimes all you hear healthcare professionals talk about is diet and exercise, and that often they are our least favourite things to do. However, they are really important – exercise in particular. If you remember the description of anxiety at the start of the book, you'll remember how anxiety is a normal response that gets the body ready to fight, flight, or freeze, but that in our modern world, there often isn't anything for our body to do. So, let's give it something to do!

For our kids, this could be going for a walk, playing with the dog, playing football, going swimming, running in a field, playing frisbee, bouncing on a trampoline, going on a climbing frame – anything that gets them out and moving their body.

I mentally break exercise into two categories. Regular exercise will help us to expand out our window of tolerance, so we can cope with more before we get pushed out of it. We tend to not notice the effects right away. In the last month, in a push to finish this book (and because it was my birthday and I ate far too much cake), I've fallen off the wagon with my running. I don't really enjoy running, but I know it helps me. After a month of not running, I've noticed I'm feeling more stressed, my mood is lower, I'm more crabby. This is my cue to lace up my running shoes again. It's a slow build-up effect – I usually don't notice feeling better when I'm doing it – but I certainly notice when I stop.

The second is 'as needed'. This is about burning off some of that anxiety in the moment, and getting some endorphins going. For our kids, it might be a lot of the same forms of exercise, but it is good to have an idea of which exercises you can access quickly as their anxiety starts to rise, and use in all weathers/environments. I might do a game of 'copy me' and we do star jumps/jumping jacks, run on the spot, pretend to be birds and flap our arms/elbows, be rabbits and do bunny hops on the floor, etc. (Joe Wicks has some great kid friendly exercise videos on YouTube you can look at for ideas.)

For adults, we can often persuade ourselves that exercise is what we need to do to feel better, but can be a lot harder for our kids, particularly when they are already close to the edge of their window of tolerance. Therefore, like all these strategies, exercise is best done when you can see they are *starting* to get stressed, but when they are still able to listen, rather than once things have got too much for them.

## Distraction

Sometimes, the best thing you can do is to be like an ostrich and stick your head in the metaphorical sand. People use this all the time, such as when getting injections and the nurse tries to distract a child (or, in my case, adult) from the giant needle that is about to impale their arm. However, we can use this day-to-day too. If there is a situation we know your child is going to struggle with, can we help to distract them so they can manage to get through it? This won't remove the fear, and there is a risk if we *always* try and distract them from this fear your child might become overly reliant on having this distraction, particular if this is a fear they face regularly. However, for some situations, this can be really useful.

I really like colouring books for this, as they are something a lot of children can do. Kids can also find tasks that involve searching for things in their environment helpful too. Things like 'how many cars can you see? How many trees can you see?' or I-Spy. Screens, favourite story books (particularly if there are pictures you can ask them to look for things in), tickles, funny faces – get creative! Lastly, having a bag of sensory toys, particularly spinny, flashy, noisy things, or bubbles and balloons!

Distraction works best when we follow it up with lots of attention. This helps them keep their focus on their distraction, but also rewards them for focusing on what we want them to focus on, not the thing we know is going to cause them to get upset.

## Comfort objects

Kids (and adults for that matter) can have comfort objects that work really well for them, like a teddy, a blanket, etc. – something that helps them feel secure and safe. Lots of kids grow out of this, but if your child is developing differently, they might not have outgrown this yet. That's ok. There might come a time when we need to try and remove the comfort object. For example, if it is causing them more problems than it is helping them with (i.e. they don't need it for anxiety and just have it out of habit, but it is causing them to be teased and they really want to make friends). However, if it isn't causing them a problem, then it's alright by me, so let's use it.

## Sensory objects

Our kids can sometimes be calmed by sensory objects. This isn't just about fidget spinners (in fact, I don't like these – they are hard and throwable!), it might be a piece of material they like to feel (top tip – sew this into the inside of a pocket so that it doesn't get lost and remains hidden at school), a smell or scent that calms them and makes them feel safe (try putting it on a collar so they can smell it by moving their head), or having something to chew on (just be careful to ensure they can't choke on whatever they are chewing, or break a bit off). A lot of kids really enjoy water play, bubbles (or bubble tubes), things they can squeeze, things that light up and have flashing colours. Play around and find what works for your child. Music can have a huge calming (or exciting) effect on mood too – just be sure you're not adding to overload by adding more noise.

There are loads of sensory toys and objects out there that are worth looking at – nhsggc.org.uk/kids has great advice on this. Just a word of warning – if you are interested in weighted blankets or vests, make sure you speak to an Occupational Therapist first, as these could cause harm if fitted or used incorrectly.

## Breathing exercises

With some kids, we are able to do some breathing exercises. Here, we're trying to breathe with our diaphragm, rather than our chest. This is also sometimes called belly breathing. When we breathe with our diaphragm, we are taking long, slow, deep breaths. When we breathe with our chest, we take short, sharp, shallow breaths – the kind we use when we are in fight or flight, or doing hard exercise. When we are anxious, our body shifts to this chest breathing to get ready to fight or run. However, it works the other way around too – if we do deep breathing, we can relax our body and reduce our anxiety. With adults, using this tends to be telling them what to do and they can go and do it. But for kids, our kids in particular, we need to make it visual. Even then, depending on a child's developmental level, this might be too much, but it can work well for some older kids, or kids with good language skills. When I try and teach these skills, I tend to use one of the following exercises:

- Get a bubble wand (or imagine one), and have a 'who can blow the biggest bubble' competition – this needs slow, deep breaths to expand the bubble slowly without popping it.

- Hold a scented candle that they like the smell of. Do a long breath to blow out the (imaginary – do not light it!) flame, then a big smell in through the nose to smell the candle.

- Get the child to lie down. Place a plastic cup on their belly. Their job is to breathe slowly to make the cup go gently up and down, trying to get it as high as they (comfortably) can, and as low as they can.

## KEY POINTS

✓ Some ways you can help your child manage anxiety are:

- Exercise – both regularly to expand their window of tolerance, and in the moment to help them burn off some anxiety.

- Distraction – things like colouring, naming or searching for things in their environment, screens etc., especially when accompanied by lots of attention.

- Comfort objects – blankets, teddys, etc. that help our children feel safe.

- Sensory objects.

- Breathing exercises – games or techniques that help your child to take long, slow, deep breaths, rather than short sharp shallow breaths that come with anxiety.

## FACING FEARS

The anxiety management strategies we just covered are ways to help kids manage their anxiety when it just all gets too much. It is good to have these in your toolbox, but they aren't perfect. Anxiety management tools are good for getting through a one off difficult event, or for helping to make something easier – **they don't stop whatever is triggering their anxiety from triggering their anxiety in the first place.** These strategies are like using duct tape to hold something together, rather than putting some nails and screws in – it will work in the short term, get you through, but it isn't going to solve the underlying problem. The best way to reduce anxiety long term is by facing fears. In fact, it is pretty much the only way to reduce anxiety long term. Let me explain why.

Anxiety works by your brain perceiving something, a trigger, and your body thinking that that trigger is something to be anxious about. Trigger = danger, so your body presses the panic button and makes you feel anxious. Here's what happens:

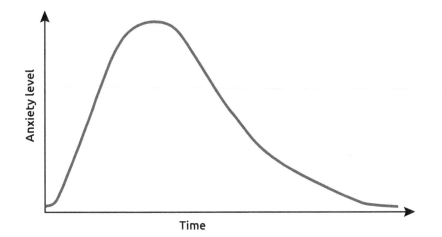

At the start, we get really anxious really quickly. Our body is pressing that panic button a few times and, if we don't get away from the trigger, it will press it more and more and more. Our body is trying to tell us to get the hell away from this trigger any way we can, and is mashing that panic button harder and harder, ramping up your anxiety more and more and more to try and get you to get away from this trigger. Your body has evolved to do this to keep you safe – it stopped you being eaten a few million years ago, so as far as your body is concerned, this trigger is the end of the world and WHY ARE YOU NOT LISTENING TO ME!

If we listen to our body's anxiety message and get away from our fears then our anxiety very quickly goes away. So, our body learns that a) that trigger is really scary because it made us feel so anxious, and b) getting away from the trigger is a great way to feel better, so let's try and do that sooner next time. So, next time our body sees that trigger it pushes that panic button even harder and even sooner.

But what happens if we don't run, if we stay and face our fears? Well, first off, our body can only feel anxious for a limited time. It turns out, being anxious is really tiring, so eventually your body will tire of pressing that big red panic button and your anxiety will start to reduce even though the situation hasn't changed. It takes a while to happen, but you can see that over time anxiety comes down.

Not running away also means our body learns something. It makes that link between the trigger and the need to press the panic button a bit weaker. Maybe that trigger isn't as dangerous as our body thought. Your body learns this because you didn't get away from what was making your anxious, yet nothing bad happened – it actually *wasn't* the end of the world. You got anxious, but that was it, and that anxiety went away. This means that next time we face our fear, we'll probably still feel anxious, but it won't be *quite* as bad – your body will press that panic button, but it won't have quite as much conviction. If we keep doing it (facing our fear and staying put), then our body will wonder if this trigger (whatever it is) is really quite as scary as it is expecting it to be? Each time we face our fear, we weaken that link between trigger and anxiety. If we stick at it, eventually (just like anything you do too much), it becomes the opposite of anxiety provoking – boring (see the diagram below – the 12 times this person faced their fear is just an example, it may take you or your child more or fewer attempts).

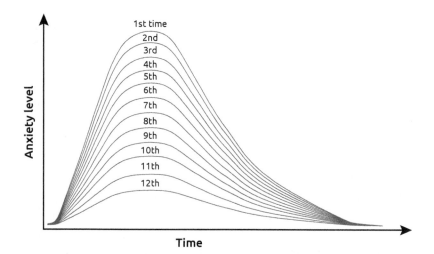

Let me give you an example. My partner loves rollercoasters. I, however, hated them for as long as I can remember. I have some vague memory of being in queues for rollercoasters as a kid at Chessington World of Adventures and Legoland. I remember seeing them go fast, flipping people over, making lots of noise and it terrified me, so I ran out of the queue. My brain saw rollercoasters (trigger) decided these were scary, so pressed that panic button. So, I became anxious, ran away, then felt better. This told my body 'yep, you were right, rollercoasters are scary, and you feel better when you avoid them'. I'm not saying my parents were wrong to let me escape the queue – it was a fear I never thought I'd have to face, so wasn't a problem for me to be scared of them. However, it taught me to be scared of rollercoasters, and I never faced that fear.

Then my partner came along, and decided that we should go to Alton Towers for a mini-break. Oh dear. Over two days, she made me ride every ride. I only had to ride each one once, but I had to ride everything. The first one, Spinball Wizzer, I could just about cope with. Then she took me on Oblivion – a ride that takes you (painfully slowly) up, trundles you to the edge, then sends you vertically straight down into a black hole. Terrifying. I saw it and felt faint.

So many times in that queue I wanted to bolt. I could feel my heart racing, my palms getting sweaty, and my stomach was in knots. It was about the most anxious I have ever felt, but I knew that if I ran out of that queue line, it would only make it worse – it would teach my body that the lesson it learned all those years ago was right. So, eventually, I did (just) manage to get on, stay on, and complete the ride (whilst holding on for dear life). It took a lot, and severely tested my willpower, but I was able to go on every ride in the park (even the teacups!). It didn't get rid of my anxiety and I certainly didn't enjoy it, but I'd started to shake that link between rollercoasters and anxiety... and I wanted to beat it!

A few years later, we returned. This time, I was determined I wanted to start to *enjoy* the rides. So, when we got in, we went straight to the back of the park, and rode a rollercoaster called Air (the one I felt least scared of as it stayed low to the ground, and you were strapped in really tightly). We rode it over and over until I wasn't anxious about it. Each time I got to the top of the lift hill and felt the lift chain release, I noticed that my anxiety wasn't *quite* as bad as the time before. Equally, after a few rides, I started to enjoy more and more of the ride as my anxiety was going down faster. I had (at least for this rollercoaster) broken that link with anxiety, and I started to have fun! I then moved onto the next rollercoaster, Nemesis, and did the same thing. I spent two days slowly going around the park getting bored of each rollercoaster (well, except Oblivion – that thing is scary!).

So, how do we do this in practice? That is what we need to think about next.

## KEY POINTS

✓ Fear is natural – it is our body's way of trying to keep us safe. However, sometimes it can be over active.

✓ If we feel anxious and then do what our anxiety drives us to do (such as run away, or take the feared thing away) it tells our body we were right to be scared and running away makes us feel better.

✓ If we face our fears and don't run away, our anxiety will eventually reduce and we are likely to be less fearful of the trigger next time we face it.

## HOW TO FACE FEARS

We've talked about expanding your child's comfort zone by every day trying to push them to do something just a little bit uncomfortable – just to near the edge of their comfort zone, as this helps keep their comfort zone where it is, or maybe even grow it a little. Having read the chapter on facing fears, you might have realised what we were doing in expanding our child's comfort zone was actually helping them face (small, manageable) anxieties and fears on a regular basis. In this section, we're going to look at how we use these principles in a more targeted way, for specific fears.

*But,* some of our kids have a *lot* of fears. Kids developing differently have a lot to manage, and we can't make them face all their fears, and certainly not all at once. Yes, this technique works, but it is *hard work* – for you and especially your child. It is not fair or correct to say 'right, Josh says face your fears, so you're going to do everything all the other kids do'. That's not what I'm saying. Rather, we need to prioritise, and make sure we are doing what is best for our child.

First – is this something that is causing a problem for *your child?* Fear of dogs – yeah, that could be a big issue. It could make it hard for them to get out and do things they enjoy. I've seen many kids with a fear of dogs where we've agreed that this is something impacting on their quality of life. Fear of rollercoasters on the other hand – maybe not so much of an issue unless your partner is an adrenaline junky. You can live a perfectly enjoyable life for 26 years without riding one. You as parents, or your child's siblings, might love them, but that is about what you want to do – not what your child developing differently wants to do, so it isn't impacting *their* quality of life.

Next, out of all the ways we could be helping your child develop, is this the most pressing and important one? Yes, they might be scared of dogs, but for most kids I'd rather conquer their fear of school first as that is probably going to have a bigger impact on them.

Lastly, and most importantly, are we sure we understand what is going on? Are we sure they are scared, rather than, say, overwhelmed? Trying to get attention? Are they missing a skill we've yet to teach them? Is this something your child does because they know if they do they'll get a favoured toy, or a bag of chocolate buttons?

If you aren't 100% sure on all three points, get professional advice before you go any further. Even if you do try to apply this technique, do so with caution, and if you are at all unsure about the technique, if it is right for your child, or if it is working correctly, stop and get professional advice.

We talked earlier about our brain seeing a trigger and linking that trigger to anxiety. If your child tries to face a fear but it gets too much and they run away from it, that will make the link between the trigger and anxiety stronger, so we'll make their anxiety worse. However, **if they can face their fear successfully, without running away or being overwhelmed, their fear will start to reduce**. By 'successfully', I mean they either leave after a set time (e.g. when a visual timer counts down), because the thing has run its course (such as the rollercoaster ride has finished), or once their anxiety has come back down to an ok level (often, about 20–30 minutes, but can be longer or shorter).

The trouble is, a lot of fears are just too big to face. For example, it took all my nerve to go on Oblivion, and I've not been back on it since because it was just too much! This was too big a fear too soon – I needed to break it down and make it more manageable. We can do this with things like:

- Time – I will face my fear for one minute vs I will face my fear for an hour.

- Proximity – I will be in the same room as a dead spider sealed in a dark Tupperware box vs I will have a tarantula walking over my face.

- Comfort objects – I will face my fear holding onto my comfort blanket vs alone.

- Support people – I will face my fear with mum holding me vs holding my hand vs being in the same room vs alone.

- Size of fear – I will go on the kiddies rollercoaster vs I will go on the biggest rollercoaster in the park.

We can use these strategies to create a ladder of feared situations. At the top is our goal – for your child to be able to tolerate walking in a park with dogs for about 30 minutes. I've not said that they need to love dogs, just to be ok walking past dogs. It is about quality of life, and as long as they can get out and about without fearing seeing a dog, that is a success. At the bottom we start with what is currently scary but tolerable. In between these ends, we want to write in lots of steps. Each step should be harder/scarier than the one before it. This could be because we've removed some level of support, increased the time, or moved from a less scary version of the fear to a scarier version. For example:

- Watching mum's friend and her friend's dog play from a safe distance, but from the car, holding onto mum, for 10 minutes. Doing this regularly until they appear less anxious.

- Hold mum's hand to go and say hello to mum's friend and her dog, with the dog staying behind a gate/fence. Doing this until able to do so without holding mum's hand.

- Hold mum's hand and go say hello to mum's friend and her dog for two minutes on the same side of the gate, with mum's friend holding onto her dog by the harness. Doing this until they appear less anxious, then repeating with the dog on a lead.

- Holding mum's hand to stroke mum's friend's dog while she holds onto the dog when you go to say hello.

- Throwing the ball for the dog in the back garden, with mum's friend handing them the ball so they don't have to touch the dog. Mum watching from behind.

And so on.

You can see I'm taking really small steps here. That is because we do not want your child to get so anxious that you have to take them away, that your child runs away, or the owner has to take the dog away. If that happens, we'll make the fear stronger and we'll take several steps backwards. We also don't want to 'flood' your child – to overwhelm them with anxiety but make them stay to show them that they are ok. That is not fair on your child and bad practice.

Instead, starting at the bottom of the ladder, we want to expose your child to that situation regularly, each time ensuring success, until the fear of that rung of the ladder has reduced. By doing so, we have hopefully made the next rung of the ladder less scary, and increased our child's confidence. We can then move up one rung of the ladder to something that previously may have been too much, but is now tolerable. This process is called graded exposure. Doing this exercise requires time, planning, and patience. We need to be doing this on a regular basis, so it is a good idea to build it into your routine (and make sure there is something really rewarding after!).

You also need to be able to read your child's anxiety levels *really* well. We are looking to get their anxiety no further than 'this is scary but I can cope', and we are looking to see it slowly reduce down to 'I don't like it but it is ok'. If you can see their anxiety is getting too much, then we need to have a plan for how we can make this exposure a little easier – comfort objects, having mum or dad hold them, owner holding the dog closer, etc. or just going back a step so we can keep their anxiety from bubbling over and taking control of them – we want our child to come away successful, even if we had to make the situation a little less scary. If we've had to add in extra supports like this, it means that next time, we may need to go back to the previous step on our ladder of fears and work on that for a while longer before we go back to the step they struggled with, or see if there is a step or two in-between we could put in instead, so there isn't as big a jump in anxiety.

This is in theory a simple strategy, but in practice getting the steps of the ladder right for your child and reading their anxiety correctly can be challenging. There is also a risk we make things worse if we do it wrong. Therefore, as always, if in any doubt about how to apply this, or if things aren't going to plan, stop and seek professional help.

## KEY POINTS

✓ Before we help your child face a fear, we need to check:

  – Is this something causing a problem for your child (is it impacting on *their* quality of life)?

  – Is it the most pressing and important thing for your child to work on right now?

  – Are we sure they are anxious (rather than, say, frustrated, upset, wanting something, etc.)?

✓ To face fears, we need to take a step-by-step approach, and every step must be manageable for our child.

✓ We take one fear and work out the least scary way your child could encounter that fear. We start here, and once they are able to manage that without it being too scary, we can move on to the next step – one step closer towards their larger fear.

✓ There are ways we can make steps more manageable and less scary.

✓ If your child becomes too scared and isn't able to cope, you need to try and make that situation more manageable (adding in extra comforts or supports), or going back to a previous step.

✓ If you are at all unsure about how to help your child face fears, get professional help.

## MANAGING MELTDOWNS

Managing meltdowns is usually at the top of parents' agenda. Usually, they tell me that when meltdowns happen, they try to calm their child down, but they can't seem to bring them out of it. The truth is, this approach is a little backwards. We want to *prevent meltdowns happening in the first place.* That is what everything we have done up to now (getting you in the right place, with the right knowledge, environment, interaction, and response) is designed to do. We can also use the tools we already have (such as STAR charts) to try to work out the triggers and functions of meltdowns, as meltdowns are just another behaviour. Yes, they are a behaviour associated with extreme anxiety/anger/upset, when the body is just in panic mode. However, they are still behaviours that are triggered, and if we can work out what those triggers and then find ways to either avoid the triggers or make them more manageable, we'll have fewer meltdowns.

Ideally, we are looking to prevent meltdowns happening. This is nicer for your child as they don't have to go through meltdowns in the first place, and it is far more effective than trying to manage meltdowns once they happen, so should always be what we try first. However, even if we cannot *prevent* meltdowns happening, we can use these same tools to work out when they are more likely to happen so we can make plans. For example, we might know that meltdowns are more likely to occur in the hour a child comes back from school. There could be lots of reasons for this, and we can try and work these out. However, until we do, knowing *when* they will happen (or are more likely to happen) allows us to make plans to help manage these, such as allowing your child some cool downtime, having a period of low demands, space to go to their room, encouraging them to get some exercise to blow off steam, sensory toys that help them to relax and calm down, etc.

Meltdowns generally have a predictable pattern. Just like other behaviours, meltdowns have smaller, low level behaviours that slowly escalate towards the 'big' behaviour that gets our attention. If we identify these early behaviours, we can get in there and do something to help our child before they get close to a meltdown. This is where having a list (mental or physical) of what works to calm your child down is really important.

Sometimes if we can't get in there early enough, or if our attempts at distraction and de-escalation don't work and our child's distress continues to escalate, then the point of no return is reached. This is when our child's distress is so great that their ability to think rationally, listen, or follow instructions starts to go as emotion takes over. For some children this includes their ability to understand language or communicate, remember what they did later on, understand other's feelings, and understand the consequences of their actions. At this point, a meltdown is unavoidable, and our child's distress will continue to escalate until they reach peak meltdown.

Before the point of no return, we can try and avoid a meltdown using all the strategies already discussed. However, once a meltdown has passed the point of no return, what do we do?

Priority number one with any meltdown is safety, for your child, and everyone around them. Ideally, we want to redirect your child to somewhere safe. Usually when at home this is their room, at school this might be a quiet room, or out and about it might be the car. If you can see that you're reaching that tipping point and your child is going to have a meltdown, or that your early strategies for calming them down aren't going to work, then we need to use this short window while we can still communicate and they can still think rationally to encourage them to get to a safe space to have that meltdown.

What do I mean by a safe space? I mean somewhere where:

- There isn't anything they could use to seriously hurt themselves (glass objects, heavy or sharp objects, drugs and chemicals, etc. are all removed).

- Windows are shut and locked (if at home – if in a car you may need windows open).

- Possible projectiles (particularly if heavy) are removed (remote controllers and small metal trains/cars are a favourite here).

- It is as quiet as possible.

- They can be alone.

- They *can* have comforting items/sensory toys/etc. that are safe with them if wanted/helpful.

- Whether you leave your child alone will depend on your child's needs, if they are safe to be left alone, and if you are safe to be with them.

While I don't put it on the list as it isn't a safety issue, clearing out valuables (either in terms of cost, or emotional value) is a good idea too. Don't expect them not to break their favourite and much loved toy just because it is a favourite and much loved toy – that 'thinking' brain may not be doing much thinking, and they may be really upset after the meltdown when they realise what has happened (potentially triggering a second meltdown).

If we can't get them to a safe space, then we need to try and turn wherever the child is into a safe space – clear the decks of any of the objects mentioned above if we can, and get people out. Over time, you'll probably also get an idea of the sorts of things your child will and won't do during a meltdown. If they aren't one for throwing projectiles, but do tend to hit things, then prioritise what you remove accordingly.

During a meltdown, you want to have *one* person in charge. This is the only person who is going to talk to your child, make decisions, who is going to keep people away, and decide whether to move to a safe space or clear the decks. This is important, as people arguing over what to do or having more than one person trying to talk to the child can add to the stress of the situation and your child.

You (or the person in charge of the situation), need to decide whether it is best to stay with your child or leave them alone. This is not an easy call, and one you/the person have to weigh up based on your knowledge of your child, and what they are likely to do. A lot of the children I work with find it easier to get through a meltdown when alone, and this also helps keep other people safe. However, other children need someone in the room for safety, or want to know someone is there in the room with them. This is different for every child and something you need to decide for yourself. However, 'alone' does not mean leave them in their room and go make dinner. It means being behind the door listening and possibly sometimes checking on them to ensure they stay safe. **Do not leave a child alone if they are not safe**.

If you are going to remain in the room, there can be a temptation to restrain your child. **Restraint should always be a last resort** – for example, when it is needed to keep a child safe from serious injury (such as because they are about to run into the road) – and be as brief as possible. The reasons for this are a) restraint often makes a child more upset, and can even be traumatising, b) restraint if done wrongly can cause serious injury or death, and c) there are legal issues around restraint. It is much better to prevent the need for restraint in the first place by working out what is causing the meltdown, or making the situation safe (e.g. lock a window and take away the key rather than restrain your child because they are trying to open and climb out the window). If you find yourself needing to restrain your child for their own safety, then after the event you need to get professional help (school, social work, and health services can all help or direct you to the right support in your area). Most of all, use your best judgement and common sense to keep everyone safe.

Here's the important thing to remember when in the middle of a meltdown. **It will end**. A meltdown is the body going into fight or flight mode. It is all pumped up, ready to fight or run away at any moment. However, the body can only sustain this level of physical effort for so long. Meltdowns are draining. Some kids are, frankly, athletes, and can have ones that go on for an hour or more, but most of the time, they don't last this long because the body simply can't keep it going. It will end. Once that exhaustion starts to hit, then you see a 'crash', often anger turns to tears, and your child may become more cuddly, or want to try and hide away. Often they'll want to sleep.

Eventually, your child may get to a point where they are able to be comforted. That isn't always an easy point to find. When a meltdown is in full swing, a lot of kids can't be comforted. Everything is so overwhelming, so scary, that talking won't be heard or understood and hugs may feel smothering or overwhelming. **That doesn't mean we shouldn't try to comfort our kids** – we absolutely should; one of our roles as parents is taking big scary emotions and making them safe. If you think your child might respond to being comforted then we should absolutely try. However, if trying to comfort your child is making things worse, or if we can predict it will make it worse, then as hard as it may be, we need to step back. This can be really hard for parents, as it goes against every instinct you have if you see your child distressed. However, if every time you try to comfort them it makes things worse, then trying to comfort them *at this point* isn't helping.

If you know from experience that, for example, in the first 15 minutes of a meltdown, or while they are hitting objects, you trying to comfort your child makes things worse, then it is ok to give them their space and not try to comfort your child. However, we want to be alert for the signs that your child is starting to come out the other side and is wanting and needing comfort. When that happens, I suggest using very little, if any, language. Language is complex, and for a lot of young kids it can be hard to process, particularly if they are still stressed or tired. Actions speak louder than words. A hug, swaddling in a blanket, stroking hair, a favourite sensory toy, singing a favourite song, are all things that, depending on what works for your child (some kids will hate these and want something else), are better than talking.

When your child is calm enough to listen, now is not the time to go over what happened, or to reprimand them for what they did in a meltdown (sometimes kids don't even remember what they did during a meltdown). Often, talking about the problem or trying to explain why some aspect of their behaviour during a meltdown was not ok can just result in a flare up again. Likewise, while *sometimes* talking about solutions may help, often these can result in another flare up too, as your solution isn't the right one, isn't good enough, or just isn't what they were wanting. I therefore suggest you avoiding talking about solutions to the problem too at this stage. Instead, talk about what is going to happen next. Our children are stressed and feeling overwhelmed. By talking about what is going to happen, we give them security, some certainty, and we ground them back into a routine they know.

Often after a meltdown, our kids are exhausted, both mentally and physically. They may want comforting (in whatever way works for them), or they may want time and space. Often kids will want to find somewhere dark and soft and sleep. Regardless, our aim is to give them time to recover, away from pressures, questions, and all but essential demands. Some kids recover quickly, while others need a good hour or two, and may be quite fragile for hours or even days after.

It is worth remembering that meltdowns can spread. For example, take a child who finds a certain class at school really challenging but is able to cope. One day, after having a really bad day, they have a meltdown in that class and get taken home. The behaviour of a meltdown has been really effective at escaping a difficult situation, and so may have increased the fear and stress of that situation, and the likelihood a meltdown will happen again. This child's feelings and difficulty with that class are genuine, as are the meltdowns, and we need to be empathically addressing this distress and finding ways for them to cope in school. Nor was it wrong to send the child home – after a meltdown, they may well have struggled to cope with school that day. However, there is a risk that our child has learned that there **is** something to fear about that class, or that they actually can't cope. This may lead them to be more fearful of school generally, or situations where there are demands placed on them, leading to heightened stress and anxiety and making meltdowns more likely. This is why if a meltdown happens, we need to take a step back and think about what caused it to ensure they don't become a repeating pattern. If you do find yourself in this situation, get in touch with your child's school and healthcare team to get some help figuring out what is causing the meltdowns, how to help your child cope, and how to break the pattern.

Sometimes, during a meltdown, kids do things that are not ok. They might break rules, damage things, or hurt people. Often, parents feel the need or want to re-establish boundaries to make it clear that some behaviour was not ok. This makes sense, however if you tell your child their behaviour is not ok in the middle of a meltdown, it isn't going to work and is likely to only make them more upset/ angry/scared. Likewise, if you do it after they have calmed down, it isn't going to have much impact – just like praise, consequences need to be immediate to be effective.

This is a particular problem for children who have trouble under-standing language or abstract concepts like time. If you try telling them their behaviour was wrong after a meltdown, then they might think you are accusing them of doing that behaviour right now, or that you are saying that whatever they are doing right now is wrong (both of which may trigger another meltdown!). In these situations, trying to explain that a child's earlier behaviour was wrong simply isn't fair to them, due to their developmental stage. Sometimes parents can find this hard, particularly if they feel pressure from other parents to tell their child that a behaviour is not ok. But there is no point you both getting frustrated and upset trying to explain something that your child can't understand yet.

Boundaries are best set day-to-day. If your child knows hitting is wrong and doesn't normally hit people, but hits during a meltdown, this is probably because of how stressed and upset they are and they are struggling to control themselves. If we can stop the meltdown happening in the first place, then they probably aren't going to end up hitting – problem solved. If, however, they hit people at other times, then that is about a boundary we need to be setting more clearly every day, in which case we'll have far better opportunities to make this boundary clear when your child isn't stressed and is in a place to learn.

## KEY POINTS

✓ Meltdowns are another (very distressing) behaviour we can use our tools to predict, understand, and prevent.

✓ When we aren't able to avert a meltdown, our children will reach the 'point of no return'. When we reach this point, we need to stop trying to prevent the meltdown, and start trying to make it safe to have a meltdown.

✓ Divert a child to a safe space, or if you can't, try and make the space safe.

✓ Have one person in charge, who is the only person who tries to communicate with your child.

✓ Some children prefer to be alone during a meltdown. However, remember safety first – only do so if they are safe, and remain by the door monitoring the situation to ensure their continued safety.

✓ Restraint should always be a last resort used when nothing else is going to keep your child safe (e.g. stopping them running into the road, or out a window), as this carries its own risks too. If you find you have needed to use restraint, get professional help to stop you needing to use it again.

✓ Meltdowns will end – they are exhausting, and can only be kept up for so long.

✓ As a meltdown starts to end, our children may become more receptive to comfort, become tired, and withdraw.

✓ As a meltdown is ending/while a child is recovering from a meltdown, do not try and talk about their behaviour during the meltdown, or solve the problem. Talk about what is going to happen, and give your child certainty.

✓ If a meltdown is becoming a regular occurrence, get professional help.

## FINDING YOUR RAG

Back in the section on 'Consistency' (in step 5), I talked about a RAG (Red, Amber, Green) chart, to help people understand and respond correctly to your child. Now, at the very end of the book, we are finally able to create it.

The reason I've waited until now to talk you through this is that it really pulls together everything we've been talking about. This RAG chart is a shorthand way to communicate to those working with your child how your child is feeling, and what they need to do based on that. It is a bit of a crib sheet that reminds people of important information in a potentially stressful situation.

I've included an example RAG chart in the downloadable appendix. I usually suggest doing RAG charts on a landscape piece of paper, and they can sometimes span a couple of pages of A4 (although try not to let them get too big, else they'll not be usable. Below is a RAG chart in a simplified form.

|  | What I look like | What I need from you |
| --- | --- | --- |
| Green | Description of what your child looks like, what they do, how they behave when they are happy, relaxed, and calm. | Information on how to keep your child in the 'green' zone. What others should do, what communication to use, what the environment should be, etc. These are preventative strategies – what your child needs day-to-day to keep them in that good place, and avoid meltdowns. |

| Amber | Description of what your child looks like, what they do, how they behave when they are getting upset, angry, frustrated, or distressed. | Information on how to move your child back to the 'green zone'. What strategies help them calm down, how to change the environment, what communication to use, etc. These are reactive strategies for when things are starting to go wrong. |
|---|---|---|
| Red | Description of what your child looks like, what they do, how they behave when they are having or are going to have a meltdown. | Information on how to keep your child and others safe in preparation for and during a meltdown. |

A good RAG plan will have lots and lots of stuff in the green section, but less in the amber section, and even less in the red section. This is because prevention is better than cure, which is why so much of this book has been about getting things right in the first place (the green stuff) to prevent our children becoming distressed, and has less about what to do when they become distressed (the amber stuff), and only one chapter on meltdowns (the red stuff).

**Green**: This is when your child is in a good place, calm, and ready to learn. This is where we are aiming to keep our child. We want to have a good description here of what your child looks like when 'green'. Remember, our kids don't always show their emotions as easily or in the same way as other kids, so we need to be really behavioural in our descriptions, just like we were for the STAR charts. So, rather than 'looks happy', we might have 'smiles, often sings, will be able to look at you for one minute or more, can sit and pay attention for at least five minutes, will follow instructions presented visually', etc. We want to keep this short and snappy, either bullet points or several short sentences – remember, this is something we want people to be able to look at on the fly, or ideally remember.

In the 'what I need from you' section is where we bullet point all the things we need to do to help keep your child in this good place. We aren't looking to give a detailed description of what their environment needs to be, exactly how to communicate with our child, or how you need to respond if they are being cheeky. You can go into that elsewhere. What we are looking for are short reminders of all the things we need to ensure we are getting right – a check-list to remind people what they need to be doing. Things like 'give choices of two things', 'use short, straightforward language', 'keep to the routine', 'use social stories to warn of changes', 'avoid loud unexpected noises', etc. Hopefully in reading this book, you'll have come across lots of things you've identified as important that you are already doing which help your child, or things you want to try out because they might help your child. If you are confident it helps your child, put it in here.

**Amber**: This is when your child is starting to get unsettled. Some-thing is wrong, and if we the adults don't step in, things could escalate. In the 'what I look like' section we need to list some of the red flags that things aren't right, particularly those which we know are good 'early warning signs' – as we want to support our children before things get worse for them. This might be things like 'starts to get fidgety, starts shouting, starts refusing to do things, takes things off the visual schedule, gets very focused on x'.

Under what to do, we want to be thinking about what strategies we've tried and tested and know help your child feel calmer. We can assume people are doing everything under 'green' already, so this section should contain additional things to do, or things that are different to what you might do in 'green'. This might be sensory strategies, things we need to change in their environment, reducing what demands we are placing on our child, offering them the chance to go somewhere we know they like and feel calm and safe in, how we might need to change (in particular, simplify) our communica-tion, etc. The latter steps of this book will hopefully have helped you identify some of the things that help your child manage tough situations, or given you ideas of things to try – if they work, then include them here.

**Red**: This is when we have reached the point of no return. A melt-down is likely going to happen, or is already happening. The focus now shifts to keeping everyone safe. Your description of your child will be the signs that we know mean that they are going to have a meltdown no matter what we do. What this looks like will be very different depending on the child. Similarly, how we respond to it will also be very different, but look to the section on 'Managing meltdowns' for pointers.

**Blue**: Some people include an extra 'blue' row. This is the period when a child has had a meltdown and is recovering from this. This is a time when your child might be feeling more fragile, tired, and needing more space in order to prevent a reoccurrence. Again, this will have a behavioural description of what this looks like (and how long it usually lasts), and a clear plan of what people need to do to help them move through the blue zone and back to green.

A RAG table isn't going to be perfect, and you'll need to change it as your child grows and develops. These are best when done with all the adults likely to be using the RAG plan involved, especially teachers, partly so you can get lots of different ideas and perspectives on what works, but also so you can ensure it will work across environments (home, school, and grandma's). Likewise, it is good to regularly review a RAG plan, so never end a meeting without deciding when the next will be.

# FINAL WORDS

One of the hardest parts of my job is managing endings. There comes a time when I have to tell parents that I've done all I can. Hopefully it is because things have really improved, and things are much more settled – the child, parents, and family are in a better place. However, when I say that it is time for me to discharge a child, this can often be met with anxiety from parents. They have had this support from me, and now I'm taking it away – what if things get worse? What if a behaviour or fear returns? What if... What if...?

This is when I remind parents that I've not changed anything. My aim as a therapist isn't to do something 'to' their child. Rather, it is to give parents the knowledge, skills, and tools they need to help their child, and together work out how to apply them. These things are rarely unique to one specific difficulty, and can usually be applied or adapted to lots of different challenges our children face. The change that has happened has come from what the *parents* have done, not me, and they will hopefully be able to use the same tools again in the future. In the same way, I hope this book has equipped you with the knowledge, skills, and tools you need to help your child, and given you some guidance on how to apply them.

You're never going to get things perfect. Even if you were able to follow this book perfectly, and have it all apply exactly to your child, then it might work for a few weeks, or even a few months. However, life moves on, you, your child, and their environment will change, and new challenges will emerge. I hope when this happens you'll be able to go back to this book and remind yourself of all the knowledge, skills, and strategies you have, and think about how they might apply in this situation. I've tried to keep each chapter (relatively) short so that you can use the contents page as a bit of a checklist, and if you think something might be relevant, or that maybe something has slipped, then it should hopefully be easy to identify it, re-read the chapter and get back on track.

Of course, not every ending is a happy one. Sometimes I discharge a family because we've come to the conclusion that actually what the child and their family need is a different set of skills or supports to the ones I can offer, such as help from social work, a Speech and Language Therapist, or an Occupational Therapist. Children developing differently have needs as unique as they are, and what I can offer is only ever part of the solution. You might have read and have tried things in the book, but either it hasn't helped, or things are still really difficult. In that case, please seek professional help – this book is not a substitute for a professional who can really get to know your child, and tailor the advice to your child and situation.

If you get professional advice, either now or later, then I strongly recommend holding onto this book and bringing it with you to your first appointment. Even if this book hasn't been helpful, or you haven't been able to put it into practice, I hope you've been able to understand some of the *theory* of what I've been talking about. The content in this book is what I and a lot of other professionals spend a lot of time going over, because it applies to so many of the difficulties the children we see face. So, if you bring this book along, you can show the professional what you have read, and what did or didn't make sense, so they don't need to spend time telling you what you already know. Equally, if you can say what did and didn't work, and what you've already tried or are doing, hopefully the professional will be able to more quickly work out how to help, or where things might need to be adapted.

Lastly, I hope this book has given you the confidence to be the parent you want to be. Parenting children developing differently can be both hard and hugely rewarding. However, it usually isn't complex – the strategies are actually pretty simple. Throughout we've talked about the same ideas: keeping communication simple and visual, praising and developing skills, consistency and routine, working to your child's developmental level, and a gradual stepped approach. None of these is rocket science, or a closely guarded secret. In fact, most of these are things that you'll naturally do as parents. Yes, they might be a bit more formal, a bit more detailed, and need to be applied in slightly different ways to other kids, but they are based on skills you already have as parents. You're a great parent, and you've got all the skills you need. This book is just about understanding how you apply your skills when your child sees the world a bit differently.

## KEY POINTS

✓ You've got this.

# Index